Video Methods

This interdisciplinary collection provides a set of innovative and inventive approaches to the use of video as a research method. Building on the development of visual methods across the social sciences, it highlights a range of possibilities for making and working with video data. The collection showcases different video methods, including video diaries, video go-alongs, time-lapse video, mobile devices, multi-angle video recording, video ethnography, and ethnographic documentary. Each method is presented through a case study, showing how it can be used in practice. The authors offer pragmatic advice and discuss practical issues, including equipment, techniques and skills, analysis, and presentation. They also show how video methods can be used in a range of different contexts—at train stations, on bicycles, in schools, outdoors, and in museums—to investigate worlds that are visible, audible, tangible, and in motion. In doing so, they illuminate the theoretical possibilities that video methods offer for researching the body, identity, everyday life, affect, time, and space.

Charlotte Bates is a Postdoctoral Research Associate in the Sociology Department at Goldsmiths, University of London, where she also gained her PhD in visual sociology.

Routledge Advances in Research Methods

Video Methods

Social Science Research in Motion

Edited by Charlotte Bates

Routledge
Taylor & Francis Group

NEW YORK AND LONDON

First published 2015
by Routledge
711 Third Avenue, New York, NY 10017

and by Routledge
2 Park Square, Milton Park, Abingdon, Oxon OX14 4RN

*Routledge is an imprint of the Taylor & Francis Group,
an informa business*

© 2015 Taylor & Francis

Library of Congress Cataloging-in-Publication Data

Video methods : social science research in motion / edited by
 Charlotte Bates. — 1st Edition.
  pages cm. — (Routledge advances in research methods ; 10)
 Includes bibliographical references and index.
 1. Social sciences—Research—Methodology. 2. Digital
video. I. Bates, Charlotte, editor of compilation.
 H62.2.V53 2014
 300.72—dc23
 2014016349

ISBN: 978-0-415-73401-1 (hbk)
ISBN: 978-1-315-83273-9 (ebk)

Typeset in Sabon
by Apex CoVantage, LLC

Printed and bound in the United States of America by Publishers Graphics,
LLC on sustainably sourced paper.

Contents

Figures

Introduction
Putting Things in Motion

Charlotte Bates

It was evident from the start that what would be missing from a book on video methods is the video. Its colour, sound, and movement resist the black and white pages of print. But something lingers in the words and stills within, a feeling of and for the vital, affective, fleeting, and sensuous intensities of video. And this is precisely why the authors of the chapters that encompass this volume have chosen to work with video as a research method. Placing video cameras between themselves and the worlds they are interested in, they have found new ways of recording and attending to the textures and rhythms of social life in motion. From video diaries and go-alongs to time-lapse video, multi-angle video recording, video ethnography, and documentary, with camera phones, minicams, handycams, and digital SLRs, as well as lapel and shotgun microphones, field recorders, batteries, tripods, and head mounts, and in homes and schools, at train stations, on bicycles and kayaks, and in the wilderness, the chapters in this volume provide an innovative and inventive inventory of the possibilities that video has opened up within the social sciences.

Over the last decade, a number of calls have been made to expand the catalogue of social science research methods. As John Law noted 10 years ago, methods of inquiry often fail to catch the texture of the world and "talk of 'method' still tends to summon up a relatively limited repertoire of responses" (Law 2004, 3). At the same time, there has been an upsurge in the popularity of visual methods across the social sciences, and a resurgence of interest in picturing social life that has helped to expand the list of devices and methods that social scientists work with (Knowles and Sweetman 2004; Pink 2012; Prosser 1998). But it is not my intention to promote video as a visual method—this would be to limit its qualities. With its sound and its movement, video exceeds the visual realm. It might better be thought of as a sensory method, not simply because it blends what we see with what we hear, but because it evokes a sense of feeling—a feeling *there* and a feeling *for* the spaces and people, the animals, things, relationships, and practices that we seek to understand through our research. Less concerned with "catching visual, visible and visibilising practices as they happen" (Laurier 2014), and more attentive to the rhythms, textures, and atmospheres of *happenings,* the video methods herein revel in the visible and the invisible sensorium of social life. So, while video might typically be associated with various practices of looking, gazing, inspecting, and surveilling, the chapters in this volume add to this list other modes of attention, including listening, sensing, and feeling. As such, they belong to a burgeoning repertoire of research methods that awaken our "sensual imagination" (Vannini et al. 2013), a phrase inspired by C. Wright Mills' call for a sociological imagination.

The chapters in this volume are testimony to the generosity of the contributors, who offer detailed descriptions of their approaches to video as the focus of their accounts. In doing so, they offer empirically grounded ways for thinking through the possibilities, and the limits, of working with video as a research method. They are also a celebration of the sheer variety and range of possibilities that video offers for the growth and development of our methodological repertoire. No two of the video methods presented here are the same, and rather than offer the reader a set of instructions or a recipe to follow, the chapters in this volume are served as tasters that issue an invitation to experiment and improvise with your own ingredients—devices, contexts, and theoretical positions—and find new ways of working with video as a research method. At the same time, they are packed with technical and practical details. This is because, as Phillip Vannini highlights in the afterword to this volume, making technological and aesthetic choices is important. Working with multimedia technologies makes these choices visible and audible, bringing into question what should be considered 'good enough' (see Gallagher, this volume). Aside from questions of quality, the time, extra effort, and cost, together with the sheer volume of material that can be generated with video means that it demands careful handling and a certain level of technical competency if researchers are to avoid being swamped by the metaphorical cutting room floor.

Two Economic and Social Research Council (ESRC) Researcher Development Initiatives have been instrumental in the composition of this volume, both for their role in nourishing ideas and for providing a meeting point. Many, though not all, of the contributors were drawn together from these two events, so I would like to give a special note of thanks to the organisers. *Live Sociology: Practising Social Research with New Media,* was a series of workshops organised by Les Back and Celia Lury at Goldsmiths, University of London. The year long programme of five workshops combined theoretical and practical training to develop skills in new multimedia techniques to collect, analyse, archive, and share ethnographic social research, as well as other kinds of social data and materials. *Experimenting with Geography: See—Hear—Make—Do,* was an international training and networking project organised by Michael Gallagher while at the University of Edinburgh. The weeklong workshop was dedicated to developing a diverse range of craft skills associated with audio, visual, and site-specific methodologies. Both events encouraged the idea of research as craft, helping researchers to develop their own craft skills and engage with the possibilities that multimedia offers as a research tool and as a form of communication and dissemination.

While grounded in different disciplines, one in sociology and the other in cultural geography, it is no coincidence that these two events eventually brought together a group of researchers with an interest in video and aligning intellectual energies. Through my own career trajectory (which has taken me from a sociology department to a department of geography, and back again to work in an interdisciplinary team of geographers and sociologists) I have been continually surprised and inspired by the discernable and indiscernible connections that I have found between the two disciplines. Put simply, within both there is a tendency to draw on ethnographic methods, a movement towards experimentation, and a swelling interest in material, bodily, sensual, and affective matters. In bringing both disciplines together in this volume, I hope not only to make these connections more immediately evident, but also to provide a common ground for cross-disciplinary exchanges and an impetus for the movement and development of video methods across and between the disciplines in new and exciting ways.

The details of these coinciding intellectual positions, and their tangled relationships with video, can be engaged with through the chapters in this volume, but it is worth briefly mentioning the two parallel movements that have informed much of this work here. Cultural geographers will be familiar with the term 'non-representational theory', which Hayden Lorimer has described as "an umbrella term for diverse work that seeks to better cope with out self-evidently more-than-human, more-than-textual, multisensual worlds" (Lorimer 2005, 83). 'Non-representational' (Thrift 2008) or 'more-than-representational' (Lorimer 2005) work insists on "expanding our once comfortable understanding of 'the social' and how it can be regarded as something researchable" (Lorimer 2005, 84). In doing so, it contains an imperative to inject life into the 'dead geographies' of representation (Thrift and Dewsbury 2000), as Lorimer writes, "What has been identified as deadening effect—the tendency for cultural analyses to cleave towards a conservative, categorical politics of identity and textual meaning—can, it is contended, be overcome by allowing in much more of the excessive and transient aspects of living" (Lorimer 2005, 83). Perhaps the greatest challenge presented by these 'more-than-' styles of working is their experimental imperative, which Sarah Whatmore has described as an "urgent need to supplement the familiar repertoire of humanist methods that rely on generating talk and text with experimental practices that amplify other sensory, bodily and affective registers and extend the company and modality of what constitutes a research subject" (Whatmore 2006, 606–607).

Sociologists, meanwhile, have also been engaging with ways of thinking that juxtapose 'lively' and 'dead' approaches to the social world. Les Back has described 'dead sociology' as "objectifying, comfortable, disengaged and parochial" (Back 2013, 18). 'Live sociology', by contrast, is "able to attend to the fleeting, distributed, multiple and sensory aspects of sociality through research techniques that are mobile, sensuous and operate from multiple vantage points" (Back 2013, 18). Like 'more-than-' styles of working, 'live sociology' is attentive to the *doing* of social life, in all its sensory dimensions and from multiple vantage points. The challenge issued, once again, is "how to find ways to represent such lives and objects that sustain rather than foreclose their vitality and ongoing life" (Back 2013, 21). Of course, there are antecedents to both these intellectual positions, and the imperative to experiment is certainly not new. As Les Back and Nirmal Puwar have noted, "invention and methodological innovation were very much part of the early days of sociology" (Back and Puwar 2013, 12). But rather than denuding the current impetus, this history provides a licence for methodological experimentation today (Back and Puwar 2013, 12).

Perhaps it is not remarkable that both disciplines have reached towards multimedia technologies, devices, and formats at the same moment in their attempts to extend their methodological repertoires and keep pace with current thinking. This experimental revival has also been propelled by the more mundane effect of our current technological climate and the availability and intensification of new multimedia devices. Yet there is something significant going on here—as our tools expand and diversify so too do the opportunities we have to expand our attentiveness and move *with* the social world. As Les Back writes, "the opportunity we have now is to enliven our methodological creativity but also to extend the scope of the 'sociological imagination' (Mills 1959) in the 21st century" (Back 2010, 16). Video is one device with which to extend and enliven both the sociological and the geographical imagination, to attune to a world that is "tentative, charged, overwhelming, and alive" (Stewart 2007, 128), and to investigate "*the happening* of the social world—its ongoingness, relationality, contingency and sensuousness" (Lury and Wakeford 2012, 2).

Although there is no companion website or DVD to this book, video from almost all of the projects can be found online, (and handily the authors have included web links in their chapters). Rather than interpreting the uptake in video, as well as other creative and multimedia methods, as a rejection of print—after all, writing too is a movement of imagination— the authors in this volume variously rise to the challenge of working with and between different formats to communicate their work. These acts of translation and modes of knowledge transmission involve taking risks, and range from writing video differently to releasing video online, showing exhibitions, and making installations and feature-length films. The possibilities are endless, and are still largely untapped (see Vannini, this volume). However the authors in this volume have begun to raise questions of how to enliven and transform their work and better communicate the results of their craft (Back 2010, 25).

ENTRÉE

The volume begins with a chapter based on my own work with video diaries. In 'Intimate Encounters: Making Video Diaries about Embodied Everyday Life', I discuss the practicalities of giving people video cameras to film their own lives. Drawing on research with people living with long-term conditions, such as diabetes, arthritis, and muscular dystrophy, I show how participant-recorded footage can illuminate seemingly mundane and ordinary, but also powerfully intimate and otherwise invisible, aspects of daily life. Featuring fragments of video diaries made by Imogen, Meghan, and Anwen, the chapter explores how their footage evokes embodied recognition through movements, textures, sounds, and aromas, and how it brings to attention emotions, memories, and other intangibles. I also experiment with writing video and share something of the experience of working with this medium and the labour of research which, in itself, produces intimacy. As such, I suggest that video offers new repertoires of emotion and sensation and allows for the incorporation of more-than-textual and multi-sensual elements of everyday life, which often elude our accounts.

Paul Simpson's 'Atmospheres of Arrival/Departure and Multi-Angle Video Recording: Reflections from St Pancras and Gare du Nord' emerges from the midst of a research project concerned with the intertwining of mobility, security, atmosphere, and ambiance. Inspired by the Panopticon, a circular architectural design for the penitentiary that forces its inhabitants into a state of perpetual self-monitoring, Simpson and his colleagues have employed multi-angle video recording at international train stations in London and Paris. 'Riffing' on the surveillant gaze and CCTV practices, they turned surveillance on itself in an attempt to apprehend the atmospheres that it is purportedly there to create and inadvertently brings about. By employing multiple video cameras to simultaneously film overlapping angles onto the same space, some maintaining a static view and others panning and zooming to mimic the actions of a CCTV camera operator, the project plays with views from on high and from in the midst, blurring the detached technological gaze with a more embodied form of vision. In his chapter, Simpson discusses the ephemeral and ethereal ambiances and atmospheres of arrival and departure that emerge, dissipate, and register differently in different bodies within the same spaces. In doing so, he shows how video draws attention to affective registers of feeling and highlights the partiality of our gaze.

In 'The Mobile Life of Screens: Digital Imaging on School Journeys in Helsinki', Kim Kullman introduces us to Anneli, Leif, Niilo, and Leila and their various encounters with squirrels, traffic crossings, and asphalt on journeys to and from school in Helsinki. Travelling with the children and discussing their images in a later interview either alone or together with friends, siblings or parents, Kullman explored the practices through which the children's daily mobilities were learned across different urban environments and modes of transport, from walking and cycling to bus, train, tram, and metro travel. In his chapter, he discusses the ways in which the children employed digital camcorders, cameras, and their screens not simply to film and photograph their school journeys, but also to expand their affective and sensory awareness of their urban environments. His work suggests that working through digital screens can help us think about our tools differently, unsettling distinctions between still and moving images and creating new engagements with the social world.

Merle Patchett recounts her video-ethnography of taxidermist Peter Summers at the National Museum Scotland in 'Witnessing Craft: Employing Video Ethnography to Attend to the More-Than-Human Craft Practices of Taxidermy'. Taking the position of 'camera-apprentice', she created an archive of video footage that enabled her to move between immersive and reflective positions and enquire into the craft techniques that it takes to separate a skin from a body and rearrange it in life-like form again. In her chapter, she presents three lessons in the crafts of taxidermy that Peter taught her. These lessons, which include interpreting the 'jizz' of the bird, teach us about the craft techniques and material assemblages of taxidermy practice. Witnessed through Patchett's embodied camerawork and developed through 'co-discovery' with Peter, these corporeal and affective 'exposures' show how video can be used to study the affective, sensory, and 'more-than-human' registers of craftwork.

In Katrina Brown and Esther Banks' 'Close Encounters: Using Mobile Video Ethnography to Understand Human-Animal Relations', a dog and its owner are out for a walk in the woods. Through a three-part mobile video ethnography, Brown and Banks explore '(ir)responsible' dogwalking practices in the Cairngorns National Park. Realising that handheld video would be fraught with difficulties in keeping up with and being involved in the fleeting moments, swift manoeuvres, and subliminal happenings of these intimate interbodily encounters, they enrolled minicams, worn by the walkers on their outings. As they note, minicam is 'already there, already rolling'. In this chapter they discuss each part of their process, from prior interview, to video outing, and post-outing video review. In doing so, they highlight the challenges of studying how people, dogs, and broader ecologies become entangled with each other, and the opportunities that video offers for developing deeper understandings of encounters between humans and other animals.

Katrina Jungnickel's 'Jumps, Stutters, Blurs and Other Failed Images: Using Time-Lapse Video in Cycling Research' introduces the use of time-lapse video to research multisensory cycling experiences. Time-lapse is an animation technique that stitches hundreds (and sometimes thousands) of still photographs together to create a sequential story via the illusion of moving image. It is conventionally used from a fixed point to record events over time, such as changing weather conditions or the construction of a building. By fixing a 'mobile lens' to the centre of her handlebars Jungnickel set time-lapse video in motion. In her chapter, she discusses videos from solo and group cycle rides undertaken as part of a mixed methods study of cycling cultures in Hull, Hackney, Bristol, and Cambridge. Focusing on the mess of blurred and distorted images from the videos, she illustrates how these 'failed' images unexpectedly provide vivid evidence of sensory experiences and the urban environment. In doing so, she presents time-lapse video as a way of 'being', 'seeing', and 'feeling there', and as a way of 'making there'.

Bradley Garrett and Harriet Hawkins' 'Creative Video Ethnographies: Video Methodologies of Urban Exploration' opens at night under the steel beams of the Forth Rail Bridge in Scotland. Based on Garrett's research on urban exploration, the practice of accessing and documenting spaces closed to public access, their chapter outlines a creative, critical account of video ethnographies. Together, Garrett and Hawkins develop thoughts on the creative possibilities and affective force of filmmaking, exploring the practical, aesthetic, philosophical, and political challenges of choosing equipment and the relations between technology, researcher, and subject. Unpicking editing as a complex and technical process, but also as an embodied and affective one, they highlight points of skilling and audiencing within the filmic process. In doing so, they argue for an explicit apprehension of the creative practices, forces, and objects of ethnographic video practices.

In 'Working With Sound in Video: Producing an Experimental Documentary About School Spaces' Michael Gallagher calls attention to the opportunities afforded by working closely with audio in video production. He reflects on the making of *Seven Primary School Spaces,* a short experimental documentary film that combined soundscape recordings and static video shots of seven empty spaces in a Scottish primary school. Images of the playground, entrance, classrooms, and hall enable close scrutiny of the physical and material aspects of the school, while soundscape recordings evoke the school's social space, a much more dynamic and noisy set of flows that ranges from bells ringing to gentle babbling and wildly out of tune recorder playing. As Gallagher notes, the disjuncture between image and audio amplifies video's more-than-representational excess, bringing to life the sensory vibrancy of the school environment. His chapter suggests intriguing possibilities for working between sound and image, and for using video to unsettle, rework, and generate new associations.

Britt Hatzius and Nina Wakeford address the challenge of creating an installation inside Intel Research offices in Portland in '"Everything Is Going On at the Same Time": The Place of Video in Social Research Installations'. Taking installation art, with its emphasis on performance, process, sensation, and experience as a source of inspiration, Hatzius and Wakeford conducted a series of visual experiments with cycle couriers and commuters in London. While studying mobile actors in such immersive environments proved to be anything but straightforward, their experiments with video caught something of the speed and risk-taking involved in navigating the infrastructure of London streets, which are often inhospitable to cyclists. Instead of showing the raw footage to Intel, they used their material to create interventions, for example two life-size prints of a London bus hung very close to each other to echo a cyclist's experience of squeezing through traffic. Their chapter points to the potential of using video to create open and generative engagements.

In 'Life Off Grid: Considerations for a Multi-Sited, Public Ethnographic Film', Jonathan Taggart and Phillip Vannini introduce us to the perils of travelling by air in a Hawker-Siddeley 748. Taggart is a trained photographer and filmmaker, Vannini a sociologist and cultural geographer. Together, they have spent two years conducting visual ethnographic fieldwork with 'off-gridders' in remote locations across Canada. The expression 'off-grid' refers to a variety of strategies through which individual households and communities disconnect from the dominant technological infrastructures that provide energy, water, and communication flows. Through their chapter, we travel with the authors to Newfoundland, where Phillip learns how to mill logs into lumber, and to Nunavut, where freezing wind and sub-zero temperatures play havoc with Jonathan's camera equipment. To close the chapters in this volume, they present their argument for a public visual ethnography—an interdisciplinary approach with multiple audiences and outputs, as embodied by their film *Life Off Grid*.

The volume comes to rest with Phillip Vannini's afterword, 'Video Methods Beyond Representation: Experimenting With Multi-Modal, Sensuous, Affective Intensities in the 21st Century'. Here, he traces the themes that flow through this book and pulls them into a tangle of trajectories, connections, and mutations. As he writes, "Video methods are moving at full speed beyond representation, finally beginning to exploit their potential to evoke, communicate multi-modally in a sensuous way, and to affect viewers in meaningful, arts-inspired ways". Yet, while video methods are certainly not what they used to be, there are, as Vannini highlights, lingering limits and still-untapped possibilities.

REFERENCES

Back, L. 2010. Broken devices and new opportunities: re-imagining the tools of qualitative research. NCRM Working Paper. Available from http://eprints.ncrm. ac.uk/1579/1/0810_broken_devices_Back.pdf

Back, L. 2013. Live sociology: social research and its futures. In Back, L. and Puwar, N. (eds.) *Live Methods*. Oxford: Wiley-Blackwell.

Back, L. and Puwar, N. 2013. A manifesto for live methods: provocations and capacities. In Back, L. and Puwar, N. (eds.) *Live Methods*. Oxford: Wiley-Blackwell.

Knowles, C. and Sweetman, P., (eds.) 2004. *Picturing the Social Landscape: Visual Methods and the Sociological Imagination*. London: Routledge.

Laurier, E. 2014. Noticing: talk, gestures, movement and objects in video analysis. In Lee, R., Castree N., Kitchen, R., Lawson, V., Paasi, A., Philo, C., Radcliffe, S. and Withers, C. (eds.) *The Sage Handbook of Human Geography*. London: Sage.

Law, J. 2004. *After Method: Mess in Social Science Research*. London: Routledge.

Lorimer, H. 2005. Cultural geography: the busyness of being 'more-than-representational'. *Progress in Human Geography*, 29(1): 83–94.

Lury, C. and Wakeford, N., (eds.) 2012. *Inventive Methods: The Happening of the Social*. London: Routledge.

Pink, S., (ed.) 2012. *Advances in Visual Methodology*. London: Sage.

Prosser, J., (ed.) 1998. *Image-based Research: A Sourcebook for Qualitative Researchers*. London: RoutledgeFalmer.

Stewart, K. 2007. *Ordinary Affects*. Durham: Duke University Press.

Thrift, N. 2008. *Non-Representational Theory: Space, Politics, Affect*. Abingdon: Routledge.

Thrift, N. and Dewsbury, JD. 2000. Dead geographies—and how to make them live. *Environment and Planning D: Society and Space*, 18: 411–432.

Vannini, P., Waskul, D., and Gottschalk, S. 2013. *The Senses in Self, Society, and Culture: A Sociology of the Senses*. New York: Routledge.

Whatmore, S. 2006. Materialist returns: practising cultural geography in and for a more-than-human world. *Cultural Geographies*, 13(4): 600–609.

1 Intimate Encounters
Making Video Diaries about Embodied Everyday Life

Charlotte Bates

I first encountered the video diary at a workshop that took place in Manchester. It was the second of five daylong workshops in the *Live Sociology* series, an Economic and Social Research Council Researcher Development Initiative organised by Les Back and Celia Lury at Goldsmiths, University of London. The workshop series explored the opportunities that new media offers for how ethnographic social research is undertaken and shared. The second workshop, entitled *Redesigning the Analyser,* focused on ways of developing dialogue with research participants. That day, Jennifer Patashnick gave a presentation on Video Intervention/Prevention Assessment (VIA), a project based at the Center on Media and Child Health, Children's Hospital Boston. The VIA project is unique. It gives video cameras to young people with chronic medical conditions, and asks them to share the stories of their lives in the form of video diaries. Each VIA participant is loaned a lightweight handheld video camcorder and asked to "teach your doctor about your life and your condition". Seeking honest portrayals rather than professional production values, a field coordinator instructs participants how to operate the camcorders, but does not teach film-making technique or visual style. The video footage is then painstakingly logged and analysed by a multi-disciplinary team, before being made accessible to clinicians[1] (see Rich et al. 2000). As Back (2006) notes:

> What is so striking in the narratives is the way they combine rich insight into unspectacular details of living with serious illness with a yearning to communicate with their audience. There is an intense sense that the participants feel that 'I need you to know this'. Participants grab the camera in the middle of a traumatic attack of breathlessness or a bloody coughing episode and record it.

The atmosphere in the small, dark seminar room where Jen showed us the VIA video diaries was palpable. Both raw and moving, the video footage demanded to be witnessed but was uncomfortable to watch. Some in the audience averted their eyes as drops of bright red blood fell from a young man's mouth and pooled into the palm of his hand, which he held out to the camera.[2] Twenty-five-year-old Jay has cystic fibrosis, and bloody cough-ing episodes like this one are part of his daily life. His testimony remained with me long after his video diary had ended. Several months later I began my own PhD fieldwork, and over the following year I worked with thirteen people who have long-term conditions, talking with them about their every-day lives and illness experiences and asking them to make their own video diaries. Inspired by the *Live Sociology* workshops and the VIA project, I hoped that these video diaries would become a version of what Back (2007) describes as sociological listening, a way to "record 'life passed in living' and to listen to complex experiences with humility and ethical care".

This chapter is presented in two parts. In the first part, I outline the pro-cess of making video diaries, using scenarios from my fieldwork to highlight the practical and methodological issues that working with video entails. As Carol Smart notes, "it is this interface between the everyday lives of ordinary people and the sociological craft of story telling where so many practical, ethical and theoretical problems arise" (Smart 2009, 3). I discuss recruitment, equipment and ethics, and transcribing, editing, and analysing footage. I also discuss how I attempted to turn participant-recorded foot-age into edited films for presentation. As such, I touch on each stage of the research process, from data gathering to analysis and dissemination. In the second part, I highlight three examples from the video diaries made by Imo-gen, Meghan, and Anwen, showing how the video camera can be used to evoke embodied recognition through movements, textures, sounds, and aro-mas, and revealing how such footage can illuminate seemingly mundane and ordinary, but also powerfully intimate and otherwise invisible, aspects of daily life. Here, I explore the possibilities of video for conveying sociological ideas and responding to "a need to incorporate a wide range of sensibilities into the creation of feminist/sociological accounts of everyday lives. These include accounting for emotions, memories, intersubjective meanings, and other intangibles" (Smart 2009, 1). In the study, video cameras were pointed at heaving asthmatic lungs and aching arthritic shoulders, and they were taken on walks and to the gym, carried on bicycles and held while running. They were also confided in at night, pointed at loved-ones, and taken for walks down memory lane. From action shots to quiet reflections, the range of footage draws attention to the more-than-textual and multi-sensual ele-ments of video as a research method.

MAKING VIDEO DIARIES

Over the year of my fieldwork I gradually recruited participants through online adverts, email lists, and personal contacts. Participation in the study was open to anyone living in London, aged between eighteen and fifty with a long-term physical or mental health condition. These parameters were set to avoid logistical issues involved in working outside of the city and to exclude issues specific to childhood and aging. I met with everyone who contacted me, eventually stopping when I felt that the sample consisted of an adequate gender mix (five men and eight women), some social class diversity, people at various life stages, and a range of conditions (asthma, bipolar disorder, chronic pain, depression, type 1 diabetes, epilepsy, joint hypermobility syndrome, muscular dystrophy, and rheumatoid arthritis).

After an initial meeting to discuss what participation in the study would involve, I interviewed participants and, as part of the interview, asked them to complete hand-drawn questionnaires. Each participant then had the choice of making a video diary and/or keeping a journal. We later met again so that I could collect the video camera and journal and discuss any issues and concerns, including how I intended to use the material that I had been given. After scanning the pages of the journals and copying the video footage that had been recorded I returned the original journals and DVDs of the unedited video footage to the participants by post. Nine of the 13 participants chose to make a video diary which they recorded with one of two video cameras, a Sony HDR-SR10E and a Sony HDR-TG7VE, which I had bought for the study with funding from the University of London Central Research Fund. Both video cameras were capable of recording high-quality footage to memory cards, and were small and easy to use. The HDR-SR10E is a typical handycam, while the HDR-TG7VE is an ultra-compact vertical camcorder, which I hoped would be easier for participants to use while performing other activities, as it is smaller and lighter to hold. One problem that I had not anticipated was that it was difficult to rest the HDR-TG7VE on a surface or put it down and continue recording, making hands-free filming impossible. I also bought a lightweight tripod, which one of the participants, who had difficulty moving around with the camera in hand, chose to use. My instructions were informal—I gave the participants basic video camera operating instructions and simply asked them to use the video camera to show and tell about their body and their condition:

> You will have one week with the handycam in which to make a video. It is up to you whether you put yourself in the frame, but try to think about both the visual and audio components and how you can show and tell about your body and your condition.
>
> (Instruction sheet)

Most of the participants recorded their video diaries over longer periods of time than a week, although in many instances filming only took place on a few days, with approximately 10 hours of video footage produced in total. Implicit in the instruction sheet was an awareness of the potential for participants to reveal or conceal themselves through the camera, something that we carefully discussed both before filming and after. The visible and audible presence of the participants on screen strongly conflicts with the presumption that good ethical practice requires automatic anonymity for participants (for example, see the British Sociological Association's Statement of Ethical Practice[3]). But as Shamser Sinha and Les Back argue, this default position "is an anxious symptom of *ethical hypochondria,* which limits the opportunities to rethink authorship and innovate new formats for research" (2014, 484). Instead of automatically ensuring anonymity and concealing all data that might have revealed the participants' identities, from on-camera shots to voice recordings and filming locations, I decided to work with what Paul Sweetman has described as an ethics of recognition (2009, 8). I found room for ethical manoeuvre in the Association of American Geographers Statement of Professional Ethics, which states: "informants should be asked whether they prefer anonymity or recognition, and the project should be implemented and its results should be presented in keeping with these individuals' preference".[4] By borrowing this definition I was able to adapt the video diary method as I worked with each participant, so that they controlled the degree to which they revealed their bodies and identities to the video camera. Some participants were comfortable on camera, others wanted to use their own identities but preferred not to film themselves directly, and one participant chose to take part using a pseudonym. In order to maintain her anonymity, Anna wrote notes to the video camera, which were then placed as subtitles on the screen. This allowed her to make a video diary without revealing her identity through the recognisable sound of her voice, and ensured her privacy without restricting her participation.

The participants also brought their own visual skills to the task of making a video diary, and found their own ways of working with the video camera and their own filmic language. They made different choices about what and how to film, and while cultural references helped them to style their video diaries, they did not appear to influence what was enacted for the video camera. The video diaries ranged from reality television to intimate personal diary, and from action shots to quiet reflections. For example, conducting a 'You are What You Eat' reality show-style shock tactic for herself, Imogen decided to record a tidy-up of her bedroom on video. She found 22 empty Lucozade energy drink bottles in her room and lined them up along the foot of her bed. The display quantified the presence of Lucozade in Imogen's body and her life and highlighted the significance of this seemingly ordinary drink. Xan used her video diary to discuss her fears in an intimate conversation with her boyfriend. Hidden behind a book, Xan's boyfriend used a camera phone to look back at the video camera while she asked him a series of uncompromisingly honest questions: "What do you think about my body? Do you think it is unusual? Do you think it is different? How do you feel about the fact that I'm barren?"

When filming was completed I transcribed the narratives from the video diaries and integrated them with interview and journal transcripts so that I could analyse the data thematically. By identifying themes across the different methods I was able to support my interpretation of the video diaries with other data and consider them in a broader context. I also wanted to attend to the seemingly mundane and ordinary details of embodied life that were recorded on video. These phenomena often escape talk- and text-based approaches (J. Lorimer 2010, 242), but were powerfully present in the video diaries. As Hayden Lorimer explains:

> At first, the phenomena in question may seem remarkable only by their apparent *in*significance. The focus falls on how life takes shape and gains expression in shared experiences, everyday routines, fleeting encounters, embodied movements, precognitive triggers, practical skills, affective intensities, enduring urges, unexceptional interactions and sensuous dispositions. Attention to these kinds of expression, it is contended, offers an escape from the established academic habit of striving to uncover meanings and values that apparently await our discovery, interpretation, judgement and ultimate representation. In short, so much ordinary action gives no advance notice of what it will become. Yet, it still makes critical differences to our experiences of space and place (Thrift, 2004).
>
> (H. Lorimer 2005, 84)

In order to re-incorporate these phenomena and the more-than-textual and multi-sensual (H. Lorimer 2005, 83) elements of the video diaries into my analysis, I rewatched the original footage, this time feeling for the less obvious sights and sounds, rather than looking for any underlying or hidden meaning. In what Back describes as a shift "from being concerned only with 'voice' to an attention to soundscape and sound image" (Back 2010, 17), I returned to the original footage to listen for the non-verbal noises that had been recorded. Acoustics have their own intimacy and they help us to see differently, working against dominant ways of looking and bringing the viewer into the experience (see Gallagher, this volume). By "turning up the background" (Back 2010, 25) I was able to pick out the bodily noises, for example breathing and footfall, that indicated the presence of bodies that were otherwise imperceptible on screen. Drawing on composer Murray Shafer's seminal book *Tuning the World* (1977), Back writes of this kind of listening as a way of taking the soundtrack of the social background seriously:

> The police siren, the children laughing in the street, the jet plane's moan overhead along with the crowing birdsong, the sounds of movement of rubber on tarmac, of internal combustion are invitations to develop a different kind of sociological imagination attentive to the rhythm and aesthetics of life.
>
> (Back 2010, 19)

As Back points out, paying attention to these sounds foregrounds the taken-for-granted aspects of everyday life and shows the potential of using sound sociologically, beyond simply recording human voices (Back 2010, 22). Along the same lines, I also 'turned up' the visual background of the video diaries. Watching them back, I began to notice things in the fragments of video—as Eric Laurier notes, "clips are usually called 'fragments' to remind the viewer that what they are looking at only appears self-contained" (Laurier 2014). Within the video diaries bodies were perceptible and imperceptible, visible and hidden. Not always shown in their entirety, the traces of bodies were present in other ways. Parts of bodies were shown to camera, shadows were trailed on pavements, and reflections were captured in windows and coffee pots. These visual traces meant that even when the participants' bodies were not directly filmed they remained sensed or felt, and by noticing them I developed a more subtle and nuanced account of embodied everyday life.

I also wanted to use the video diaries to present the study in a more experimental, experiential, and embodied way. To do this, I edited some of the video footage into a series of split-screen clips using Final Cut Express (see Figure 1.2 and Figure 1.3). The process of editing the footage helped me to become fully immersed in the video data and, as outlined above, develop a heightened attention to both the audio and the visual components of the video diaries (which can be edited as independent tracks in Final Cut). As I manipulated the video I drew attention to particular moments, zooming in on some elements, cutting others out, and laying sound down over footage in different places (see also Garrett and Hawkins, this volume). As Michael Guggenheim has argued, visual sociologists tend to view the manipulation of images negatively, as though any kind of interference might detract from the social scientific value of the material. With Guggenheim, I would suggest, "there is no representation without manipulation" (Guggenheim forthcoming). In fact, my manipulation of the video resonated with the ways in which I similarly edited and conceptually framed textual material from the interview, journal, and video transcripts. As such, the work of editing and sequencing video footage can be seen as paralleling the more standard academic task of selecting and framing quotes from discursive sources when writing up research. Textual and visual data present similar difficulties, and "it is as easy to select a particular quotation that supports the point one is making as it is to manipulate the framing, lighting or tone of a photograph to present the desired effect" (Knowles and Sweetman 2004, 13).

The end result of this editing process was an hour-long film composed of 16 short clips framed through a double or triptych split-screen. Some clips show two or three scenes from one video diary playing simultaneously, others show a single scene split using the same format, but all have a single audio track. I have shown these clips in academic presentations—as Jamie Lorimer notes, videos "provide lively materials for subsequent presentation and evocation" (J. Lorimer 2010, 251)—and have also uploaded two to Vimeo, a community for storing and distributing video content online, to accompany a printed article (Bates 2013).[5] At the same time, I have been cautious not to let the edited video diaries go public in their entirety or without written companionship. While video offers untapped possibilities for reaching a much wider audience (see Vannini, this volume) the video diary footage was not made for this purpose, and just as interview transcripts should not be left to 'speak for themselves' (Back 2007), the video diaries need to be situated in sociological analysis and interpretation.

The unsettled and unsettling question once a study has ended is how to translate video into academic text, or how to write video without it wilting and dying on the page. As Smart points out, "many discussions of developing new, sensitive or innovative methodologies focus on the practices of collecting data and/or the problems of how to analyse the data. But there is a third phase which needs consideration and that is how then to present the worlds and experiences that have been witnessed" (Smart 2009, 9). The next part of this chapter highlights three fragments from the video diaries, using video stills, thick descriptions, and verbatim quotations. These fragments are both a way of illustrating the video footage in print and an experiment in writing video (see also Jungnickel, this volume). My approach to this challenge focuses on seeking ways in which writing and video might work together, so that they inform, inspire, and enliven each other.

INTIMATE ENCOUNTERS

Elsewhere, I have written about the possibilities that video offers for the sociology of the body, a field in which the issue of methodology is under-explored. As Phillip Vannini writes in the afterword to this volume, "the evocation of experiences and practices of the human body—in all their non-representational excesses—is precisely where traditional methods, with their excessive emphasis on the discursive or the causative, have left much to be desired". I suggested that the video camera is beautifully sensate and can be used to record a wide range of bodily sensations, activities, and practices, but also pointed out that while video is a useful tool for recording the sensual and affective qualities of bodily experience, these recordings can sometimes be at odds with the embodied sensation they seek to evoke (Bates 2013, 31). The end result is a dissonance between experience and playback, suggesting that video is much more than a simple or straightforward recording device. The footage documents but it also confounds, it has a life of its own and a relationship with its viewers—as W.J.T. Mitchell writes, images exert their own power over the living (Mitchell 2005). Here, my focus is less on the materiality of embodiment and more on the emotions, memories, and other intangibles that are lived through the body and which saturate the video diaries. In the study, video cameras were pointed at heaving asthmatic lungs and aching arthritic shoulders, and they were taken on walks and to the gym, carried on bicycles and held while running. But they were also confided in at night, pointed at loved-ones, and taken for walks down memory lane. From action shots to quiet reflections, the range of footage draws attention to the potential of video to incorporate a wide range of sensibilities into the creation of sociological accounts of everyday lives.

The following pages lay bare three fragments from the video diaries made by Imogen, Meghan, and Anwen, showing how the video camera can be used to evoke embodied recognition through movements, textures, sounds, and aromas, and exploring how such footage can illuminate seemingly mundane and ordinary, but also powerfully intimate and otherwise invisible, aspects of daily life. At night, in rituals of care, and in memories and reflections, these fragments offer a series of intimate encounters with the sensuous, the tangible, and the intangible 'sensation of living'. In essence, they pursue the precarious relationship between the tangible and the intangible, or what Jennifer Mason terms the *in/tangible,* highlighting "a seam in the sensation of living that is both familiar and extraordinary" (Mason 2011, 14). Along similar lines, John Law has noted, "much of the world is vague, diffuse or unspecific, slippery, emotional, ephemeral, elusive or indistinct" (Law 2004, 2). Video is one way of coming to know these elusive, sensory, and emotional aspects of social life.

The fragments, composed using video stills, thick descriptions, and verbatim quotations, are also an attempt to share something of the experience of working with video and the labour of research which, in itself, produces intimacy (Fraser and Puwar 2008). As Mason writes, "it is striking to what extent one gets 'raw' and 'deep', and sometimes quite uncomfortable, insights" by presenting audio and visual data alongside text (one has only to remember the reactions of the audience to Jay's bloody coughing episode in the VIA video diaries). She continues, "as a researcher one suddenly feels almost too close to the living and breathing experience of one's respondents, as though an unspoken and unseen boundary has inadvertently been crossed" (Mason 2011, 15). Presenting this 'raw' data might well be construed as such a boundary crossing, as sensational and unnecessarily fleshed out. But the sensory and emotional intimacies afforded by the video diaries, as research material, are precisely what I want to highlight. Closeness seeps through the video diaries with affective intensity, and needs foregrounding in debates about methods and methodology.

Each composition is ordered in the same way, a still, followed by a description, ending with a quotation—the voice audio transcription that originally accompanied the video clip which the still is taken from. The descriptions are intended to briefly introduce the participant and put the still in motion, foregrounding the details that are otherwise lost from the voice audio transcripts. These layered compositions are a form of portraiture (Miller 2008), an account of life as it unfolds on screen, and a way of evoking intimacy and writing video.

* * *

Imogen is 25 and has type 1 diabetes. The condition is difficult to manage and her nights are often disturbed. In order to fend off a night-time hypo— a hypoglycaemic episode—she can drink some Lucozade or eat a crumpet

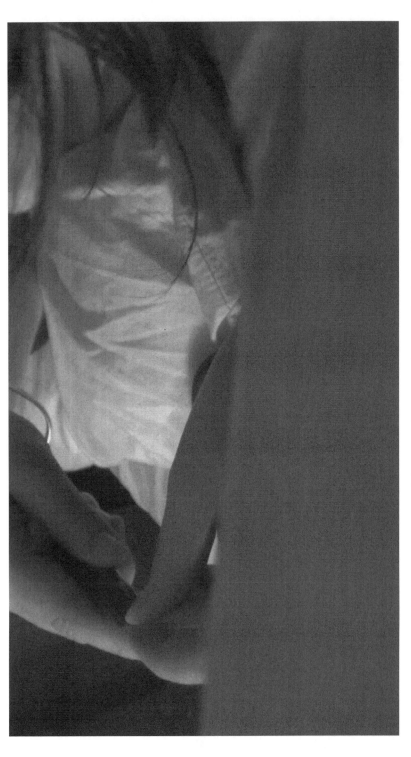

Figure 1.1 "I don't really check in the middle of the night when I hypo, because why else would I wake up in the middle of the night, other than because my sugar level has dropped. Let's find out." (Imogen, Video Diary)

before going to bed, but these measures do not always prevent her blood glucose level from dropping while she is sleeping, triggering a hypo which will then wake her up. The sensation starts to come through in a dream, a faint, shaky, sluggish feeling that muddles her thoughts and later makes her stumble over her words. One of these interrupted nights was recorded on video. In the video, Imogen describes the sensation of being woken by a hypo, checks her blood glucose level, and tries to work out the chain of events that have led to this moment. A bedside light dimly lights the room and shines on Imogen, who is lying in bed, eyes half open, her voice soft and slightly quivering. Her head is resting on a white pillow and her arm is outstretched, holding the camera out in front of her so that she can speak to it. At this moment I am looking at her, but it also feels like she is looking at me, showing me, bringing me into her night through the camera. She decides to check her blood glucose level, not because she needs to check it but because she wants to show me the evidence, the reason why her night has been ruptured. The sheets rustle as she moves around in bed, and the camera swings round with her body before coming to rest on the bed sheets, leaving her hands free to perform the test. A quick click to the tip of her middle finger, which she then holds to the blood glucose monitor, it reads 3.4 (under the normal low of 4). Both Imogen and the camera swing round again so that she can lie down, tired, frustrated, and confused. The minutes pass as Imogen tries to figure out the cause of this drop, and as she works through the possibilities her voice becomes steadier, clearer, and brighter. The hypo is fading, leaving her hungry and needing the loo, but instead of climbing out of bed she smiles, turns the light and the camera off, and drifts back to sleep. Imogen's narrative runs over this sequence:

> I don't know what time it is, I've just woken up in the middle of the night, a few minutes ago. My top lip tingles, and I'm clearly hypoing but I don't know what my sugar level is, it was 9.8 when I went to bed, which is fine. I've hypoed a lot lately. Anyway, I just drunk what was by my bedside without even thinking, which was half a bottle of lemon Lucozade. So I'm just waiting for it to come up. My top lip still feels a bit dead, but it definitely feels like it's getting there. I feel kind of like tingly around my head, around my fingers, which is always a sign. I don't even know what my level is, I probably should check it. In fact, I'll film it and check it. I don't really check in the middle of the night when I hypo, because why else would I wake up in the middle of the night, other than because my sugar level has dropped. Let's find out. This is after drinking the Lucozade, yes, its 3.4. This happened last night . . . It must be my background insulin, because, what's the time? The time is 1:30am. Is that all? I wish it was later. I went to bed this evening because I felt really tired after hypoing last night. After hypoing last night, I felt really tired the next day, because I'd gone to bed late and then hypoed, and had to get up at like 6:45am . . . This is a horribly rambled message, isn't it. I thought I should take you through how

Figure 1.2 "There's something about the sound of a coffee maker, it just makes you feel like your day is off to a really good start!" (Meghan, Video Diary)

my brain works, when I'm hypoing in the middle of the night. Anyway, funnily enough, I can feel my top lip has stopped tingling, just about, and there isn't the general feeling of tinnitus which happens when I hypo, at night anyway, that's disappeared, at 1:34am, that's how I'm feeling. The problem is I'm really hungry, it's probably just my body going feed me, eat sugar, but if I do that, I mean I've already had enough sugar now to raise my sugar level to around 10 tomorrow morning, so I can't really eat anything . . . Anyway, I'm going to go back to sleep, night night.

(Imogen, Video Diary)

* * *

Meghan is 32 and has rheumatoid arthritis. One of the ways that she manages her condition is through her diet. Foods she should avoid, or at least not overindulge in, include: caffeine, sugar, alcohol, red meat, dairy, citrus fruits, vegetables in the nightshade family, and saturated fat. The consequences of consuming these foods are manifested in swollen and sensitive joints, so that simple pleasures have become indulgences that have an acutely felt price. Yet through her love of food, Meghan has made up for the instances when she feels deprived by the foods she should not eat by creating food rituals that give her pleasure. One of these rituals transforms coffee, which strictly speaking she should not drink, into a special act of care. Recorded on video, the sounds of coffee brewing—the electric buzz of the machine, the gurgling water, and the drip of the coffee pot slowly filling up—evoke the smell of freshly brewed coffee filling the room and bring the intimacy of the ritual to the screen. The camera is fixed on the coffee maker with its orange on light glowing warmly, and as the minutes pass the black coffee froths and rises inside the glass jug while an empty mug waits expectantly beside it. With Meghan, I am patiently waiting for the coffee to finish brewing, and, as I wait, I begin to understand the significance of this seemingly ordinary start to the day, which connects Meghan to childhood memories, and through the small acts of others makes her feel cared for:

> I love coffee; I love its flavour, its warmth, it's very comforting to me. There's something about the sound of a coffee maker, it just makes you feel like your day is off to a really good start! When I do research about diet and arthritis, coffee is one thing that you're really supposed to avoid. But I feel so deprived without a cup a day, and sometimes I have two. Sometimes I have thought that making coffee is a meaningless ritual, and that I could just substitute it with something else. Instead of turning on the coffee maker I could make a cup of tea. But tea doesn't have the same texture to me, or the taste. The funny thing is, I don't know how to work this coffee machine, and my housemate sets it up the night before. And maybe that's a bit of what it's about, somebody looking after me in a way. My grandmother always had a coffee pot set to

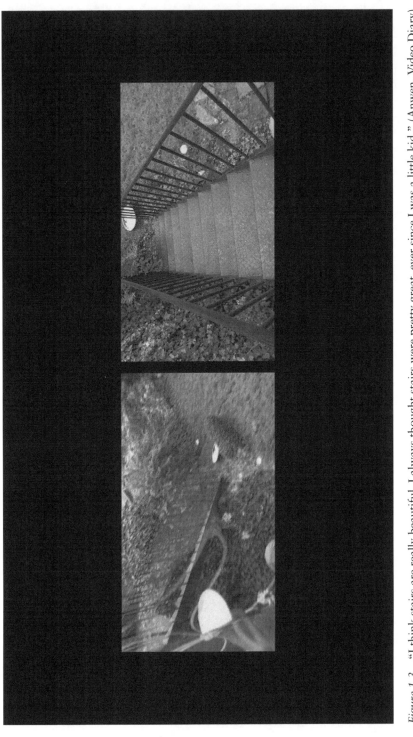

Figure 1.3 "I think stairs are really beautiful. I always thought stairs were pretty great, ever since I was a little kid." (Anwen, Video Diary)

automatic; she didn't even have to hit the switch, it was just ready when she woke up. Making a cup of coffee this way takes so much longer than a cup of tea, you really have to be patient.

(Meghan, Video Diary)

* * *

Anwen is 31 and has a rare form of muscular dystrophy that affects the muscles in her arms and legs. It is a condition with no medication or treatment, and Anwen does not know what the future holds. For now, she is able to walk independently with the help of a cane, but her mobility is limited and she risks falling. Crossing the road, popping to the local shops, and negotiating the post that lies scattered on the floor of the communal hall in her building all require thought and care. A flight of stairs takes on new significance when it presents itself as an obstacle, and in the opening shot of her video the camera peers down a steep metal staircase, issuing a sense of vertigo. The stairs lead down to a small concrete landing and into the back garden of Anwen's flat, which is laid to lawn. A sense of stillness permeates the screen, then the camera suddenly zooms across the garden to track a city fox trotting by, getting lost for a moment in the greenery then finding focus again on a garden table and chairs which lie fallen on the grass, before returning to rest on the staircase. Anwen is talking, but the noise of a helicopter passing by above interrupts and forces her to pause for a moment. The drone seems to fill the screen as we both wait. She swings the camera left to the garden next door, taking in a sideways shot of a staircase like her own. Stairs pose a problem for Anwen, and she rarely risks the descent into the garden:

> Stairs are a big problem, there are stairs everywhere you go, that's how most people manage buildings. But they're a real part of me negotiating whether I can go places. Sometimes I can manage stairs well enough on my own, I've been feeling pretty fit lately. I'd probably make more of an effort with these stairs if it wasn't so bloody cold, and in any case there's this bit down the bottom, down there you can see there's a bit of a landing and there's nothing for me to hold onto to get onto the grass, and even with my stick it's a bit tricky to get down into the yard . . . This is also the way that I have to think about how I get about every day, how I'm going to get there, get inside, get myself out, especially on my own. If Simon is with me and we're travelling or whatever, there's always the unexpected flights of stairs and hills and things that are hard to manage, and we hire cars or, well, we've hired a car before, and he carries me up the stairs, which is lovely, and we manage that way. But obviously it can get a bit tricky . . . I think stairs are really beautiful. I always thought stairs were pretty great, ever since I was a little kid. I grew up in an area where it was pretty flat, and we never had stairs in our houses when I

was a kid, except for the house when we lived in the Northern Territory, all the houses there were on stilts, for cyclone reasons. But most of the houses in Perth, Western Australia, all the other houses I lived in, they didn't have stairs. So when I was tiny I used to get really excited by stairs. And of course even now I see places that have got a spiral staircase in them, and I snap out of my usual attitude, which is oh fuck, a set of stairs, and think how beautiful they are, how nice they are.

(Anwen, Video Diary)

* * *

ENDINGS AND BEGINNINGS

The confusion of an interrupted night, the morning sounds of coffee brewing, a moment of afternoon reverie, all evoke the intimacy that saturates life as it is lived throughout the day. This intimacy is embodied and affective, material and ephemeral, tangible and intangible. Tangled up in everyday movements, textures, sounds, and aromas, such more-than-textual and multi-sensual moments can be difficult to know through conventional methods of inquiry. As an audiovisual medium that resonates with multiple registers of feeling, video is an ideal method for illuminating the seemingly mundane and ordinary, but also powerfully intimate and otherwise invisible, aspects of daily life, and evoking "sensory and corporeal worlds" (Mason and Davies 2009, 590) on the screen and in print.

In coming to know these details through the video camera, I have been taken into personal and otherwise inaccessible moments of the participants' lives, and in writing about them I have shared them with a much wider audience. But in sending the camera into the lives of others, my intention has not been to stalk anyone with "360 degree enquiry" (Mason 2011, 16). It would be simplistic to think that intimate data is necessarily intrusive. Instead, with Mason, I am arguing for "gentle, inquisitive and politically astute knowledge practices that seek insight and appreciation rather than capture and singular truth" (Mason 2011, 17).

The beauty of video is that it shows us things that are elusive without trying to hold them still. It revels in the fleeting and affective, offering a mode of evocation that does not immobilise or flatten that which it seeks to know. As Jennifer Mason and Katherine Davies write, "Too often social science research and knowledge is oddly abstracted and distanced from the sensory, embodied and lived conditions of existence that it seeks to explain" (Mason and Davies 2009, 600). Through live footage and thick evocative descriptions, video offers the opportunity to overcome a "conservative, categorical politics of identity and textual meaning" by "allowing in much more of the excessive and transient aspects of living" (H. Lorimer 2005, 83), and to extend the "range, texture and quality of what passes as academic representational practice and writing" (Back 2013, 28). It suggests new repertoires of emotion and sensation, pointing the way towards cultivating a version of what Paul Stoller has called a sensuous scholarship (Stoller 1997) for the 21st century.

ACKNOWLEDGEMENTS

I would like to extend my heartfelt thanks to Anwen, Imogen, and Meghan whose video diaries have featured in this chapter. Thanks to each of you for your time, candidness, and trust.

NOTES

1. This information was taken from: http://www.cmch.tv/via/ourwork/datacollection.asp
2. This clip from Jay's video diary can be watched online at: http://www.cmch.tv/via/video/pop.asp?video = jb_coughs_up_.mov
3. The British Sociological Association statement of ethical practice is available online at: http://www.britsoc.co.uk/about/equality/statement-of-ethical-practice.aspx
4. The American Association of Geographers statement of professional ethics is available online at: http://www.aag.org/cs/about_aag/governance/statement_of_professional_ethics
5. The two video clips that accompany my article (Bates 2013) can be watched online at: http://vimeo.com/videodiaries/videos

REFERENCES

Back, L. 2007. *The Art of Listening*. Oxford: Berg.
Back, L. 2010. Broken devices and new opportunities: Re-imagining the tools of qualitative research. NCRM Working Paper. Available from http://eprints.ncrm.ac.uk/1579/1/0810_broken_devices_Back.pdf
Back, L. 2013. Live sociology: social research and its futures. In Back, L. and N. Puwar (eds.) *Live Methods*. Oxford: Wiley-Blackwell.
Bates, C. 2013. Video diaries: audio-visual research methods and the elusive body. *Visual Studies*, 28(1): 29–37.
Fraser, M. and Puwar, N. 2008. Introduction: intimacy in research. *History of the Human Sciences*, 21(4): 1–16.
Guggenheim, M. Forthcoming. The media of sociology: tight or loose translations? *British Journal of Sociology*.
Knowles, C. and Sweetman, P. (Eds.) 2004. *Picturing the Social Landscape: Visual Methods and the Sociological Imagination*. London: Routledge.
Laurier, E. 2014. Noticing: talk, gestures, movement and objects in video analysis. In Lee, R., Castree N., Kitchen, R., Lawson, V., Paasi, A., Philo, C., Radcliffe, S. and Withers, C. (eds.) *The Sage Handbook of Human Geography*. London: Sage.
Law, J. 2004. *After method: mess in social science research*. London: Routledge.
Lorimer, H. 2005. Cultural geography: the busyness of being 'more-than-representational'. *Progress in Human Geography*, 29(1): 83–94.

Lorimer, J. 2010. Moving image methodologies for more-than-human geographies. *Cultural Geographies,* 17(2): 237–258.

Mason, J. 2011. Knowing the in/tangible. Realites Working Paper 17. Available from http://www.socialsciences.manchester.ac.uk/morgancentre/realities/wps/17–2011-11-realities-intangibles.pdf

Mason, J., and Davies, K. 2009. Coming to our senses? A critical approach to sensory methodology. *Qualitative Research,* 9(5): 587–603.

Miller, D. 2008. *The Comfort of Things.* Cambridge: Polity Press.

Mitchell, W. 2005. What Do Pictures Want? The Lives and Loves of Images. Chicago: University of Chicago Press.

Rich, M., Lamola, S., Gordan, J. and Chalfen, R. 2000. Video intervention/prevention assessment: A patient-centred methodology for understanding the adolescent illness experience. *Journal of Adolescent Health,* 27: 155–65.

Sinha, S. and Back, L. 2014. Making methods sociable: dialogue, ethics and authorship in qualitative research. *Qualitative Research,* 14(4): 473–487.

Smart, C. 2009. Shifting horizons: Reflections on qualitative methods. *Feminist Theory,* 10(3): 1–14.

Stoller, P. 1997. *Sensuous Scholarship.* Philadelphia: University of Pennsylvania Press.

Sweetman, P. 2009. Just anybody? Images, ethics and recognition. In Leino, R. (ed.) *Just Anybody.* Winchester: The Winchester Gallery/Winchester School of Art.

2 Atmospheres of Arrival/ Departure and Multi-Angle Video Recording
Reflections from St Pancras and Gare du Nord

Paul Simpson

INTRODUCTION

This chapter emerges from the midst of a research project concerned with the intertwining of mobility, security, and affective atmosphere and ambiances. This research deployed what we [1] have come to call 'multi-angle video recording' as one means of considering the experiences of arrival into and the departure from two mobile spaces connected by the international rail link between the UK and France: St Pancras, London and Gare du Nord, Paris. Multi-angle video recording refers to a practice whereby multiple handheld and tripod-mounted digital video cameras were set up to simultaneously film overlapping angles onto the same space. These videos were combined into a montage of camera angles on a single screen. This provided multiple points of view, something akin to a 'panoptic' form of vision, onto these spaces and the social interactions that occurred within them. By deliberately riffing on CCTV surveillance practices, picking up their classic motifs but also playfully reorienting them to produce a more embodied form of vision, this approach deliberately blurred the detached technological gaze often associated with video-based practices of observation. Instead, mixing camera angles allowed for a view from the ground and from above; from in the midst of bodies and from multiple points in between.

This research in St Pancras and Gare du Nord illustrates the utility of multi-angle video recording and presentation techniques along two intersecting lines. It shows how they presented one means of approaching (though not necessarily 'capturing') the ephemeral and ethereal ambiances and atmospheres of arrival and departure that emerge and dissipate in and out of such mobile spaces in the interactions of bodies, technologies, materialities, and movements (see Adey et al. 2013). Furthermore, in combining these multiple camera angles into a single matrix, they raise questions about the orientation and perception of the situated researcher/observer, flagging the partial and fragmented nature of these positions/perspectives and so the role the research plays in constructing the field itself (Dewsbury 2010).

In reflecting on this, the chapter unfolds as follows. First, the chapter contextualises the research project by reviewing recent work on ambiances and affective atmospheres. Second, the chapter provides details on what the multi-angle filming actually entailed, the technical aspects of undertaking this, and reflects on the practical and ethical challenges faced in using this filming technique. Third, the chapter turns to the video output and reflects on the ways this montaged video material, and the research process itself, helped the researchers become attuned to the ambiances and atmospheres of arrival and departure present in the two stations. Finally, the chapter concludes by summarising the contribution this technique can make to attempts to attend to affective experiences and the ambiances and atmospheres they find articulation within.

CONTEXTUALISING AMBIANCES, ATMOSPHERES, AND SECURITY

The use of multi-angle video recording discussed in this chapter formed one part of a larger ethnography-based collaborative research project between geographers, urbanists, and architects from the UK and France. This collaboration was motivated by a desire to explore the intersections between recent Francophone research on ambience and Anglophone research on affective atmospheres, and specifically what combining these traditions might offer to understandings of contemporary surveillance and security practices. While holding much in common, these two bodies of work have, until very recently, developed largely independently of one another. It is not possible here to exhaustively outline them. However, there are a number of key commonalities and contrasts between these two literatures that are important to draw out given their influence on how we approached our research.

First, in working in the wake of the corporeal turn in the social sciences, atmosphere- and ambiance-based research are both concerned with the relationships between bodies and the environments they inhabit. As such, talking of atmospheres, Bissell (2010, 272) argues that such atmospheres "form part of the ubiquitous backdrop of everyday life" that forcefully affects the ways in which individuals and collectives inhabit space as embodied beings. Further, Edensor (2012, 1114) contends that "all atmospheres entangle affect, emotion, and sensation" and so highlights the interconnections that exist between the sensory experiences of bodies and the social situations they move through. Similarly, in talking of ambiances, Augoyard (2007) suggests that ambiances form a sort of climactic mood that surrounds bodies and, in so doing, qualifies their social milieu. We do not experience these kinds of settings in a detached, objective way, but as having certain qualities that impact upon our bodies. The common metaphor that is used within this literature is: who hasn't walked into a room and *felt* the atmosphere/ambiance therein (Brennan 2004).

Second, sensory perception plays a key role for much of the work on both ambiances and atmospheres. We apprehend ambiances and atmospheres through our bodies in a multisensory way. For example, Anderson (2009, 79) notes that affective atmospheres, while holding an ambiguous position regarding the specific origin, "require completion by the subjects that 'apprehend' them". This means that, to a degree, they can be seen to 'belong' to the subjects that perceive them. Further, in talking of ambiances, Thibaud (2002a) suggests that pre-reflexive perception is central to any theory of ambiance. It is the perceiving/feeling body-subject that is enveloped by the ambient situation and so ambiances must be sensed through their immediate contact with them. It is not possible to 'step back' from the ambiance or to get outside of it to consider it through more objective measures. Instead, Thibaud (2002a) proposed a more 'ecological' approach to thinking about perception based on the situation of the sensate body in a specific ambient environment (also see Simpson 2013).

Third, both approaches variously propose a 'vibrant' form of materialism (Bennett 2010). Both of these approaches recognise the agential role that materiality can have in shaping experiences and in the formation of ambiances and atmospheres. 'Solid' material forms impact upon the ambiance and atmospheres and such ambiances and atmospheres in turn hold the capacity to shape the conduct of various bodies that reside within them. As such, affective capacities and an agential liveliness are taken to be "internal to, rather than in supplement or opposition to, the taking place of matter and materiality" (Anderson and Wylie 2009, 319). Talking of atmospheres Anderson (2009, 79) suggests that, in addition to the role of the perceiving subject discussed above, "atmospheres 'emanate' from the ensemble of elements that make up the aesthetic object" and so, in this sense, they also belong to the object. While subjects are necessary to perceive atmospheres, it is important to recognise that they are not the sole source of these atmospheres; they are not a feature of the subject's mental life but rather emanate from the world of objects and entities that the subject inhabits and interacts with. Similarly, in talking of ambiances, Thibaud (2011, 43) suggests that ambiances involve a specific mood that is "expressed in the material presence of things". This approach requires us to endow urban space with specific qualities and properties that impact upon the urban populace; they are not just neutral containers for the playing out of social life. As such, ambiances are both subjective in their relation to embodied sense-perception as discussed above but also objective as "it involves the lived experience of people as well as the built environment of the place" (Thibaud 2011, 43).

Finally, both are concerned with how ambiances and atmospheres can be shaped. For work on ambiances, this should not be confused with approaches that take an objective approach in simply experimenting with specific 'ambient parameters' such as light, heat, smells, and so on, in pursuing positive ambient environments. Instead, the ambiance-based research discussed here takes ambiances to be a far more dynamic, diffuse, and distributed phenomena and so "ambiance does not appear to be something that is easy to build or to circumscribe" (Thibaud 2002b, 198). This means that the design of ambiances needs to move beyond a focus on the rational planning of spaces, and the instrumental adjustment of their objective qualities as just mentioned, towards an engagement with their sensuous experience and so a more experiential form of design practice. For work on atmospheres, this has been approached largely in terms of the politics of affect and how certain affective experiences are being increasingly engineered into (largely urban) spaces. As Thrift (2004, 68) has claimed, while there is also a level of contingency to this, it is in fact possible for "affective responses [to] be designed into spaces, often out of what seems like very little at all". Spaces are designed to captivate us, and so manipulate us, in different ways (Ash 2010), often with an emphasis on consumption (Thrift 2008).

It is here that an interest in surveillance and security becomes significant. Recently, there have been a number of prominent discussions of the affective feelings often engendered by securitised public space. We read of 'panic', 'fear', 'terror', and 'neurosis' as underlying contemporary experiences of a variety of forms of public space (De Goede and Randalls 2009; Füredi 2005; Isin 2004). These spaces have been increasingly policed and monitored through various bodies and technologies which in turn connect back into such affective states in a form of feedback loop; the very presence of the bodies that are meant to secure such spaces become a source of anxiety in drawing attention to the need for their presence. However, other affective states are arguably also produced, or at least sought, in these sorts of spaces and out of these presences. These are by no means as obviously pressing or distressing as the relatively extreme states mentioned above. For example, Allen (2006) has outlined the subtle ways in which power operates through the space itself, its seductive ambient characteristics, which act to produce a particular mood "that affects how we experience it and which, in turn, seeks to induce certain stances which we might otherwise have chosen not to adopt" (2006, 445). Furthermore, elsewhere in this research we have considered the ways in which practices of surveillance articulate (though not necessarily succeed in producing) more positive moods within the spaces they monitor, such as tranquillity or welcome (Adey et al. 2013). The use of multi-angle video recording discussed in this chapter was then devised precisely as a means for thinking through the sorts of ambiances and atmospheres—understood as a form of immersive and affective volume which radiates from the diverse range of material and immaterial bodies and in which the mobile bodies find themselves—present in our station spaces for those that arrive into and depart from them.

However, it is important to flag that there is at least one key point of distinction between ambiance- and atmosphere-based approaches and that this was fundamental to the methodological techniques and disposition assumed in this research project. The distinction lies in the respective interest of each approach in the methodological development necessary to engage with these various themes.

One the one hand, research interested in affect has been somewhat limited in its development of appropriate research methods, only having started to consider this relatively recently. While there have been a range of largely suggestive gestures towards sources of methodological inspiration in other disciplines such as performance studies (Thrift 2003), work here has been far more interested in theoretical developments (Latham 2003). That said, there have been some recent signs of change. For example, in thinking about embodied practices in general there has been an increasing level of interest in video methods (Brown and Spinney 2010; Garrett 2011; Simpson 2011) and mobile methods (Buscher et al. 2011; Fincham et al. 2011; Merriman 2013; Spinney 2011). However, within these discussions there has also been at times a somewhat troubling emphasis on trying to 'capture' affective experiences and intensities using various technologies which in many ways contradicts the understandings put forward within the aforementioned theorisations of such phenomena. As Davies and Dwyer (2007, 258 and 261 [emphasis added]) suggest, in response to the realisation that "the world is so textured as to exceed our capacity to understand it" there have been "attempts to *capture* the ephemeral, the fleeting, the immanence of place". In light of this, others have responded to such initial methodological developments and the languages they have adopted in a more muted way. For example, in critical response to early developments around video methods Paterson (2009) argues that while such a medium can show the detail of bodily motility and non-verbal interactions between bodies, as well as verbal communication and sounds, it nonetheless gives a very limited sense of the felt aspects of such movement and interaction. Or as Dewsbury (2010, 325) more pithily notes "it is a video camera, it records moving images with different effects for sure which can then be edited and superimposed in imaginative ways but still". The thrust of such critiques is that we should not so much turn towards technologies, such as video, as presenting 'the answer' for engaging the ever expanding epistemological realms opened up by interests in corporeality and embodied practices, but rather that we should reconsider our (often scientific) methodological mindset and question whether the fleeting and ephemeral phenomena we research can in fact be 'captured' and somehow 'brought back in' in the first place.

On the other hand, work researching ambiances has more extensively engaged in methodological experimentation and developing means for apprehending ambiances. These hold some affinities with such calls for what could be thought of as a more performative mode of research in the ways they mix relatively 'standard' social sciences methods (like semi-structured interviews) with innovative, *exploratory* mobile and multimedia informed approaches. For example, in researching the sonic qualities of underground spaces, Rémy (1999, 2001) employed a methodology based on the examination of the transitions that occur in these qualities when moving between different spaces rather than focusing on singular spaces. Here, alongside architectural analysis and the consideration of various measures of acoustic character, sound-walk recordings were made through the stations and these were used in interviews with people using the station to help them describe features of these soundscapes that are not necessarily easy to describe. This sort of elicitation-based transition analysis allowed for the creation of a sort of sonic reference tool for future architectural projects that was attentive not just to objective, measurable sonic parameters but rather subjective perception and cultural contexts. Equally, in researching pedestrian practices in urban environments, Thomas (2008, 2010) employed a novel 'three-person walk' that entailed auto-ethnographic walking through the city ('I-walk'), walking and talking with other walkers ('you-walk'), and then an observation of other walkers at a distance ('he-/she-walk'). In combination, this walking-talking-watching approach, of researching in the first, second, and third person singular, allowed a wide range of insights into the practical, social, and affective aspects of walking experiences to emerge and particularly how these were impacted upon and shaped by the ambiances and atmospheres of the urban environment.

In carrying out the filming discussed in this chapter we wanted to embody these sorts of experimental dispositions towards our research field. We hoped that adopting such dispositions in producing the multi-angle filming montages discussed in this chapter would help us come to in some way register the vibrant materialities of our fieldsites and the ways they impacted upon the people that moved through them.

MULTI-ANGLE FILMING IN THE SURVEILLANCE SOCIETY

Befitting the geography of our collaboration, to understand our development of multi-angle filming it is necessary to turn to 18th century London via 20th century Paris. In *Discipline and Punish* Michel Foucault (1979) reflects on Jeremy Bentham's vision for the ideal penitentiary: the Panopticon. By way of circular architectural design this building was to force its inhabitants into a state of perpetual self-monitoring. Through backlighting and minimal furnishing, the cells allowed for the production of an absolutely transparent space with no hidden corners beyond the (potential) gaze of those in charge. The relation of the central observation tower to the cells meant that inmates perpetually saw themselves as being seen by others without knowing if they were in fact being watched. This, ideally, meant the surveillant gaze was internalised such that the inmates self-policed.

However, Foucault suggests that such a model for the automatic functioning of power through pervasive vision and the internalisation of the surveillant gaze was not meant to be confined to the design of houses of correction alone. Rather, the Panopticon . . . must be understood as a generalizable model of functioning; a way of defining power relations in terms of the everyday life of men . . . : it is a diagram of a mechanism of power reduced to its ideal form; its functioning, abstracted from any obstacle, resistance or friction, must be represented as a pure architectural and optical system: it is in fact a figure of political technology that may and must be detached from any specific use. . . . Whenever one is dealing with a multiplicity of individuals on whom a task or particular form of behavior must be imposed, the panoptic schema may be used.

(Foucault 1979, 205)

In this sense, the Panopticon represents a technology designed to solve the problem of surveillance, a problem that has been seen to pervade much of contemporary urban life. As Koskela (2003, 293) highlights:

The idea of video surveillance is almost literally the same: a technological solution designed to solve the problems of surveillance in urban space. People under surveillance are—as in the Panopticon—to be seen but to never know when or by whom; under control but without physical intervention.

Such discussions around the intersection of architecture and forms of surveillance and security, alongside our related supposed contemporary immersion within an all encompassing panoptic urban environment, inspired our method of multi-angle filming (also see Adey 2007).

There are, however, a few important caveats to make here. First, this 'method' was not a pre-existing one that we sought to employ in our research having read about its use by others. Rather, and tying into the methodological disposition of ambiance research outlined above, the general idea and its ultimate form emerged from our encounter with our field-sites and our discussions that took place within it. Like so many public and mobile spaces, our two stations are surveilled by a comprehensive network of CCTV cameras. Given debates over the loss of civil liberties in light of the proliferation of such technologies (see Lyon 2007) and debates over the negative atmospheres and ambiances the increasing presence of such technologies can create mentioned above, this seemed to us to be a particularly pertinent area of tension to consider when thinking about and trying to research the atmospheres and ambiances of arrival into and departure from our sites. 'Riffing' on some of the key motifs of CCTV surveillance seemed to be an appropriate way to proceed; we wanted to turn the CCTV Panopticon and its product on itself in an attempt to apprehend the atmospheres they are purportedly there to create (tranquillity as stated in Gare du Nord), or inadvertently bring about (fear, suspicion, paranoia) rather than to monitor, and induce the self-monitoring of, the conduct of passengers.

Second, our use of multi-angle video recording was also connected to the range of intended outputs we had in mind in doing the research. An integral outcome of our research project, and so of this filming technique, is to be a multimedia exhibition based upon the audio and visual materials generated during our research. While still in the planning stages at the time of writing, the intention is for such materials (including the montages presented here) to be displayed and/or interacted with our station spaces and so to engage users of those spaces.[2] Our orientation in employing this method was then both social-scientific and artistic. As such, we were not necessarily just trying to produce 'data' that would be subsequently analysed and 'written-up' in traditional publishing outlets such as this one. Rather, there was also an aesthetic element to our research design and 'output'. We were also concerned with what the research process itself, as well as the product, allowed us to see and how this could feed into some kind of video-installation work that would tell something about our research project's themes. This is, in turn, reflected in aspects of our discussion of the research materials below.

Moving to the specifics of what the method actually entailed, there were a number of components to this. Initially we chose a suitable site within each of our stations. These sites were chosen to allow some of the filming to take place from an elevated view to mimic the overhead positioning of many CCTV cameras. This entailed filming from on a staircase or mezzanine level. At each site we situated four or five cameras, each operated by a member of our research team. The camera angles overlapped but did not film exactly the same area. There were, nonetheless, some blind spots that the cameras did not cover (for example, views obscured by signage or pillars). Some of the cameras maintained a static view throughout the duration of the filming while others, particularly the elevated ones, panned and zoomed to mimic the curiosity and enquiries of a CCTV camera operator. We attempted to film simultaneously by agreeing on a start and end time given both the distance between camera operators and the need for subtlety at times (see below).

One of the 'artistic' elements of our chosen camera angles is that, as well as the classic CCTV view from on high, we also wanted to include filming from ground level. This was included both to disrupt the traditional perception of what CCTV should look like but also to get a sense of the feeling of actually being in that space of arrival/departure. Often video cameras, and particularly CCTV cameras, are perceived to be somewhat detached from the sensuousness of embodied experiences. However, we wanted to play between this sort of detached observational gaze and a more embodied, on-the-ground view from within the social life of the spaces that would give a sense of their vibrancy and bustle; a sense of the density of bodies and the feelings and moods that circulated between them.

We used little in the way of specialist equipment. The video cameras were standard digital video cameras recording to internal hard drives or memory cards. The video from these cameras was later downloaded to an iMac and synchronised and combined onto a single-screen view using Adobe Premier Pro. This synchronisation presented some challenges given both the number of video streams to sync but also the slight differences in the starting time of each video and the difficulties of coordinating this precisely across a relatively distributed space. To allow for the accurate synchronisation of the various video streams a key event was found in each of the video collections that could be seen in multiple cameras. For example, for our Gare du Nord filming we used the stopping of a man who was looking at an announcements board to synchronise two of the camera streams (see Figure 2.1) and then used a luggage cart passing a specific pillar that one of these cameras and the other two remaining unsynchronised cameras could see for orientation. Each video stream was cued based on these common points and the footage synced from there.

There were a number of practical challenges when it came to undertaking the filming itself. Most prominent was gaining permission. For St Pancras, while taking some time to arrange, this was fairly unproblematic. We sought and received formal permission from the station's management group to undertake research in the space. As part of this, our chosen filming locations had to be agreed in advance and we had to acquire health and safety clearance for these specific locations; the station's management wanted to ensure that our activities were not going to cause a risk to those passing through the station. For example, when it came to the filming itself, if using a tripod, we had to cordon-off our cameras using official St Pancras station bollards to ensure that our tripods' legs were not going to cause issue. This obviously had implications for our visibility as researchers. While at times this impacted upon how people behaved in frame, for the vast majority it appeared to have a limited impact. Further, each day we arrived to carry out our field research we had to register with the station, receive photo-ID badges, and show these to any employees of the station on request.

For Gare du Nord our experience was more complex and frustrating. Despite trying to contact the station management through various means and on a number of occasions, we received no response. Having found information on the SNCF website (one of the companies that manages parts of Gare du Nord) stating that in normal circumstances amateur photographers and film makers were welcome in the station and that only commercial filming required specific permission, we decided to carry out our filming. However, when we started filming we were, on a number of occasions, approached by security staff and questioned about our activities. While in most cases we were met with a slightly suspicious reaction and given begrudged permission to continue, on one occasion a member of our team was told that we were not allowed to be there and that we had to leave immediately.

Given the SNCF website information mentioned above we decided to go back into the station, but this time made sure we were armed with the webpage open on our various smart phones in case we were told to leave again. However, one of the French members of our research team was, upon

Figure 2.1 Man with suitcase standing looking at departures sign. The man dressed in black holding the wheeled suitcase was used to synchronise the top two video streams. From there, a second event visible in three of the video streams was used to synchronise all four video streams.

re-entering the station, immediately shadowed by undercover security staff. This meant our filming was both increasingly pursued with a covert edge— we did not use tripods, we filmed from a more dispersed arrangement within the station, had cameras running while hanging from straps around our neck, and so on—and ultimately curtailed when we realised that the site was being so actively policed for the use of cameras. This meant the filming we managed to undertake in Gare du Nord was to a greater degree 'naturalistic' (Laurier and Philo 2006) but also, ironically given our research project's focus, pursued amid an atmosphere of uncertainty and insecurity.

The challenges we met in Gare du Nord do raise ethical questions regarding undertaking this sort of filming in public and semipublic spaces. While often deemed to be a benchmark of ethical research, clearly for our filming it is simply not practical to seek written consent from all the people we recorded. However, there has been a fairly limited discussion of what, if any, alternative models should be used in such a situation. Equally, on the rare occasion that this is discussed, there has been a tendency to assume an interactive mode of research practice whereby the researchers filming will also personally engage with those being recorded, at times entirely dismissing the validity of more observational methods, and therefore assuming consent would be gained through fairly traditional means (Prosser et al. 2008). There are, however, some sources we can turn to for guidance here. For example, Laurier and Philo (2006) displayed signs in their research spaces (cafes) and offered 'participants' both further information and the right to opt out. Also, in presenting material, Laurier et al. (2012) have edited their images to significantly reduce the ability to actually identify participants without losing the content of the images. In our research we adopted the sentiment of these latter approaches. In general, we were open with anyone who approached us and provided explanations of what it was we were doing, making consent practical on the basis of opting out. Equally, for all of our footage we have ensured that care has been taken in the selection of any visual materials so that the identity of participants (knowing or not) is not easily discerned.

ARRIVING INTO AND DEPARTING FROM ST PANCRAS AND GARE DU NORD

Having provided this context, the chapter will now turn to the output of the filming itself. In approaching our video materials we did not employ any formal model of data analysis. Instead, we were more generally interested in the ways in which the montaged video material, and the process that lay behind the collection of the video they are based upon, may (or may not) give us a sense of the ambiances and atmospheres experienced in arriving into and departing from those spaces. To gain a sense of this, we engaged in a process of iterative viewing whereby we watched and rewatched the clips a number of times (Simpson 2012). During this process we allowed different events to gain our attention or for different patterns of movement or interaction to emerge. Sometimes this came from individual camera angles and other times this came as a result of a particular constellation of angles and events bringing something to the fore either by showing a common emergence or by making something distinctive stand out from the rest of the camera angles. When something did catch our attention our viewing often became non-linear; we scanned backward and forward through the clips to, for example, establish when a person that caught our attention entered, double check the lead up and follow up from the event, and so on. We jumped to earlier points to check back on something previously noticed or jumped forward to see subsequent implications of what we noticed. We also compared the perspectives given by our various camera angles. This was not a pre-planned process but one that emerged organically and intuitively as our viewing unfolded.

Furthermore, the fact that we each approached the video, and so the ambiances and atmospheres of our station spaces, from different perspectives and positions had a bearing on how and what we perceived (see Adey et al. 2013). Different events in the video caught each of our attentions to differing degrees, if at all. Each of us saw the space presented in the montaged video differently and ended up pursing these interests in differing directions. No specific pattern emerged within this in terms of, for example, our identity-position (i.e. according to nationality or gender). Rather, a more micro-level play of differences appeared to play out based upon our own, singular, orientation in being (and having been) in the world (Ahmed 2010a). It is important to note then that the discussion below is just one of many possible engagements with the video material collected and by no means the definitive one.

In the space available here there are three main themes that this section will pick up on: the issue of orientation in passengers' arrival into the stations; the simultaneous presence of multiple atmospheres/ambiances in such spaces; and the issue of how we can in fact go about sensing ambiances and atmospheres in carrying out this sort of research.

ORIENTATION IN ARRIVAL

One of the key things that our multi-angle video montage drew attention to in terms of the ambiances and atmospheres of arrival and departure into and out of our spaces was feelings of orientation and disorientation. Our station spaces each provide quite distinctive experiences of arrival and departure. In Gare du Nord the station is relatively traditional in layout (when focusing on the ground floor station). There are a series of parallel platforms that terminate into the station which presents a perpendicular concourse with information displays and shopping kiosks/cafes. Arriving into the station is therefore fairly straightforward—you get off the train, carry on along the line of its arrival, and then find an exit amongst these retail units. The main distinctive feature of this area of the station is the raised check-in and waiting area for the Eurostar service from which a clear view of this layout is provided (two of our cameras were situated in this area—see Figure 2.1 and Figure 2.3). In St Pancras, the arrival is a little more disorientating. While passengers again arrive onto platforms that run perpendicular to a concourse in front of them and access to the city beyond, passengers on Eurostar trains arrive on the upper level of the station before descending to a lower level on escalators. This results in the passengers turning a number of corners (and doubling back on themselves) before appearing on the lower level in a direction perpendicular to that of their arrival.

The area passengers arrive into is also quite confined and lacks the grandeur of the upper level's period facade or Gare du Nord's voluminous structure. Instead, passengers are faced by a relatively confined space that looks directly onto the side of a stairwell (see Figure 2.2). There is little in the way of sight lines to either outside the station or the area the passengers initially arrived into. In fact, it looks more like they have arrived into a shopping mall (or airport, given the line of drivers waiting) rather than a train station, as there are no trains or platforms anywhere nearby. Other than the suspended signs facing them, there is relatively little for the arriving passengers to orientate themselves in relation to. Also, while in Gare du Nord it is possible to see the check-in area from where passengers arrive and the arrival area from the check-in desks and departure lounge, in St Pancras the two are not visible to each other.

The respective layouts here appear to have implications for the sort of atmosphere/ambiance that starts to emerge from the combination of arriving and departing passengers and physical/sonic architecture when a Eurostar train arrives. Focusing on St Pancras, while many passengers appeared visibly excited upon arriving—they used animated gestures or emotionally hugged awaiting friends and relatives as they appeared through the arrival doors out into the station—this was often quickly countered or contrasted by the confusion that emerged when they tried to find their way through the public area of the station. The arrival doors are opaque and so the arriving passengers do not necessarily know what is awaiting on the other side, nor those waiting on the passengers arriving. This means that passengers walk out from the arrival gate and stand in the middle of the passageway. Sometimes passengers spin round on the spot in looking for something that would tell them which way to go or where to exit. Often, a number of passengers congregate and so block the flow of people through the space. The man to the right in Figure 2.2 looking over his left shoulder, for example, had just arrived and stopped directly in the path of the hatted person carrying a coat with the back to the camera.

During an arrival, then, while arriving passengers come in a relatively steady flow, there can be quite heavy congestion[3]. There is commonly a

Figure 2.2   Orientation in arriving in St Pancras (detail from St Pancras multi-angle filming). Passengers arrive to the right of the pillar on the far right of the image/beneath the sign that is partially visible here. To the top left of the image the staircase that partially obscures passengers' views can be seen.

prominent and speedy flow of people going from the bottom of Figure 2.2 to its top as both Euston Road and one exit from the underground station is located to the bottom and the check-in gates (as well as other train services) are located beyond the top of the image. This then risks turning the general atmosphere of disorientation into one more conflictual. We witnessed passengers walking through the space become visibly frustrated as they tried in vain to get past the static/spinning arrivals and to their destination. These sentiments of excitement, confusion, disorientation, and urgency mixed in the specific situation that the space that arriving and departing passengers were presented with.

MULTIPLE ATMOSPHERES/AMBIANCES

This suggests a further feature of the ambiances and atmospheres of arrival and departure that emerged from our montage film: the way in which multiple atmospheres and ambiances can exist in relative proximity to one another. Or rather, how the ambiances and atmospheres present in a space can be sensed and registered differently in and by different bodies within those same spaces.

This was best illustrated in one event that occurred during our filming in Gare du Nord (see Figure 2.3). Here, following a station announcement, a number of station staff in orange fluorescent bibs and other security staff rushed to the platform of a boarding train. As this happened the departure board (visible as white in the top left and bottom right images) changed from a black background displaying the departure information in yellow to the white background with red writing that can be seen here. Significantly, the red writing reads 'Acces Interdit' (Access Forbidden). It was not clear what actually occurred from the video but it appeared that there was some kind of security alert at the platform resulting in it being shut down and the train being held in the station. This effected a tangible change in the mood in this part of the station. This can be seen in the increasing number of people who stopped and stood at the entrance to the platform and looked on/occasionally spoke to one another. From the busy bustle of a train boarding the atmosphere suddenly changed to one of confusion and concern.

However, this shift in ambiance/atmosphere did not permeate throughout the entire station. It was not registered in all the bodies present. As can be seen in the bottom left image, people continued to walk through the station having passed the site of the emerging incident. In fact, the vast majority of station inhabitants that passed by it did so without paying much attention at all or they just glanced over with limited interest as they moved on to their own platform or wherever else their business was taking them. The angle of their arrival, their specific disposition, was directed enough so that this event did not distract them from what it was they needed or wanted to do.

Figure 2.3 'Acces Interdit'. The top left image shows the platform sign saying 'Acces Interdit' (Access Forbidden). The bottom right image shows a growing crowd of people who have stopped to see what is going on and/or waiting to access the platform. The top right image shows a young couple affectionately playing and occasionally embracing.

This limited scope of the security-event atmosphere can also be seen in the image at the top right of Figure 2.3. As the announcement was made, the couple visible at the left of the image were in an embrace. Following this, they playfully circled each other, touched each other, and kissed. They took no notice of what was going on. Their own situation of amorous encounter was not impacted upon by the emerging feeling of concern spreading only twenty yards away from where they stood. While they cannot not have heard the precipitating announcement, this was not registered in any significant way in their corporeal disposition or their subjective mood. They just carried on as before in their own intersubjective bubble. Eventually, with the platform still closed and the event carrying on, the couple's train arrived at the platform they were waiting by and they walked off to board it, entirely oblivious to the nearby commotion and concern.

Through viewing these various angles onto the space it became very evident that bodies, therefore, do not arrive into or find themselves in an atmosphere/ambiance in an entirely passive or neutral way. Nor does such an atmosphere exist as an objective product of certain ambient parameters. The situation is not simply to be understood in terms of the objective outside acting in on the body (Dyson 2009). Rather, the lively and affected nature of bodies means they bring with them a specific affective disposition which impacts upon the ways in which ambiances and atmospheres are registered (Ahmed 2010b); the same situation can be registered in multiple ways, or not at all. While we can walk into a room and 'feel the atmosphere' we also have to think about the body itself that arrives and each body's singular susceptibility to being affected at any given time (Bissell 2010).

SENSING AMBIANCES AND ATMOSPHERES?

Having discussed these video montages in terms of the sense of the ambiances and atmospheres of arrival and departure they gave in these two spaces, it is also important to note a further function of this videoing and so a quite different key output in terms of our more creative agenda. In doing this filming our interest was not only in the content of the video produced. It was also to gain an understanding of how it is we sense the sorts of ambiances and atmospheres present in these spaces—with how we look, see, hear, and listen—or potentially with how we *fail* to sense them. Looking at these videos draws attention to this tension in our (in)ability to attend to what is going on around us, to the partiality of our gaze and our comprehension. When so much of what happens in the world is missed and/or apprehended only through fleeting looks, glances, or fragments of things heard (Casey 2007), our understanding of the environments we inhabit, while often very practically sophisticated, nonetheless exceeds our capacity to exhaustively know it.

In this sense, our multi-angle video montage specifically highlights our partial perspective onto these spaces and the limited nature of our comprehension. While we started from the panoptic ideal of complete vision and all-encompassing monitoring, we have, in fact, ended up highlighting nearly the opposite. Looking at the video brought about a somewhat disorientating and even overwhelming sensation rather than a comprehensive view, and we found ourselves primarily looking as opposed to listening, never mind smelling or touching. While looking at a single video clip presents us with an immense amount of detail and information, much more than we can pay attention to either through a single or a number of viewings, being faced with multiple clips increases this exponentially. It becomes impossible to exhaust this place (Perec 2010).

This, in turn, presented us with a number of very simple yet fundamental questions. First, where to look? It did in fact take several viewings to simply apprehend where the cameras were filming relative to each other. Finding common reference points was not easy and it was, at least initially, hard to re-place ourselves into the station spaces (especially with our Gare du Nord video) and make sense of what we were seeing. Further, we then have to ask: what should we look at or for? What is worth looking at? What counts as 'normal'? What counts as 'suspicious'? These are questions we never clearly found an answer for.

Ultimately, this returns us to the point that ambiances and atmospheres cannot be understood in any sort of objective and clearly measurable sense. Our attempts at using this videoing approach explicitly highlight that to apprehend such ambiances and atmospheres it is not simply a case of mapping out a space, of measuring the relative levels of light, noise, smell, or temperature that might contribute to the feel of the space. It is not simply a case of noting the specific movements made by individuals, recording their patterns and frequencies, or of noting who in fact those individuals are. Instead, such atmospheres and ambiances are to be experience in their midst, in the middle of these events and parameters. Our situation outside them as viewers only provides a partial and limited sense of what was in fact taking place. This is *a* sense nonetheless, but certainly not the final word.

CONCLUSION

This chapter has sought to give an insight into the use of multi-angle video recording in researching the ambiances and atmospheres of arriving into and departing from two surveilled and securitised mobile spaces. It has argued that this videoing and the related presentation allowed us to approach (though not necessarily 'capture') the ephemeral and ethereal ambiances and atmospheres that emerge and dissipate in and out of these mobile spaces in the interactions of bodies, technologies, symbols, materialities, and movements. Here we saw how a particular constellation of architecture, vision, social interaction, and movement produced a particular atmosphere of excitement, disorientation, and, at times, agitation in moving through St Pancras.

Further, building from this, it became evident through using this filming technique in Gare du Nord that ambiances and atmospheres are sensed differently by different bodies depending on their own specific disposition in moving into and out of any given space. While in the same setting, bodies will experience that setting differently.

This chapter has also suggested that combining these multiple camera angles into a single matrix allowed us to raise questions about the orientation and perception of the situated researcher/observer, flagging the partial and fragmented nature of these positions/perspectives and so the role the research plays in constructing the field itself. Looking at these multiple images arrayed side-by-side starts to give us an insight of the plurality of perspectives and perceptions on the space and so on any kind of ambiance or atmosphere that may emerge and be apprehended by those inhabiting the space (or equally by those researching it). Ambiances and atmospheres become much more than constellations of particularly ambient qualities (of light, sound, smell, and so on) or the outcome of specific material-architectural configurations. Instead they are dynamic and emerge and deform in a multiplicity of ways amid the more-than-human ecology of that situation.

That all said, one of the key messages of this chapter is not so much tied to what this method allowed *us* to do and see, to sense and feel. This chapter has not been written with the aim of engendering a desire to copy the specific format of multi-angle filming discussed here *per se*. Rather, the intention here has been to encourage a more general reorientation of the traditional disposition towards social science research, particularly when it comes to researching in light of recent developments around new forms of materialism, practice, experience, affect, and so on. The use of video methods (and research methods in general) discussed here suggests a situated approach to engaging with video (and other) recording technologies that is based upon the specific questions, concerns, and field of enquiry being engaged. Furthermore, this also encourages such developments to move away from trying to 'capture' such phenomena and bring it back from the field for further analysis. The disposition outlined in this chapter would suggest a more performative ethos when it comes to methodological endeavours (Dewsbury 2010). Perhaps approaching the field with the disposition of an artist rather than a scientist will allow for the world to appear differently, to allow researchers to become caught up in the onflow of everyday life, and better understand their ever-evolving situation within this. It is a case of finding the means of amplifying intensities and helping us learn to see the world differently from our habitual ways of looking and feeling.

NOTES

1. The video data collection and editing discussed in this chapter is derived from an Agence Nationale de la Recherche-funded project 'Sensory Enigmas of Contemporary Urban mobility', ANR 'Espace & Territoires', decision

#ANR_10_ESVS_013_01. The material from the project discussed here was produced in collaboration with Peter Adey (RHUL), Laure Brayer (CRESSON, Grenoble), Damien Masson (Cergy-Pontoise, Paris), Patrick Murphy (Goldsmiths, London), and Nicolas Tixier (CRESSON, Grenoble). Thanks also go to Peter, Laure, Damien, Patrick, and Nicolas for commenting on an earlier version of this chapter.

2. To date, we have experimented with this by hosting a range of soundwalks and audio tours in St Pancras as part of a conference event we organised in February 2013. Details of this event can be found at: http://www.ambiances.net/seminars/london-2013-ambiances-and-atmospheres-in-translation.html

3. One of the reasons we have chosen to show a single camera angle as opposed to one including views also from the ground is because of this congestion. While the lower views give a strong sense of this congestion in the density of bodies they show, this very density renders the illustrative capacities of the images relatively useless. All that can be seen in some of these images is the head and back of the person directly in front or also, raising ethical issues, extreme close ups of individuals that would be hard to anonymise without entirely blurring the image.

REFERENCES

Adey, P. 2007. 'May I have your attention': airport geographies of spectatorship, position, and (im)mobility. *Environment and Planning D: Society and Space,* 25: 515–536.

Adey, P., Brayer, L., Masson, D., Murphy, P., Simpson, P. and Tixier, N. 2013. 'Pour votre tranquillité': ambiance, atmosphere, and surveillance. *Geoforum,* 49: 299–309.

Ahmed, S. 2010a. Orientations matter. In Coole, D. and Frost, S. (eds.) *New Materialisms: Ontology, Agency, and Politics.* London: Duke University Press.

Ahmed, S. 2010b. Happy objects. In Gregg, M. and Seigworth, G. J. (eds.) *The Affect Theory Reader.* London: Duke University Press.

Allen, J. 2006. Ambient power: Berlin's Potsdamer Platz and the seductive logic of public spaces. *Urban Studies,* 43: 441–455.

Anderson, B. 2009. Affective atmospheres. *Emotion, Space and Society,* 2: 77–81.

Anderson, B. and Wylie, J. 2009. On geography and materiality. *Environment and Planning A,* 41: 318–335.

Ash, J. 2010. Architectures of affect: anticipating and manipulating the event in processes of videogame design and testing. *Environment and Planning D: Society and Space,* 28: 653–671.

Augoyard, J. 2007. *Step by Step: Everyday Walks in a French Urban Housing Project.* Minneapolis: University of Minnesota Press.

Bennett, J. 2010. *Vibrant Matter: A Political Ecology of Things.* London: Duke University Press.

Bissell, D. 2010. Passenger mobilities: affective atmospheres and the sociality of public transport. *Environment and Planning D: Society and Space,* 28: 270–289.

Brennan, T. 2004. *The Transmission of Affect.* London: Cornell University Press.

Brown, K. and Spinney, J. 2010. Catching a glimpse: the value of video in evoking, understanding and representing the practice of cycling. In Fincham, B., McGuinness, M. and Murray, L. (eds.) *Mobile Methodologies.* Basingstoke: Palgrave MacMillan.

Buscher, M., Urry, J. and Witchger, K. (eds.) 2011. *Mobile Methods*. London: Routledge.

Casey, E. S. 2007. *The World at a Glance*. Indianapolis: Indiana University Press.

Davies, G. and Dwyer, C. 2007. Qualitative methods: are you enchanted or are you alienated. *Progress in Human Geography*, 31: 257–266.

De Goede, M. and Randalls, S. 2009. Precaution, preemption: arts and technologies of the actionable future. *Environment and Planning D: Society and Space*, 27: 859–878.

Dewsbury, J. D. 2010. Performative, non-representational, and affect-based research: seven injunctions. In DeLyser, D., Aitken, S., Craig, M., Herbert, S. and McDowell, L. (eds.) *The SAGE Handbook of Qualitative Research in Human Geography*. London: Sage.

Dyson, F. 2009. *Sounding New Media: Immersion and Embodiment in the Arts and Culture*. London: University of California Press.

Edensor, T. 2012. Illuminated atmospheres: anticipating and reproducing the flow of affective experience in Blackpool. *Environment and Planning D: Society and Space*, 30: 1103–1122.

Fincham, B., McGuinness, M. and Murray, L. (eds.) 2010. *Mobile Methodologies*. Basingstoke: Palgrave MacMillan.

Foucault, M. 1979. *Discipline and Punish: The Birth of the Prison*. Penguin, London.

Füredi, F. 2005. *Politics of Fear*. Continuum, London.

Garrett, B. 2011. Videographic geographies: Using digital video for geographic research. *Progress in Human Geography*, 35: 521–541.

Isin, E. F. 2004. The neurotic citizen. *Citizenship Studies,* 8: 217–235.

Koskela, H. 2003. 'Cam Era'—the contemporary urban Panopticon. *Surveillance & Society,* 1: 292–313.

Latham, A. 2003. Research, performance, and doing human geography: some reflections on the diary-interview method. *Environment and Planning A, 35*: 1993–2017.

Laurier, E., Brown, B. and Lorimer, H. 2012. What it means to change lanes: actions, emotions and wayfinding in the family car. *Semiotica*, 191: 117–135.

Laurier, E. and Philo, C. 2006. Natural problems of naturalistic video data. In Knoblauch, H., Raab, J., Soeffner, H.-G. and Schnettler, B. (eds.) *Video-Analysis: Methodology and Methods*. Oxford: Peter Lang.

Lyon, D. 2007. *Surveillance Studies: An Overview.* Cambridge: Polity.

Merriman, P. 2013. Rethinking mobile methods. *Mobilities,* 9(2): 167–187.

Paterson, M. 2009. Haptic geographies: ethnography, haptic knowledges and sensuous dispositions. *Progress in Human Geography,* 33(6): 766–788.

Perec, G. 2010. *An Attempt at Exhausting a Place in Paris*. Adelaide: Wakefield Press.

Prosser, J., Clark, A. and Wiles, R. 2008. Visual research ethics at the crossroads. Realities Working Paper no 10.

Rémy, N. 1999. Coming in and coming out underground spaces. In *8th International Underground Space Conference of Acuus Xi'An. Agenda and prospect for the turn of the century: papers of the conference*. Eighth International Underground Space Conference of Acuus Xi'An, China, 27–30 September.

Rémy, N. 2001. Sound qualities in railway stations. In Drever, J. L. (ed.) *Sound practice: the 1st UKISC, United Kingdom and Ireland Soundscape Community Conference on Sound Culture and Environments*. First UKISC Conference on Sound Culture and Environments, Dartington Hall Conference and Dartington College of Art, England, 16–20 February.

Simpson, P. 2011. 'So, as you can see . . .': Some reflections on the use of video methodologies in the study of embodied practices. *Area*, 43: 343–352.

Simpson, P. 2012. Apprehending everyday rhythms: rhythmanalysis, time-lapse photography, and the space-times of street performance. *Cultural Geographies,* 19: 423–445.

Simpson, P. 2013. Ecologies of experience: Materiality, sociality, and the embodied experience of (street) performing. *Environment and Planning A,* 45: 180–196.

Spinney, J. 2011. A chance to catch a breath: using mobile video ethnography in cycling research. *Mobilities,* 6: 161–182.

Thibaud, J-P. 2002a. From situated perception to urban ambiences. *First International Workshop on Architectural and Urban Ambient Environment,* February 6–8, Nantes.

Thibaud, J-P. 2002b. L'horizon des ambiances urbaines. *Communications,* 73: 185–201.

Thibaud, J-P. 2011. The three dynamics of urban ambiances. In LaBelle, B. and Martinho, C. (eds.) *Sites of Sound: Of Architecture and the Ear.* Berlin: Errant Bodies Press.

Thomas, R. 2008. The power exerted by urban atmosphere over our choice of walk. In *Barcelona Walk 21* [CD-ROM], Barcelona, 8–10th October.

Thomas, R. 2010. Architectural and urban atmospheres shaping the way we walk in town. In Methorst, R., Monterde i Bort, H., Risser, R., Sauter, D., Tight, M. and Walker, J. (eds.) *Pedestrians' Quality Needs Final Report: Part C Executive Summary.*

Thrift, N. 2003. Performance and . . . *Environment and Planning A,* 35: 2019–2024.

Thrift, N. 2004. Intensities of feeling: towards a spatial politics of affect. *Geografiska Annaler B,* 86: 57–78.

Thrift, N. 2008. The material practices of glamour. *Journal of Cultural Economy,* 1(1): 9–23.

3 The Mobile Life of Screens
Digital Imaging on School Journeys in Helsinki

Kim Kullman

This is my first meeting with 7-year-old Anneli and her mother. We are sitting in an empty classroom inside the school building of Anneli, who is smiling hesitantly and answering my questions in a reserved tone. However, when I take the camcorder out of my bag, she suddenly lights up. Anneli is clearly drawn to the sleek and diminutive design of the digital camera, looking at it intently and asking me how we are going to use it. I switch on the camera and Anneli lifts it carefully from my hand. Her mother prompts her to walk with it a bit, and Anneli begins to carry the camera around the classroom, navigating between the desks and looking steadily into the screen, saying that the camera shakes when walking. As we gather to watch the footage on the display screen, Anneli begins to laugh.

* * *

This empirical vignette, stemming from a collaborative research project on the school journeys of 7–12-year-old children in Helsinki, Finland, describes a mundane encounter between a digital camcorder and 7-year-old Anneli, whose initial reservations about my presence are replaced by a sense of curiosity when introduced to the camera, which she begins to transport around the classroom, as if anticipating our journeys together. For Anneli, as well as for most of the children who took part in the project, the visual equipment became synonymous with research: it framed daily situations as extraordinary by implying new modes of looking and new ways of engaging with the environment.

The project, which involved 23 children from the Helsinki Metropolitan Area (population 1.4 million), set out to explore children's daily mobilities across different urban environments and modes of transport, from walking and cycling to bus, train, tram and metro travel. The study was based on the idea that a closer exploration of the actual settings where children learn and refine their mobility skills and sensibilities not only lends important insight into their agencies and sociabilities in urban spaces, but contributes to wider efforts to support their everyday movement, which has become a tension-laden issue in Euro-American settings, mostly due to an exponential growth of automobility and changing cultural conceptions of childhood, risk and well-being (Barker et al. 2009; Skelton and Gough 2013). At the same time, the study sought to address a peculiar gap in the diversifying work on all things mobile (Adey 2009; Cresswell 2006, 2010; Peters 2006; Sheller and Urry 2006; Urry 2007), where the practices through which mobilities are learned in the first place have attracted considerably less attention. The study was particularly interested in exploring whether children's experiences of learning mobility could point to alternative modes of engagement with the city and everyday urban travel practices.

The set-up of the project was relatively straightforward: the participants were encouraged to photograph and film any features of their school journeys that they felt were interesting, and they were told that these images would be discussed in a later interview, which the children could take part in alone or with their friends, siblings or parents. The choice of equipment— the camera was a Canon Ixus 400 with a 128-MB memory card, and the camcorder was a Sanyo Xacti C40 with a 1-GB memory card—was mainly shaped by practical considerations: the camera was found in a cupboard at home and the camcorder was acquired specifically for the project, mainly picked due to its lightness, small size and affordability. After my first meeting with the families, during which we tried out the cameras and talked about how we would use them, I travelled with each participant to school and back home between two and four times, assisting with the filming and photographing as well as engaging with the children and the specificities of their everyday journeys.[1]

The children were already familiar with digital media, and, during our first meeting, I often found them sitting by the computer, using their phones or playing with games consoles. Nonetheless, travelling between home and school with two cameras and a researcher was a new experience for everyone, and this necessarily turned our journeys into experimental encounters, whose purpose was not only to represent children's mobilities as they appeared but to bring out their unexplored potential. It was particularly the digital screens of the two cameras that seemed to encourage this kind of experimentation, as the children began to employ them as "material probes" for "churning up events" (Simone 2012, 208). Indeed, for the participants, screens were framing devices, microscopes, telescopes and platforms for sharing experiences—anything that could be used to expand their affective and sensory awareness of the everyday city.

Inspired by these intensive engagements, this chapter discusses the medium of the screen and its role in children's mobile photography and filming during school journeys in Helsinki. There are several reasons for this foregrounding, the primary among them being that screens are expressive of recent shifts in visual cultures and practices brought about by digital technology (Coleman 2013; Simone 2012; Thrift 2005; Wasson 2007). Apart from allowing people to view and edit images on the move (Larsen 2008; Larsen and Sandbye 2014), screens facilitate experimentation with relations between still and moving images by opening a space where both can interact (Ash 2009; Campany 2008; Røssaak 2011). Screens also constitute sites for affective and multi-sensory engagements with images that generate all kinds of situated relations between bodies, visual materials and the world, inviting exploration of how people *both* mobilise *and* become mobilised by images in different everyday settings (Lisle 2010; Marks 2000, 2002; Witmore 2004). As digital technology has further complicated the permeable boundaries between photography and video filming, visual researchers increasingly find themselves working *between* still and moving images. Rather than seeing such complications as a problem, this chapter indicates that they create useful crossovers between photographic and videographic methods that can only diversify the expressive and participatory possibilities of visual research. Images, whether still or moving, have always been characterised by a certain flexibility and undecidedness as they shape and become shaped by embedded moments of production and consumption. This chapter argues that thinking and working through screens might help researchers to make better use of the multiple mobilities and immobilities of images as they go about studying the daily lives of children and adults alike.

Developing this argument, the remainder of my chapter proceeds in the following manner. First, I explore the particularities of visual research with children by presenting some earlier work within this inventive and interdisciplinary area. Second, I discuss the ubiquity of screens and how they have altered understandings of still and moving images, and their relations to bodies and worlds. Third, I engage with the ways in which the children in Helsinki employed digital cameras to make sense of their mobilities. This discussion comes in two parts, the first exploring how children learned to move with the screens and use them for mapping new composites of "affects" and "percepts" in urban environments (Deleuze and Guattari 1994, 164; see also Grosz 2008), the second examining how these affects and percepts were shared and discussed during mobile and sedentary interviews with participants and their friends, siblings and parents. Lastly, I provide an overview of the issues raised throughout this chapter and point to some future challenges for visual research.

VISUAL RESEARCH WITH CHILDREN

Visual research with children is interdisciplinary by inclination and encompasses everything from drawing (MacRae 2008; Mitchell 2006) and painting (Askins and Pain 2011) to all kinds of elaborations of analogue and digital photography, videography, visual interviews and film-making (e.g. Aarsand and Forsberg 2010; Luttrell 2010; MacLure et al. 2010; Murray 2009; O'Loughlin et al. 2013; Orellana 1999; Rasmussen 1999; Thomson 2008; Young and Barrett 2001), as well as, more recently, mobile phone imaging and GPS mapping (see Mikkelsen and Christensen 2009; Pyyry 2013; Walker et al. 2009). While it is impossible to do justice to this work here, it has opened new directions for my own research that I will continue to develop in the following sections, which is why an outline will have to suffice for the moment.

First, childhood researchers have become ever more suspicious of methods that claim to offer easy access into the everyday experiences and environments of children. This also applies to visual methods, such as drawing, painting, photography and filming, which, as students of childhood maintain, cannot be seen as automatically contributing to the expressive and participatory potential of research with children (Cook and Hess 2007; Mitchell 2006). As Christensen and James (2008, 2) write:

> Although some research techniques may sometimes be thought to be more appropriate for use with children, with regard to particular research contexts or the framing of particular research questions, there is, we would argue, nothing particular or indeed peculiar to children that makes the use of any technique imperative.

These authors are not arguing against child-friendly research, but stress instead that the suitability of a method is a precarious outcome of a process of adaptation, where researchers and children are collectively exploring the available methods and tools to adjust both the study and daily practices better to one another. This adaptation is often based on the idea that the prior qualities of methods are less important than the ways in which they can actually be made more interesting and relevant for everyday lives (see Kullman 2013, 887–889). Approaching visual research as a process of adaption suggests that its limits and possibilities are negotiated on an ongoing basis, not least as issues such as ethics, expression and participation are often interrelated and situated (Aarsand and Forsberg 2010)—for example, by allowing children to use visual media in different (unplanned) ways, researchers may expand the ethical scope of their study, as children have more opportunities to convey their experiences of the project (Askins and Pain 2011; Gallacher and Gallagher 2008; Thomson 2007). While working in this manner entails accepting that visual research is, to a certain degree, an unpredictable event, it also brings out the importance of continuous collaboration among the involved adults and children.

Second, many childhood researchers work in an experimental vein, because they do not approach methods and materials, whether these are cameras, paint or clay, as standard equipment that need to be used in one prescribed way or another, but rather as adaptable and transformative entities that allow for different modes of expression and participation (see Askins and Pain 2011; Gallacher and Gallagher 2008; MacRae 2008). This might simply entail being aware of the fact that there is no single right way of studying the world or that research

> can be a sensual experience. Paint and clay bring tactile pleasures; experimenting with line, shape, angle, perspective and colour are interesting

experiences in their own right. . . . Children given a camera may become
interested in exploring and representing light, or in trying to capture the
intricate patterns made by clouds.

(Thomson 2008, 14)

Researching in a more experimental manner, then, involves fostering
a process that allows more space for children to explore what a method
can actually *do* in daily settings, and how they might use it to open new
possibilities in the world. This also involves recognising that the materials created and shaped by participants are often more than data or direct
representations of everyday life—they can serve all kinds of aesthetic and
transformative purposes, which are valuable in and of themselves, not
least as they chart areas of experience that might otherwise escape attention, such as affective and multi-sensory engagements (see Askins and Pain
2011; Gallacher and Gallagher 2008; MacLure et al. 2010; MacRae 2008;
Pyyry 2013).

Third, there is a long tradition in visual research of involving children
in mobile picture-making by inviting them to explore their daily environments with cameras (Orellana 1999; Rasmussen 1999). More recent
studies have employed methods such as participatory photography, videography, GPS and visual group interviews to explore, for example, children's interactions with spaces inside and around schools or during the
school journey (Mikkelsen and Christensen 2009; Murray 2009; Ross
2007; Walker et al. 2009). These studies share an interest in encouraging children to actively move around in their daily settings with visual
equipment in order to produce images of the experiences, practices and
spaces that are important to them. Ross (2007, 388; original emphasis),
among others, has used participatory photography to give "prominence
to the *meaning* of [children's mobilities], highlighting the ways in which
children's agency is expressed in their movement through and engagements in their localities". These kinds of methods demonstrate the value
of combining visual research with the actual mobilities of children as they
participate in the intricate arrangements of bodies, materials and spaces
that make up their everyday lives.

The following section will continue to elaborate on these methodological insights by discussing how digital screens have reconfigured picture-
making practices. Current visual research with children appears to direct
relatively little attention to the possibilities raised by digital picture-
making, such as viewing images on the move, which has created new
embodied and collective ways of engaging with still and moving images.
Likewise, few researchers have explored how moving with digital screens
entails diverse expressive actions that do not always result in images but
may still be significant for participants and their encounters with everyday environments.

SCREENS, BODIES AND IMAGES

Although digital screen-based media have long been researched and theorised across the human and social sciences, there is a widespread tendency in this work to approach the screen itself as a passive medium:

> It is commonly assumed that screens do not call attention to themselves. Rather, they subsume their materiality and status as objects to the need to reflect, enchant, engross, or incite. That they are objects of a particular kind is much less important than the images they 'carry', transmit and arrange.
>
> (Simone 2012, 208)

Recent work, however, has begun to rethink the relations between screens, images and worlds (see Ash 2009; Coleman 2013; Larsen 2008; Marks 2000, 2002; Simone 2012; Thrift 2005), arguing that screens, understood in the widest possible sense, have always been essential for aesthetic and expressive practices, from architecture to painting and cinema, because they stand for the gesture of "framing" that captures and recomposes the intensities of the world to create a "space in which sensations may emerge, from which a rhythm, a tone, coloring, weight, texture, may be extracted and moved elsewhere" (Grosz 2008, 12; see also Deleuze and Guattari 1994, 163–199). Authors such as Thrift (2005, 233–234) have claimed that the proliferation of digital technology has further enveloped life in a "complete ecology of screens . . . which can be thought of as a vast geographical web of perception". Screens, from mobile phones and camcorders to tablet devices and interactive advertising, cannot be seen as neutral media but rather as active elements that potentially transform our engagements with the world. As Wasson (2007, 90) writes, through "dynamics of size, colour, shape, clarity, and blurred abstraction, screens are not blank frames but active forces"—they are intensive entities that we constantly interact with and that function as "a surface that animates, that *brings images to life*" (Coleman 2013, 12; original emphasis).

For the present argument, foregrounding digital screens will offer us a better understanding of different aspects of children's mobile picture-making in Helsinki. First of all, screens direct attention to the spatial and temporal situatedness of visual practices by working as sites through which images are produced, consumed and shared in present digital cultures. They constitute an arena for the exploration of actual encounters between bodies, images and environments, thereby inviting us to adopt a practice-orientated approach to visual research with children and to explore more closely the "*material compositions and conduct* of representations" (Dewsbury et al. 2002, 438; original emphasis). Ash (2009, 2107), among others, argues that it is essential to attend to the "spatiotemporal conditions under which images appear", including the material specificities of screens, because these shape "the sensual appearance of images and their phenomenal interpretation" (Ash 2009, 2109).

Second, screens highlight the affective and multi-sensory qualities of children's engagements with visual materials, suggesting that "images are themselves navigated through specific kinds of movement and interaction" (Coleman 2013, 17). Screens work as a "portable sensorium" (Marks 2000, 243), mobilising images that contain not only pre-coded meanings in need of interpretation, but "blocs of sensation", that is, composites of "affects" and "percepts", or different types of pre-personal intensities, that have the potential to set bodies in new kinds of motion as they engage the attention of viewers (Deleuze and Guattari 1994, 164; see also van Alphen 2008; O'Sullivan 2001). The notions of affect and percept do not refer to individual affections or perceptions, but rather to the "mobile and mobilizing forces" (Grosz 2008, 76) that expressive materials, such as photographs and video, bring into their encounters with viewers. Addressing viewers across sensory modalities, before they are able to consciously register these effects, affects and percepts open human beings to unexplored dimensions of experience by intensifying mundane colours and shapes, sounds and rhythms, in ways that "may summon up and generate future sensations, new becomings" (Grosz 2008, 75). Screens are one of the arenas where such intensive encounters between bodies and expressive materials are played out, often inviting unexpected responses in those who they bring together for the making and viewing of images.[2]

Third, screens turn picture-making into co-experimentation. Through their viewing and editing features, screens are spaces for the elaboration rather than the mere representation of the world (Ash 2009; Coleman 2013; Simone 2012; Thrift 2005; Wasson 2007). Screens remind us that visual technologies can generate new "modes of engagement" with others and the environment (Witmore 2004, 58), as, for example, indicated by digital tourist photography, which often takes the shape of a

> collaborative event because 'onlookers' can also monitor the screen when picturing takes place and the result is immediately available for inspection and therefore for comments from 'onlookers' (who may turn into 'co-producers') and 'posing actors', and they may demand that the image must be deleted and re-taken, perhaps several times.
>
> (Larsen 2008, 148)

Consequently, as Larsen (2005, 429) argues, picture-making "does not so much reflect 'geographies' as produce them, new bodies and new 'ways of being together'". Screens are sites for the shared exploration and elaboration of experiences that allow images to be mobilised as potentially transformative entities.

Fourth, screens bring into focus the varied qualities that still and moving images assume as they circulate in daily settings. The relations between still and moving images, particularly in photography and cinema, are a topic of longstanding debate (Campany 2008), and digital technology has added more complexity to the ostensible stillness or motion, stability or mutability of images (Ash 2009; Røssaak 2011) by, for example, fostering a more serial approach to picture-making, as people mobilise the still by creating cascades of images that flow into one another (see Latham and McCormack 2009). Similarly, one can use screens to pause video footage and turn it into a focus of microscopic study—all of this while viewers are on the move. It could also be argued, to press this argument further, that any encounter with a still or a moving image entails one or another kind of mobility, whether this happens on the level of affection and perception (Lisle 2010). We move *with* the images that we carry around on digital screens and, as we do so, we in turn become moved *by* these images.

This section has argued that highlighting digital screens offers researchers an opportunity to explore how people engage with still and moving images in various embodied ways, employing them to experiment with different styles of relating to the world. The following sections will continue to elaborate this argument empirically by discussing children's digital imaging practices during school journeys in Helsinki, concentrating on two aspects in particular. First, I explore how children deployed the two cameras and their screens to create alternative ways of sensing and interacting with the urban environment, allowing novel affects and percepts to emerge as a result. Second, I will discuss the diverse forms of collective engagement that screens—both camera and computer—facilitated among the children, parents and me, allowing us to conduct interviews both while being mobile and (seemingly) still.

SENSING WITH SCREENS

As the episode with Anneli at the outset of this chapter suggested, learning to move around with a digital screen entails adjustment and practice. Children soon realised that navigating spaces with a camera requires a new kind of attentiveness, as one has to look at the screen, keep the camera steady and make decisions about what to film or photograph, while also being mindful of the surrounding environment, so that one does not bump into persons and things or, when moving in traffic, put oneself at unnecessary risk. Different practices of mobility also shaped our picture-making in diverse ways, which meant that the filming and photography had to be adapted to the varying formations of bodies, materials and spaces that characterised the daily city—for example, public transport introduced certain conditions for the picture-making, because our movements were constrained by the architecture of buses, trains, trams and the metro, and also because we had to avoid photographing or filming other passengers directly, so as not to interfere with their privacy.

As the cameras proved constitutive of field relations, I gradually became more interested in the situated specificities of children's engagements with the visual technology. Michael (2004, 19–20; see also Aarsand and Forsberg 2010; Hutchby 2001) argues that leaving unexplored the mediating role of artefacts and technologies during research can easily mask the fact that both the "researcher" and the "participant" are "heterogeneous, situated, embodied, and emergent" entities, whose abilities to express and share experiences and understandings are co-shaped by the materials that facilitate this process in the first place. For the children in Helsinki, the screens assumed such a role, opening new ways for them to engage with their surroundings and enabling them to share experiences with co-travellers.

Instead of having to engage with the world through a viewfinder, the screens allowed children flexibility, as they could, for example, run with the equipment, or make all kinds of gestures and movements, but still be aware of what they were filming and photographing through quick glimpses at the screen. As a consequence, the children developed intricate bodily relationships to the screens, using them to amplify diverse affective and sensory possibilities in their surroundings. This sensing "with" screens became a crucial part of field relations and children's visual work (Kullman 2012, 7; see also Murray 2009; Pyyry 2013). At the same time, the screens constituted collective arenas for visual exploration that allowed children to replay images on the move, as 10-year-old Leif and his friend Niilo, demonstrate in the following empirical vignette,[3] based on the images produced by the boys, field notes, and interview transcripts.

* * *

As we are walking in a park near the school, Leif notices a tiny squirrel chewing away on a pine nut on the ground. The boys become animated by this sight and begin to film and photograph the animal from all possible angles. Leif, who is holding the camcorder, tells Niilo to be careful, so that we do not scare away the squirrel: "Niilo, you can just use the zoom, you don't have to go closer!" Then Leif softens his voice and zooms into the fur of the squirrel, almost as if stroking it, calling the animal "cute" and "brave". The squirrel becomes disturbed by our presence and scurries up a nearby tree, where it soon disappears amidst the branches.

After our brief encounter with the squirrel, Leif and Niilo cannot stop thinking about it, and the intensity of their engagements with the animal seems to spill over into the remainder of our walk. Niilo is replaying his photographs of the squirrel on the display screen of his camera, and each time Leif and Niilo see a glimpse of the animal, they become visibly energised. This intensity appears to be echoed in the excitement whereby the boys move around with the two cameras, pointing them in all thinkable directions and zooming in and out of different details in their daily environment, such as planes in the afternoon sky and flowers on the ground. Niilo even

Figure 3.1 Left: Still image from the footage that Leif, a 10-year-old boy, produced of the squirrel that we encountered on the school journey. Right: Still image from the footage that Leif produced of Niilo, a 10-year-old boy, who was watching his photographs of the same squirrel on the display screen of the camera.

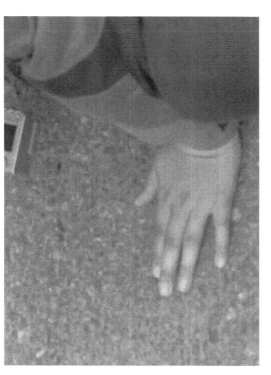

Figure 3.2 Left: Photograph that 10-year-old Niilo took of his 10-year-old friend Leif, who is using the camcorder to examine a flower that he has picked up from the ground. Right: Still image from the footage that Leif produced of Niilo as he touched and photographed a patch of asphalt.

stops momentarily to take pictures of the pavement, holding the camera in one hand and using the other to touch the rugged surface that he is photographing. Then the boys gather around the screen to view the photograph, concluding that, when explored up close, asphalt does not really look like asphalt but rather like the texture of a rock.

And so our shared walk continues, Leif and Niilo working with their cameras as if they wanted to cover every square inch of their journey. But the brief encounter with the squirrel stays with the boys, and, during our next walk, Leif zooms into the place by the pine tree where we had seen the squirrel, saying: "This is where the squirrel was last time".

* * *

From this account it is clear that Leif and Niilo are mobilising cameras not only to represent their walk between home and school but also to elaborate new ways of engaging with the diverse bodies and materials that make up the city, from patches of worn asphalt to skittish squirrels. Leif and Niilo are employing their cameras as "modes of engagement" that enable them to experiment with alternative ways of relating to their surroundings (Witmore 2004, 58). As Pink (2007, 245) argues, moving with a camera can facilitate "a process through which people, things and sensory experiences are drawn together." This is exactly what Leif and Niilo are doing as they dance around with the visual equipment, their gestures weaving together bodies, materials and spaces along the way, highlighting how all of these often unrecognised elements play a role in the shaping of their journey.

It is also clear that the screens of the two cameras occupied a central position in this act of drawing together. Consider, for example, the way Leif uses the camcorder to engage with the squirrel—cautious of startling the animal, Leif zooms into its fur and moves the camera back and forth, as if carefully stroking the squirrel through the medium of the screen. A comparable gesture is performed by Niilo, who inspects a patch of asphalt by using his screen as a microscope, while simultaneously feeling the rough ground with his bare hand. Together these moments point to the "haptic visuality" of children's mobile photography and filming by bringing out "the material presence of the image", as the participants engaged with screens using the whole body (Marks 2000, 163; see also Marks 2002). The children, in other words, were sensing with screens, employing these to frame as well as amplify details in their environments. For brief periods, the children would even stop filming or photographing altogether and simply explore the world through the screen, which reminds us, once again, that cameras are not only picture-making tools, but framing devices, probes, microscopes, telescopes, amplifiers and much more.

Leif and Niilo also indicate that screens are arenas for collaborative and site-specific engagement with images. The participants were not simply generating images as data or representations for the researcher but as expressive materials for their own doings—for example, the boys reviewed the series of images that Niilo produced of the squirrel, allowing the affects and percepts stored into previously taken images to enter into the present moment and inspire our moving bodies into new kinds of actions. As Grosz (2008, 75–76) writes, affects and percepts are "extracted from the energetic forces generated between subjects and objects that are arrested, as it were, in flight, where they live as pure movement or transition". For Leif and Niilo, the images of their encounter with the squirrel clearly served as a repository of "pure movement and transition" that they could draw on to intensify their experiences of the school journey. At the same time, the boys complicated the relationship between still and moving images by indicating that one can actively move and sense with a still, letting it modulate one's engagements with the surrounding world. As Lisle (2009) argues, "the origin point of a photograph is potential mobility, [and] mobility is never completely vanquished when it is turned into a still image".

Travelling with still and moving images, then, the children cultivated new possibilities for employing visual materials as part of research—for example, they would sometimes produce rapid series of stills of specific practices and spaces, approaching these not so much as a "sequence of representations" as "an index of the intensity and consistency of attending to and through the everyday" (Latham and McCormack 2009, 256). Such series of stills carried their own rhythms that could be reanimated when the images were later viewed one after the other, in this sense enacting some of the intensities that went into their making. Likewise, some children created both still and moving images with the camcorder or reviewed and paused their footage, thereby slowing down moving images to gain more insight into how their travel practices were composed—for example, this was something that 11-year-old Anni and her 8-year-old sister Enni did during their metro journey: they filmed short sequences of all kinds of micro-practices involved in using the metro, such as waiting for the train, boarding a carriage and finding a seat. After this, the girls would watch these sequences together on the camera screen.

Above all, by actively exploring their mobilities through the screen, the children brought out their affective and sensory reflexivity in relation to the urban environment. This points to children's heightened awareness of their surroundings, and suggests that the school journey offers them ample opportunities to become more attuned to the everyday city. The intensive engagements with screens discussed here demonstrate that the children in Helsinki navigate images as they navigate urban spaces— through "haptic perception" that involves the whole body and attends carefully to the particularities of environments (Marks 2002, xiii). Next we will explore how this attentiveness was expressed during visual interviews.

SHARING WITH SCREENS

While my initial plan was to conduct interviews after fieldwork, we were already engaging in mobile visual interviews during the school journeys by gathering around the screens to share our thoughts on their still and mobile framings of the world. Such sharing "with" screens could take place when travelling in buses, trains or the metro, or while walking on the street or running through a park, each of these practices creating responses to images, ranging from quick glances to closer explorations (Kullman 2012, 10–12). These moments around the screens were significant—regardless of whether they resulted in verbal exchanges, gestures, movements, murmurs, exclamations or simply more picture-making—because they added to the sense of bodily togetherness that gradually emerged during fieldwork.

The intensities of our mobile interactions with the images also found their way into the later sedentary interviews, most of which lasted between 45 and 60 minutes and took place in homes, where the participants and, as was often the case, their friends, siblings and parents, would assemble around the screen of my laptop. During such instances, it became clear how well the children knew their images—for example, even if some of them had created almost 100 photographs and filmed long sequences, the children could still ask me to find a specific image that they remembered producing, or to replay a certain part of their footage. One reason for children's familiarity with their images was that they had already reviewed them on the move. Another was that the affects and percepts of our journeys had been stored in the materials, which addressed children's bodies directly and brought them "into contact with the material forms of memory" (see Marks 2000, 243; also Marks 2002).

The atmosphere of the visual interviews was in many ways continuous with the school journeys in that children's immediate reactions to their images were often embodied, as they became variously animated by the photographs and footage, laughing, pointing at details or simply expressing amazement at how everything looked. Indeed, the computer screen turned into an arena for intensive engagements with the visual materials, as we would collectively work with the images, pausing, rewinding or fast-forwarding their flow, or turning the volume up and down—anything that would bring them alive to us (see MacLure et al. 2010; Spinney 2011). According to Ash (2009, 2110), the materialities of screens have an important role in these engagements, as they "trace out a territory of affects and create a material *umwelt* for the human viewer" by conditioning relations between bodies and images. As the laptop that I brought along to each interview had a relatively small screen, 13-inches, it invited all those present to cluster around the computer. While we were all facing the screen, watching and listening intently, we formed an assemblage of co-sensing bodies, whose responses to the visual materials were perceptible to others and therefore created a space for the sharing of affects and percepts.

There was an underlying deliberateness to our improvised way of using visual materials, as it entailed looking for patterns of affects and percepts that could move children and parents into new understandings of the school journey. This suggests that an "affective reading" and "reading for meaning" are not opposed approaches to visual interviews (van Alphen 2008, 29). Rather, it is precisely because images move viewers—sometimes pleasantly, at other times unpleasantly—that they encourage participants to think and express themselves in new ways about their experiences: "A hasty flight to . . . meaning can only end up in the already known, . . . whereas the affective operations and the way they shock to thought are what opens a space for the not yet known" (van Alphen 2008, 30). To explore this issue more closely, let us turn to the following empirical vignette of 8-year-old girl Leila and her parents, assembled from the footage of Leila, fieldnotes and interview transcripts.

* * *

We are sitting around the kitchen table, watching a clip where Leila, her friends and I are walking from school along a pavement on a quiet side street that leads to a busy four-lane road. As we reach the road, we need to stop by the edge of the pavement and wait for the lights to change. Standing there, we are overtaken by something much larger than us: endless flows of cars, buses, lorries and trams that pass us at considerable speed just a few feet away, and whose noises drown out our conversation on the video almost entirely.

As we are watching this intense scene, full of movement and noise, unfold across the screen, a certain tension builds up in the kitchen, and Aila and Asko, the mother and father of Leila, appear slightly shaken by the footage, particularly as it later shows a girl, who Leila does not recognise but who cannot be much older than her, barely making it across the street before the oncoming vehicle traffic. I ask Leila a few questions about her footage:

> Kim: Do you feel that it's difficult to cross here?
> Leila: Well, quite difficult.
> Kim: What makes it difficult?
> Leila: Well, sometimes cars jump the light.
> Kim: Have you seen things like this happening?
> Leila: Yes. . . . Even today when we were coming from school.

Later during the interview, Asko points out that he was startled to witness the moment of crossing as it was being replayed on the computer screen. He explains that he is worried about this crossing, and that he has repeatedly practised using it with Leila. Disturbingly enough, despite this careful and

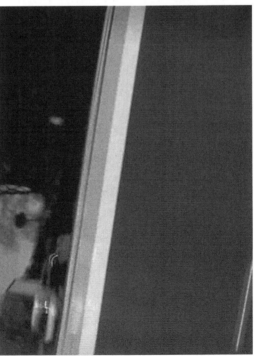

Figure 3.3 Left: Still image from footage that 8-year-old Leila produced of a bus driving through a busy crossing on her way home from school. Right: Still image from Leila's footage of a car passing through the same crossing.

continuous training, the crossing seems to fail Leila, because it cannot prevent vehicles from jumping the light, therefore needlessly putting Leila and her friends in a vulnerable position in traffic.

* * *

This episode demonstrates what Harper (2002, 21) calls "breaking frames": a moment when images, through their capacity to show events in an alternative light, offer "a new framing of taken-for-granted experiences". Here, the different affects and percepts that composed the event of crossing—stored as an arrangement of colours, shapes, rhythms and sounds in the video footage as a result of the attentive camera work of Leila—were carried over into the kitchen of her family, not only causing a sense of unease but raising broader questions about the challenges that children encounter as they travel around in the daily city. The moving images intensified what might otherwise have been a mundane instance of crossing through the way they transmitted the overpowering affective and sensory presence of the vehicle traffic that passed close to Leila and her camera, appearing as swooshing lines and shapes on the screen. The disturbing noise from the accelerating vehicles also played into this intensification, not only silencing the conversation on the screen but interrupting our interview in the kitchen. And then there was the girl running across the street, and her similarity to Leila, who could have been crossing herself. Sitting in the kitchen, these intensities elicited bodily responses in those present, such as silence and gasps, only afterwards translating into attempts to verbalise and interpret.

The interview with Leila and her family indicates that an important task of visual research, whether one works with stills, moving images or both, is to animate the participants by channelling some of the affects and percepts that pass through their daily practices and spaces, so as to generate new ideas and insights about them. As I have argued, this effect may be accomplished collaboratively with participants by working through the available materials and then focussing on images that are conducive to novel reactions and thoughts. All of these details and decisions matter, because people encounter images with the whole body (Marks 2000, 2002). Even while being confined to a seat in a room, the viewing body is moving, although here "movement becomes a matter of internal qualitative shifts in degree, rather than shifts in kind as when moving through extended space" (Ash 2009, 2114; see Lisle 2010). This poses a specific challenge for researchers, and especially those who employ participatory methods, as the seeming stillness and mobility of images becomes less important than the "qualitative shifts in degree" that they can create in others. As this chapter has suggested, one productive forum for such experimentation with the affects and percepts of still and moving images is the digital screen, which has the potential to bring bodies, images and worlds into new relationships and, in doing so, transform understandings of the everyday.

CONCLUDING THOUGHTS

This chapter has argued that experimenting with screens offers a useful way for visual researchers to engage with children's digital filming and photography. Working through screens has a series of advantages, among them the possibility to inspire recursive processes of picture-making that enable participants to actively explore their still and moving images, as well as to try out alternative modes of incorporating these images into different practices in order to develop awareness of new features in everyday environments. At the same time, screens highlight the affective qualities of visual materials by serving as sites for intensive and situated encounters between bodies, images and worlds, in this sense directing attention to the varied ways in which images, whether ostensibly still or moving, participate in mundane settings.

Being aware of the multiple mobilities of images creates new opportunities for expanding the potential uses of still and moving images as part of research. For example, equipped with a screen, participants and researchers can arrange visual interviews on the move, and thereby contribute rich situated knowledge not only about daily practices but the moment-to-moment unfolding of a method, as participants are encouraged to reflect on their visual work in real time, which, in turn, adds to the adaptability of a method, because the researchers and participants can rearrange their approach to picture-making whenever required. Most importantly, in multiplying the possible modes of image production and consumption, screens ask for greater attention to the unexpected ways in which images may become mobilised and immobilised as part of the everyday practices of research. They remind us that visual researchers often operate in a space *between* still and moving images, where the still can be mobilised and the moving image stilled on the very same device. For this reason, screens suggest that photographic and videographic methods can and often need to be deployed and elaborated in dialogue with one another. Apart from unsettling distinctions between still and moving images, screens invite researchers to think about their equipment beyond mere generators of visual data. As we have seen, a screen is a mobile playground for all kinds of intensities that pass through the world.

Since my fieldwork with the children in Helsinki ended, the number and size, affordability and connectivity of digital screen-based devices has increased rapidly, opening all kinds of possibilities for mobilising visual research. However, this chapter has not sought to celebrate digital picture-making or recent technological advances by claiming that these automatically make visual research easier or more inspiring and productive (for a critique, see Savage et al. 2010). Instead, through offering a detailed discussion of children's engagements with screens, it suggested that the value of any method or medium depends on whether participants manage to use these to express themselves and their experiences. This means accepting that participants may also employ methods and media in unexpected but still meaningful ways—for example, many children in Helsinki enjoyed using the visual equipment for other practices than picture-making, such as looking at the world framed by the screen or circulating cameras among friends. One possibility of allowing more space for this kind of experimentation is to adopt a "post-medium" (O'Sullivan 2001, 130) approach to visual research, which entails strategically suspending prior ideas about the specifics of media, and focussing instead on how they are actually used and, crucially, transformed in encounters with participants (see Kullman 2012).

Still, there remains a particular challenge that concerns not only those who work with children but all visual researchers. Through the proliferation of digital technologies, and especially the possibility to circulate images through interconnected devices and online environments (see Larsen 2008; Larsen and Sandbye 2014), visual researchers are faced with the ever-complex mobility of images that have been generated during the course of research. If participants have co-created the visual materials and feel that they have a right to ownership, researchers need to find a way, if not to immobilise images, then at least to manage their future mobility. My attempt to deal with this challenge involved agreeing with the children and parents—through a verbal and written contract—that I could use images produced by children in my research as long as the participants remained unrecognisable. Likewise, the families agreed that they would use their images only privately. However, more than such quasi-legal contracts, I would like to stress the importance of cultivating ways of working and thinking that, instead of seeing images as mere data or representations for research, starts to take them seriously as active entities that have an impact on bodies and worlds. What the children's intensive experiments with screens seem to suggest is that attending to the affective mobilities and immobilities of images might also help to foster more ethically aware ways of making, using and sharing visual materials—ones that recognise the true force of images, both for good and bad.

NOTES

1. Some of my initial fieldwork with the children was conducted using one digital camera, as I did not manage to obtain a digital camcorder during the early stages of the project. Once I also borrowed a VHS-C camera of an older make from my institution, but ended up operating it myself due to its size and the complexity of functions. This experience brought out the advantage of allowing children to film their journeys with a lighter digital camcorder. The effort to incorporate a larger camera into our mobile interactions was highly distracting, not simply because I had to focus all my attention on manipulating the camera but also because it effectively excluded children from filming.
2. There is a perennial debate around the definition of affect in the human and social sciences (van Alphen 2008, 23–25). Here, I draw on a Deleuzian understanding, which has been adapted from the work of Spinoza, where affects, according to Deleuze (1988) and later elaborations of his thinking (e.g. Anderson and Harrison 2010; Grosz 2008; Massumi 2002; O'Sullivan 2001), are seen as pre-personal intensities that emerge in encounters between the entities populating the world—intensities, furthermore, that either decrease

or increase capacities to act by bringing about transformations in the bodies they pass through and connect to other bodies. Apart from directing attention to the emergent, relational and open-ended aspects of human experience, the notion of affect advances an ethics that strives to move thinking towards a greater recognition of the infinite potential of the world to become otherwise. If affects are irreducible to individual emotions and move bodies to feel the world in new ways, percepts are irreducible to individual perceptions and move bodies to perceive the world in new ways. Affects and percepts, then, are independent from human subjects—they are intensities that art and other practices create and mediate to transform experience (see Deleuze and Guattari 1994, 164; Grosz 2008, 78).

3. I have briefly discussed the school journeys that I shared with Leif and Niilo in an earlier paper (Kullman 2012, 7), where I did not concentrate on the encounter with the squirrel.

REFERENCES

Aarsand, P. and Forsberg, L. 2010. Producing children's corporeal privacy: ethnographic video recording as material-discursive practice. *Qualitative Research* 10: 249–268.

Adey, P. 2009. *Mobility*. London: Routledge.

Alphen, E.J. van. 2008. Affective operations of art and literature. *RES, 53/54*: 20–30.

Anderson, B. and Harrison, P. 2010. *Taking-Place: Non-Representational Theories and Geography*. London: Ashgate.

Ash, J. 2009. Emerging spatialities of the screen: video games and the reconfiguration of spatial awareness. *Environment and Planning A,* 41: 2105–2124.

Askins, K. and Pain, R. 2011. Contact zones: participation, materiality, and the messiness of interaction. *Environment and Planning D: Society and Space,* 29: 803–821.

Barker, J. A., Kraftl, P., Horton, J. and Tucker, F. 2009. The road less travelled? New directions in children's mobility. *Mobilities,* 4: 1–10.

Campany, D. 2008. *Photography and Cinema*. London: Reaktion Books.

Christensen, P. and James, A. (eds.) 2008. *Research with Children: Perspectives and Practices,* 2nd ed. London: RoutledgeFalmer.

Coleman, R. 2013. Sociology and the virtual: interactive mirrors, representational thinking and intensive power. *The Sociological Review,* 61: 1–20.

Cook, T. and Hess, E. 2007. What the camera sees and from whose perspective. Fun methodologies for engaging children in enlightening adults. *Childhood,* 14: 29–45.

Cresswell, T. 2006. *On the Move. Mobility in the Modern Western World*. London: Routledge.

Cresswell, T. 2010. Towards a politics of mobility. *Environment and Planning D: Society and Space,* 28: 17–31.

Deleuze, G. 1988. *Spinoza: Practical Philosophy*. San Francisco: City Lights Books.

Deleuze, G. and Guattari, F. 1994. *What is philosophy?* London: Verso.

Dewsbury, J.-D., Harrison, P., Rose, M., and Wylie, J. 2002. Enacting geographies. *Geoforum,* 33: 437–440.

Gallacher, L.-A. and Gallagher, M. 2008. Methodological immaturity in childhood research? Thinking through 'participatory methods'. *Childhood,* 15: 499–516.

Grosz, E. 2008. *Chaos, Territory, Art. Deleuze and the Framing of the Earth*. New York: Columbia University Press.

Harper, D. 2002. Talking about pictures: a case for photo elicitation. *Visual Studies,* 17: 14–26.

Hutchby, I. 2001. The moral status of technology: Being recorded, being heard, and the construction of concerns in child councelling. In Hutchby, I. and Moran-Ellis, J. (eds.) *Children, Technology and Culture. The Impacts of Technologies on Children's Everyday Lives.* London: Routledge, 114–132.

Kullman, K. 2012. Experiments with moving children and digital cameras. *Children's Geographies,* 10: 1–16.

Kullman, K. 2013. Geographies of experiment/experimental geographies: a rough guide. *Geography Compass,* 7: 879–894.

Larsen, J. 2005. Performativity of tourist photography. *Space and Culture,* 8: 416–434.

Larsen, J. 2008. Practices and flows of digital photography: an ethnographic framework. *Mobilities,* 3: 141–160.

Larsen, J. and Sandbye, M. (eds.) 2014. *Digital Snaps. The New Face of Photography.* London: I.B. Tauris.

Latham, A. and McCormack, D. 2009. Thinking with images in non-representational cities: vignettes from Berlin. *Area,* 41: 252–262.

Lisle, D. 2009. The 'Potential Mobilities' of Photography. *M/C Journal,* 12. http://journal.media-culture.org.au/index.php/mcjournal/article/viewArticle/125.

Lisle, D. 2010. Moving encounters: the affective mobilities of photography. In Bissell, D. and Fuller, G. (eds.) *Stillness in a Mobile World.* London: Routledge, 139–154.

Luttrell, W. 2010. 'A camera is a big responsibility': a lens for analysing children's visual voices. *Visual Studies,* 25: 224–237.

MacLure, M., Holmes, R., MacRae, C. and Jones, L. 2010. Animating classroom ethnography: overcoming video-fear. *International Journal of Qualitative Studies in Education,* 23: 543–556.

MacRae, C. 2008. Representing space: Katie's horse and the recalcitrant object. *Contemporary Issues in Early Childhood,* 9: 275–286.

Marks, L.U. 2000. *The Skin of the Film. Intercultural Cinema, Embodiment, and the Senses.* Durham: Duke University Press.

Marks, L.U. 2002. *Sensuous Theory and Multisensory Media.* Minneapolis: University of Minnesota Press.

Massumi, B. 2002. *Parables for the Virtual: Movement, Affect, Sensation.* Durham: Duke University Press.

Michael, M. 2004. On making data social: heterogeneity in sociological practice. *Qualitative Research,* 4: 5–23.

Mikkelsen, M.R. and Christensen, P. 2009. Is children's mobility really independent? A study of children's mobility combining ethnography and GPS/mobile phone technologies. *Mobilities,* 4: 37–58.

Mitchell, L.M. 2006. Child-centered? Thinking critically about children's drawings as a visual research method. *Visual Anthropology Review,* 22: 60–73.

Murray, L. 2009. Looking at and looking back: visualization in mobile research. *Qualitative Research,* 9: 469–488.

O'Sullivan, S. 2001. The aesthetics of affect. Thinking art beyond representation. *Angelaki,* 6: 125–135.

O'Loughlin, J., Chróinín, D.N. and O'Grady, D. 2013. Digital video: the impact on children's learning experiences in primary physical education. *European Physical Education Review,* 19: 165–182.

Orellana, M.F. 1999. Space and place in urban landscape. Learning from children's views on their social worlds. *Visual Sociology,* 14: 73–89.

Peters, P.F. 2006. *Time, Innovation and Mobilities. Travel in Technological Cultures.* London: Routledge.

Pink, S. 2007. Walking with video. *Visual Studies,* 22: 240–252.

Pyyry, N. 2013. 'Sensing with' photography and 'thinking with' photographs in research into teenage girls' hanging out. *Children's Geographies.* doi: 10.1080/14733285.2013.828453

Rasmussen, K. 1999. Places of children—children's places. *Childhood,* 11: 155–173.

Ross, N. 2007. 'My journey to school. . .': foregrounding the meaning of school journeys and children's engagements and interactions in their everyday localities. *Children's Geographies,* 5: 373–391.

Røssaak, E. 2011. *Between Stillness and Motion. Film, Photography, Algorithms.* Amsterdam: Amsterdam University Press.

Savage, M., Ruppert, E. and Law, J., 2010. Digital devices: nine theses. *Centre for Research on Socio-Cultural Change Working Paper no. 86.*

Sheller M. and Urry J. 2006. The new mobilities paradigm. *Environment and Planning A,* 38: 207–226.

Simone, A. 2012. Screen. In Lury, C. and Wakeford, N. (eds.) *Inventive Methods. The Happening of the Social.* London: Routledge, 202–218.

Skelton, T. and Gough, K. V. 2013. Young people's im/mobile urban geographies. *Urban Studies,* 50: 455–466.

Spinney, J. 2011. A chance to catch a breath: using mobile video ethnography in cycling research. *Mobilities,* 6: 161–182.

Thomson, F. 2007. Are methodologies for children keeping them in their place? *Children's Geographies,* 5: 207–218.

Thomson, P. (ed) 2008. *Doing Visual Research with Children and Young People.* London: Routledge.

Thrift, N. 2005. Beyond mediation: three new material registers and their consequences. In Miller, D. (ed) *Materiality.* Durham: Duke University Press, 231–255.

Urry, J. 2007. *Mobilities.* Cambridge: Polity Press.

Walker, M., Whyatt, D., Pooley, C., Davies, G., Coulton, P. and Bamford, W. 2009. Talk, technologies and teenagers: understanding the school journey using a mixed-methods approach. *Children's Geographies,* 7: 107–122.

Wasson, H. 2007. The networked screen: moving images, materiality, and the aesthetics of size. In Marchessault, J. and Lord, S. (eds.) *Fluid Screens, Expanded Cinema.* Toronto: Toronto University Press, 74–95.

Witmore, C. L. 2004. Four archaeological engagements with place. Mediating bodily experience through peripatetic video. *Visual Anthropology Review,* 20: 57–71.

Young, L. and Barrett, H. 2001. Adapting visual methods: action research with Kampala street children. *Area,* 33: 141–152.

4 Witnessing Craft
Employing Video Ethnography to Attend to the More-Than-Human Craft Practices of Taxidermy

Merle Patchett

INTRODUCTION

> No book description can adequately convey all that should be known. To learn what is necessary the personal instruction of a good teacher, and the smallest modicum of experience, are worth more than any printed course of instruction, however ostensibly complete.
>
> (Ward 1880, 3)

A video-ethnographic study of a practicing taxidermist opens up new spaces of enquiry into the more-than-human geographies of craft and craftwork. In an attempt to witness the non-representational and more-than-human aspects of taxidermy craftwork in my doctoral research I undertook a video ethnography of taxidermist Peter Summers based at the National Museum Scotland (NMS; see Patchett 2010, 2012b). Using a discreet HD video camera I filmed Peter performing various aspects of the craft during a number of workshop visits that took place over a three-year period. The resulting archive of video footage offers a "portfolio of ethnographic exposures" (Dewsbury 2009, 326), enabling enquiry into the craft techniques it takes to separate a skin from a body and rearrange it in life-like form again. In this chapter I aim to elaborate on, and present aspects of, this video ethnography in order to emphasise its potential for witnessing and exposing the sensory, affective and more-than-human registers of taxidermy practice.

To do so, I will first elaborate on the more-than-human research arguments and methods that framed my decision to undertake a video ethnography of a practicing taxidermist. I will then discuss my crafting of a form of sensory video ethnography to get at the more-than-human practices, embodiments and materialities associated with taxidermy craftwork. In terms of analysis, I present three lessons in the crafts of taxidermy that Peter taught me during the video ethnography: Rehabilitation, Mimetic Reproduction and Becoming-Bird. The immersive position that the video camera affords offers a highly instructive context in which to enquire into the more-than-human craft techniques and material assemblages of taxidermy practice. At the same time it also offers a reflexive position, enabling critical reflection on the practice and utility of video ethnography for these purposes. Overall the chapter aims to highlight video ethnography as an effective tool for witnessing and studying craft practices, emphasising the serious empirical involvements required of researchers when engaging with the practices, embodiments and materialities of craftwork.

CRAFTING MORE-THAN-HUMAN GEOGRAPHIES

> Taxidermy, which is derived from two Greek words, a literal translation of which would signify the "arrangement of skins".
>
> (Browne 1896, 1)

Taxidermy is the craft or process of preparing and mounting animal skins so that they appear "lifelike" (Star 1992). Considerable academic attention to date has been paid to the 'finished' form and display of taxidermy specimens inside cabinets, behind glass—in other words, to their representation (Alberti 2011; Haraway 1989; Poliquin 2008; Wonders 1993). In contrast my research has sought to focus on the relationships, practices and geographies behind the making of specimen animals and displays (see Patchett 2008, 2012b, Patchett and Foster 2008, Patchett et al. 2011; Patchett et al. 2012). These efforts are aligned with non-representational and more-than-human research arguments and approaches in cultural geography that seek to revalue the place of life in its multiplicity of human and non-human forms, processes and connectivities through a prioritisation of practice (see Thrift 2000, 2007; Thrift and Dewsbury 2000; Whatmore 2002, 2006). For those unfamiliar with such discipline-specific concerns, Sarah Whatmore (2006) and Jamie Lorimer (2010) have separately set out the key research agendas that have informed and shaped more-than-human research within geography. These can be synthesised into three interwoven strands that overlap with those of non-representational theory.

First, more-than-human geographies draw on post-human and new materialist critiques of the current ontologies of humanism "to draw attention to the diverse objects, organisms, forces and materialities that populate an emergent world and cross between porous bodies" (J. Lorimer 2010, 238). This has led to the redistribution of subjectivity as something that "does not live inside, in the cellar of the soul, but outside in the dappled world" (Whatmore 2006, 603), and to the recognition that 'the human' emerges as no less a subject of ongoing co-fabrication than any other socio-material assemblage. Whatmore thus prefers the signature 'more-than' over 'post' to suggest it is "what exceeds rather than what comes after the human" that should be of pressing concern (Whatmore 2004, 1361), as post-human writings can end up recentring or periodising the human as "the human being that once was, but which has been 'eclipsed' or 'transcended'" (Braun 2004, 1354).

Second, rethinking humanism has led to a revaluing of the excessive and unpredictable nature of life. For example, as Lorimer outlines, "a great deal of work has been done to unpack the category of 'the animal' to recognise the difference this subsumes and the diverse and familiar modes of lively being it contains" (J. Lorimer 2010, 238). This in turn has led to a rethinking of what forms of intelligence, truth and expertise count and as a result "attention has turned away from cognition to issues of embodiment, performance, skill and affect understood as relational and distributive forces and competencies that cut across any ley-scientist and human-nonhuman divides" (Ibid).

Third, there is a distinct experimental politics and methodological ethos to these modes of thought. In order to extend the company and modality of what constitutes a research subject and conceive of the research process as communal, more-than-human researchers emphasise working as a "collective experimental politics, not a critical endeavour intent on positioning others as representative of a peculiar or particular species, interest, belief or practice" (Hinchliffe et al. 2005, 655). The aim of more-than-human research thus becomes enacting "affective, micropolitical experiments, less certain about what a body can do or become and how humans and animals can and should live together" (J. Lorimer 2010, 239).

Accordingly much of more-than-human research thus far has focused on animal cultures and the refiguring of human/non-human relations (Braun 2006; Greenhough and Roe 2011; Hinchliffe 2008; Lorimer 2006; Philo and Wilbert 2000; Roe et al. 2011; Whatmore 2002). I would like to argue that a study of taxidermy practice opens up new spaces of more-than-human enquiry into the geographies, materialities and embodiments of craftwork. To date, craft and craftwork have been theorised as processes conducted by active human agents upon inert and passive materials (Crawford 2009; Frayling 2011; Gane and Back 2012; Sennett 2008). Given the recent more-than-human ontological and epistemological developments outlined above, such static, anthropocentric approaches to craft are in need of critique. To counter an overly humanistic craft tradition, my doctoral thesis developed a post-human ontological approach to argue for recognising the distinctive more-than-human craft techniques and material agencies involved in taxidermy craftwork, an approach that seeks to rethink human intentionality during craftwork more broadly (Patchett 2010). To develop this rethinking in this chapter, my focus is on witnessing the more-than-human craft techniques of taxidermy practice, and while, much like the criticism levelled at post-human writing, this could lead to a continuing focus on the human (i.e. the human plus . . .), thus negating a full encounter with the decidedly nonhuman agencies of the dead animal bodies involved in taxidermy practice, this emphasis is important in this chapter as I am specifically interested in, as will become apparent, how the craftsperson becomes 'more-than-human' by working with non-human materials and agencies during craftwork.

One thing is certain: whichever way you frame these more-than-human styles of thought they necessitate a rethinking of the orthodox methodologies of the social sciences and humanities. Whatmore (2006) argues that in order for academic researchers to embody and enact more-than-human modes of working they must develop and follow an explicitly experimental methodological imperative. The first aspect of this imperative, according to Whatmore, is to supplement "the familiar repertoire of humanist methods (which generate text and talk) with experimental practices that amplify other sensory, bodily and affective registers and extend the company and modality of what constitutes a research subject" (Whatmore 2006, 606–607). The second aspect demands actively redistributing expertise "beyond engaging with other academic disciplines or research fields to engaging as well with knowledges, practices, vernaculars beyond the academy" (Ibid, 607). More-than-human researchers must therefore commit to research as 'a co-fabrication' or 'working together' with the worldly phenomena enjoined in the research process.

This overlaps with the concerns of non-representational theorists who, much like more-than-human geographers, seek to harness and experiment with the mainstay of qualitative research methods by developing approaches such as 'observant participation' and 'performative ethnography' (Anderson and Harrison 2010; Dewsbury 2009; Lorimer 2005; Thrift 2000). This type of enquiry requires researchers to immerse themselves in the phenomena being studied to the point that they are becoming the phenomena. However, as Dewsbury cautions, this "is not an argument for losing ourselves in the activity and deterritorializing ourselves completely from our academic remit" (2009, 326). Rather than immersing ourselves in the space and becoming the phenomena, the aim is to gather a "portfolio of ethnographic 'exposures' that can be thought of as 'a series of testimonies to practice'" (Ibid, 326–327). Elsewhere Dewsbury (2003, 1923) has called this stance a form of 'witnessing', a stance that is orientated towards being "in tune to the vitality of the world as it unfolds".

The experimental and immersive demands of more-than-human and non-representational geographies thus framed my decision to place myself in the position of apprentice to taxidermist Peter Summers of the National Museum Scotland (see Figure 4.1), recognising the position of apprentice, or 'learner', as a highly instructive context in which to enquire into the complex practices, embodiments and materialities of taxidermy craftwork. This apprenticeship included learning 'how-to-do' certain aspects of the craft (like making a cabinet skin) to crafting a form of sensory video ethnography to produce a series of testimonies to the practice of removing a skin from a body and rearranging it into a life-like form, testimonies that were infused with a certain fidelity to the more-than-human craft techniques performed.

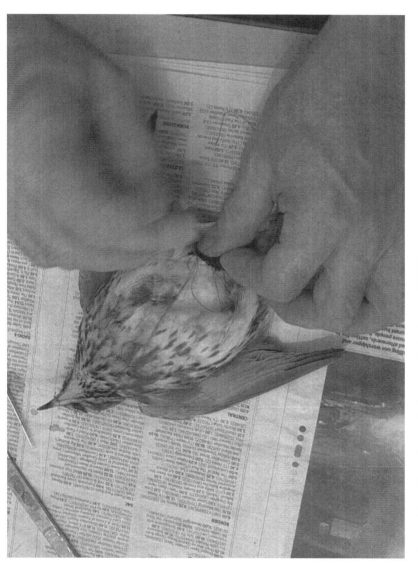

Figure 4.1 Witnessing craft. Image: Merle Patchett/NMS.

OBSERVANT PARTICIPATION: CRAFTING VIDEO ETHNOGRAPHY

> Do not let a scanty supply of tools stop your progress. I have seen wonderful pieces of taxidermy done with a sharp pen-knife, some wire, tow, needle and thread and some arsenic.
>
> (Davie 1894, 23)

Jamie Lorimer emphasises video as a useful supplement for the field observations of the more-than-human geographer as moving images offer "a means of witnessing various forms of knowledge, skill and embodied practice that can escape text-and talk-based approaches" (J. Lorimer 2010, 242). Lorimer cites the work of Eric Laurier and his co-authors as example, illustrating how they have used video to examine "skilful negotiations with objects (like fishing rods), embodied and situated practices (such as seeing fish or communicating), reciprocal human-animal interactions (like walking and playing with dogs) and relational forms of canine mind and movement" (Ibid). Furthermore, Bradley Garrett (2011) emphasises the ethnographic and performative possibilities of videographic methods. Here the emphasis is on making rather than simply using video to acknowledge and explore ethnographic and sensory experience beyond the audiovisual,

> threading in more of the multiple subjectivities and interests that exist in every project, capturing the 'sensuous interrelationship of mind-body-environment' (Howes, 2005, 7) in the peculiar moments of the present tense.
>
> (Garrett 2011, 11)

Here Garrett makes the point that there is a great deal of sensory experience beyond the audiovisual that video footage can also capture and thus why it makes a particularly effective medium for exploring the non-representational and more-than-human aspects of craft practices (for similar see MacDougall 2006; Pink 2006, 2009). However, as Paul Simpson outlines in this volume, there has also been "a somewhat troubling emphasis on trying to 'capture' affective experiences and intensities using various technologies". Here Simpson makes the point that in reference to image-making 'capture' carries representational connotations of fixity and stasis, a detached mediation between subject and world, in contrast to the way that 'witnessing' has been taken up as a trope in non-representational theory (see Dewsbury 2003). What I will come to argue through my analysis is that what non-representational and more-than-human geographies offer is a way of thinking moving images, and specifically video ethnography, less in terms of a representational logic of 'image-capture', and more through a material and affective logics of 'exposure-witnessing'.

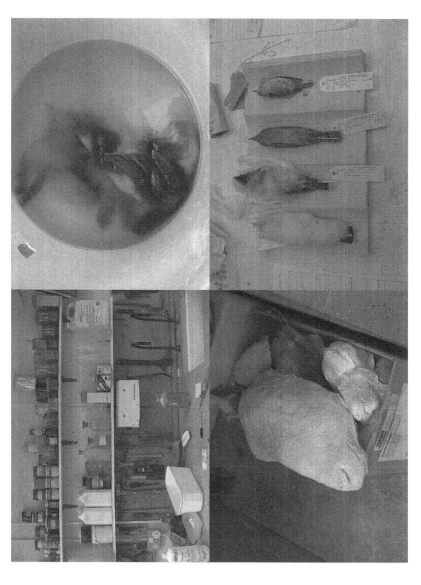

Figure 4.2   Workshop scenes at the NMS. Image: Merle Patchett/NMS.

Specifically for my doctoral research this meant developing a form of video ethnography that would witness the 'sensate'—"that which is felt, experienced and sensed" (Harrison 2000, 498)—and 'more-than-human' aspects of taxidermy craftwork of Peter Summers. Developing a form of sensory video ethnography demands rethinking the ethnographic process through reflexive attention to what Sarah Pink terms the 'sensoriality' of the experience, practice and knowledge of both the researcher and those who participate in their research (Pink 2009, Pink and Mackley 2012). The taxidermy workshop at the NMS is an intoxicating and disorientating assemblage of bodies (live and dead), sounds and smells (see Figure 4.2). The immersive position that the video camera afforded offered a highly focused and instructive context in which to enquire into the more-than-human craft techniques and non-human material agencies of taxidermy.

Using a discreet HD video camera I filmed Peter performing various aspects of the craft during a number of workshop visits that took place over a three-year period. The resulting archive of video footage offers more than just a record of past practice, however, as video records "hold the promise that the researcher might examine past activities not as past but rather as '*formerly present*'" (Raffel 1979, quoted in Laurier and Philo 2006 [italics original]). As such video footage can be understood as offering a portfolio of ethnographic exposures, or "a series of testimonies to practice" (Dewsbury 2009, 326) that can enable a researcher to revisit and immerse themselves in a craft practice as it unfolds. This type of witnessing is in tune with Thrift's (2000) flipping of 'participant observation' to 'observant participation', and emphasises the serious empirical involvement involved in more-than-human engagement with the practices, embodiment and materiality of craft work.

In the following analysis I present three lessons in the crafts of taxidermy that Peter taught me during the video ethnography: Rehabilitation, Mimetic Reproduction and Becoming-Bird. The immersive position that the video camera affords offers a highly instructive context in which to enquire into the more-than-human craft techniques it takes to separate a skin from a body and rearrange it in lifelike form. The immersive video also offers a reflexive position, enabling critical reflections on the practice and utility of sensory video ethnography for these purposes. For example, on watching the footage back I realised that the footage on its own failed to fully describe or disclose some aspects of what was going on. By watching the footage back with Peter and asking him to elaborate on aspects of the craft I was unsure of, I was able to build up a commentary to accompany the video footage. This dual process of analysis, termed 'co-discovery' by Pink (2007), often took place in Peter's workshop, and on watching back the footage together I would ask Peter to explain, in his own terms, what was going on to corroborate or contradict my interpretations. I often recorded these sessions, and Peter's responses, in an ethnographic notebook which I took with me to the workshop sessions. These exchanges also ended up featuring in the video footage itself as due to the nature of my repeat visits Peter would in turn be repeating certain procedures and thus was able to reflect on any questions I had in relation to a procedure as he was doing it. Thus in this instance, rather than relying on playback, 'co-discovery' often happened during the event of practice. Both forms of 'co-discovery' add additional layers of ethnographic narration to supplement my presentation and enquiry into the video footage in the following analysis sections.

AN APPRENTICESHIP IN TAXIDERMY

Lesson 1: Rehabilitation

> The reason birds are always selected is because of easiness of treatment for the student's first lessons in taxidermy, before his teacher allows him to "try his apprentice hand" on the more difficult branches of the art.
>
> (Browne 1878, 125)

Peter had decided my first lesson would be the craft of preparing an avian study-skin, as this was the first method that he had been taught as an apprentice taxidermist. While Peter's preoccupation as a specialist bird taxidermist would necessitate his choice of a bird, historically birds were thought to suit the purpose of the amateur best because fresh specimens were easy to procure. Nowadays the NMS only source their specimens through ethical means and thus are dependent on donations from the public (in the form of found dead animals) and from recognised institutions like zoos and animal sanctuaries. This means that there is little in the way of 'quality control' for the taxidermists working there, and Peter would not be able to pre-empt what specimens he would receive or indeed what state of preservation they would be in. The specimens with which Peter worked were often in poor states of preservation and did not always come as whole cadavers, or even with the expected appendages like the skull or skeletal frame. Even when they did come as whole cadavers they would be put straight into the freezer to prevent further decay. Thus when Peter chose a specimen from the freezer it was often a 'lottery' as to the quality of the mount he would have to prepare.

In Lesson 1: Rehabilitation,[1] Peter selects a Sparrow Hawk and demonstrates aspects of the rehabilitation process. The 'rehabilitation' process, as Peter calls it, is an important yet not well documented aspect of taxidermy practice. This process begins as soon as a specimen is selected from the freezer. The first clip in the video depicts Peter opening the freezer, which is full to the brim with specimens, and then opening a bag at random to see what specimen he is going to work with. The bag contains a Long-Tailed-Tit, which Peter identifies before even taking it out of the plastic bag, and a Sparrow Hawk. It is clear that on taking out and handling the Sparrow

Hawk cadaver Peter is much more keen to work on this specimen and so decides to skin this first. Peter's responsiveness to the material and affective agencies of the Sparrow Hawk is indicative of the distinctive more-than-human material agencies that play a vital collaborative role in taxidermy craftwork. Peter is not working on inert and passive materials; rather, he is working with, and even to an extent being led by, the corporeal, material and affective affordances of the specimens.

After the Sparrow Hawk has been taken out of the freezer and has been given time to thaw, the first task in the rehabilitation process is to work out the rigor mortis so that the specimen can be teased into a malleable working state. In the second clip of the video we witness Peter's warm hands loosen the wing and leg joints and generally soften the body and skin. Working out the rigor mortis also affords Peter the opportunity of inspecting the specimen for broken bones or tears in the skin. At this point the role of the taxidermist is not that far removed from that of a pathologist, as they can often establish cause of death. In the case of the Sparrow Hawk, the left eye is full of blood, indicating that it has been killed by a blow to the head, which Peter surmises was probably caused by the hawk flying into a window.[2]

Once cause of death has been identified, the next task before the skinning can commence is addressing a condition known in the craft as 'freezer burn'. Skins often dry out after being in the freezer and it is vitally important to wet the skin throughout the procedures of skinning and setting-up to keep the skin pliable and prevent tears. This again highlights that Peter must be ever responsive to the material qualities of the skin he is working with. The third clip in the video demonstrates Peter injecting one of the Sparrow Hawk's eyes with water, to bring it back to its natural pressure so that it can be measured and replaced with accurate replacement glass eyes later on in the procedure. Although some may find this to be a particularly gruesome procedure to witness, I reasoned it was important to include and discuss for two main reasons. First, it reveals how Peter is able to rejuvenate and work from the dead matter of the Sparrow Hawk. By injecting the eyes with water Peter is able to measure accurate replacements, thus illustrating how he works from and with the body parts of the Sparrow Hawk to guide his recreation of the specimen. This again highlights how the material agencies and corporeal capacities of the bird skins play a vital role in taxidermy craftwork. Second, it is important to show the eyes being inflated to expose and accustom viewers to the unsettling sensate and material assemblages experienced during taxidermy. The video retains a level of fidelity to the dual experience of revulsion and compulsion I experienced, and theorists of and commentators on disgust argue takes place (Kolnai 2004, Miller 1997), when confronted with entopic materials like congealed blood, oozing bodily fluids and decaying flesh which are both present and exert themselves on Peter (the craftsperson) and the witness (cameraperson/audience) during the rehabilitation process.

The ability of the footage to capture this underlines the potential of video ethnography to acknowledge and explore the complex corporeal and material affordances of taxidermy craft assemblages. Ethnographic film-maker MacDougall argues that video can generate 'corporeal images' in that videographic images "are not just the images of other bodies; they are also images of the body behind the camera and its relations with the world" (2006, 3). Following this, I would argue my video produces 'corporeal images' in that the clips convey the corporeal and sensory negotiations and relations between Peter and the Sparrow Hawk body, but also between these more-than-human bodily negotiations and myself as cameraperson.

We might therefore rather understand the video clips as 'corporeal exposures' to the relations and negotiations between the taxidermist and bird bodies but also between my relations and negotiations with this process from the immersive position of the handheld camera. My use of the word 'exposure', following Dewsbury (2009), over 'image' here expresses my desire to move away from the rather static representational visual politics suggested by the latter to instead emphasise the performative, haptic and affective dimensions of images (both still and moving). Pink argues that video should also be understood as "a reflexive research tool, and understood in relation to the recording position of the researcher" (Pink and Mackley 2012, 4.3). I too attempted to be reflexive about and be responsive to the task as it unfolded, using the freedom the hand-held camera afforded to move position in order to best witness, record and convey the procedures being carried out. This makes evident my body behind the camera and its relations with the more-than-human craft assemblages taking place in Peter's workshop. The aim in presentation is for the viewer to feel, through my body-positioning, like they too are in the position of apprentice, open to being affected by the more-than-human corporeal processes witnessed. This offers a way of rethinking moving images, and specifically video ethnography, less in terms of a representational logic of 'image-capture', and more as a material and affective logics of 'exposure-witnessing'.

Lesson 2: Mimetic Reproduction

> The normal movements of the articulations of the skeleton and the ligaments that control them should receive the most careful consideration . . . no opportunity should be lost to studying such matters using animal cadavers.
>
> (Browne 1896, 9)

Peter's great skill as a taxidermist is underlined when he makes replacement body parts when mounting specimens. To make highly accurate replacement parts, Peter insists on making his own replacement parts from scratch so that he can more faithfully sculpt and thus reproduce the unique form of the particular specimen he is working with and from. Rather than throw away all the fleshy parts after skinning,[3] Peter retains the main body cavity and skeletal parts as referents from which to sculpt replacement parts.

In Lesson 2: Mimetic Reproduction,[4] Peter is making a replacement body out of balsawood for a large Eagle Owl.[5] In the video we see that far from discarding the body, Peter uses it as a vital referent for making the replacement body out of a block of balsa wood he has cut specifically for this purpose. Much like with the eye of the Sparrow Hawk, Peter works from and with the dead matter of the Eagle Owl to create a mimetic replacement. For example, in the first clip Peter marks the shape of the carcass onto a piece of balsa wood, using the body directly rather than taking measurements. On placing the carcass on the block of balsa wood, he cautions that this has the disadvantage of flattening the upper and under surfaces of the carcass. To take the foreshortening of the back into account, Peter lifts up the pelvis in order to curve the back and mark the natural vertebrate length. On asking him how he knows what the 'natural curvature' would be, he puts it down to understanding the natural curvature of the muscles through his experience. In asking Peter, during 'co-discovery', to elaborate on this he explained that a taxidermist is required to have not only an intimate understanding of material, corporeal and anatomical compositions of the bird in death, but also the behavioural and corporal embodiments of the bird in life if they are to reproduce this faithfully when mounting.

This experience is illustrated when Peter pulls out the pectoral muscles to their 'natural profile', before marking their position on the balsa wood block. This demonstrates Peter responding to what he termed in co-discovery as 'sag' in death, which is when muscles relax and stiffen in death, thus losing their natural form. This illustrates Peter is not just working from the dead matter of the Eagle Owl, but is also calling on his understanding of the corporeal embodiments of live birds. While this might overemphasise Peter's impetus and intentionality during this process, at the same time it also demonstrates the more-than-human creative and mimetic techniques Peter draws on when sensing and interpreting the referent body and creating a replacement. Peter is drawing on his experience as a craftsperson, but that experience reaches beyond his own embodiments to incorporate the embodiments and sensibilities of other beings, which in this case happens to be an Eagle Owl. This again challenges our understandings of human intentionality within craftwork as it highlights how more-than-human corporeal capacities are incorporated into taxidermy craftwork.

This is further evinced in the video when Peter has started to carve the balsa wood body and is marking on the wood where indentations for the humerus and pelvic joints need to be carved out. In the clip Peter is continually referring to the carcass, using it to guide his crafting of the replacement body, allowing us to witness the practical, sensual and affective relations maintained between Peter, the referent carcass and the unfolding balsa wood body. The essence of skilled practice, according to Tim Ingold, lies in the craftsperson's ability to achieve this type of "sensory correction": their ability to adjust their movements/actions in relation to their tools and materials as the task unfolds (Ingold 2006, 76). A fluent craft performance thus has to be 'felt', and 'feeling' according to Ingold lies in this synergy between practitioner, tools and materials.

We certainly see this synergy at work in Peter's practice in the video when Peter is carving anatomical details into the balsa wood body. Here he is again drawing on more-than-human creative and mimetic technique and capacities to carve a replacement. What is remarkable about this procedure is that Peter never once measures the referent body and yet, on using the callipers we see that his 'more-than-human' sensing has produced almost exact measurements. When asked how he knows how much to carve off the balsa wood Peter explains he is working from "eye and feel". This again highlights the synergy between practitioner, tools and materials during the craft process.

However, where Ingold draws on a more humanistic phenomenological tradition of thought to argue that this process of sensing is led by the practitioner, in that during this process their body is "both biographer and auto-biographer" (Ingold 2006, 72), I would like to argue that 'sensing' here connotes a more-than-human synergy between practitioner, tools and materials. While Peter's intentionality and creative impetus is certainly guiding aspects of this process, this is always in relation to the tools and materials he is working from, with and against. In this way the process can be understood as a co-fabrication rather than autobiographical. Here I am drawing on Whatmore's redistribution of subjectivity (Whatmore 2006) to argue that craftwork is a co-fabrication of practitioner, tools and materials, encompassing distributed and relational socio-technical and corporeal agencies.

This lesson also highlights how I as 'camera-apprentice' was becoming responsive to the synergy of practitioner, tools and materials. Instead of focusing solely on the hands and body parts like in Lesson 1, the camera and my bodily position begin to zoom out to accommodate more of Peter's body, workbench and the surrounding workshop itself. During the footage you witness Peter using his own body to describe how he mimetically interprets the embodiments of a living Eagle Owl so he can both impute them into his sensing of the dead matter and when carving the replacement. While the camera's zooming out to incorporate Peter's full body may again emphasise his role as biographer of this craft process, I would argue that this shows Peter calling on his understanding of the corporeal embodiments of live birds, thus demonstrating the more-than-human intentionalities and sensibilities co-fabricated into this process. It is important to qualify here that I do not want to downplay Peter's skill as an exceptionally talented taxidermist, rather I seek to emphasise that Peter's skilful embodiments during the craft process depend on more-than-human techniques for sensing and mimetically reproducing the body and embodiments of other beings.

The repositioning of the camera also highlights my presence as camera-person. In line with Ingold's (2006) argument above it could be argued my positionality is close to that of biographer, in that I am telling, through my use of the camera, the story of taxidermy craft practice. Yet in reframing my role here as 'apprentice camera-person' I want to emphasise how I too was attempting to be responsive to not only the tasks as they unfolded and but also to the distributed agencies of taxidermy craft work that permeated into and animated my positioning and embodied camerawork. This highlights my attempts at learning to be affected and thus led by the practical, sensual and affective dimensions and agencies at play in taxidermy craftwork.

Lesson 3: Becoming-Bird

> The job of the taxidermist is to reproduce the forms, attitudes and expression of animals as they appear in life.
>
> (Davie 1894, ii)

Once a replacement body has been made, the next stage when setting-up a specimen for display is to fit the skin over the replacement body parts and thus begin the reassembly. Turning the skin back over the skull and replacement body can be considered a critical moment in this process since it is the point at which the formless skin begins to 'take shape' as a recognisable bird (see Figure 4.3).

Put crudely, the process of taxidermy is one of "dismemberment and reart-iculation" (Desmond 2002, 161). However, as Peter stressed to me during co-discovery, taxidermy requires more than just the rearticulation of form through the making of mimetic replacement parts. Here Peter conveyed that in order to rearrange the skin in 'life-like' form, the taxidermist must impute a sense of the animal's 'character' or 'essence' into the mount through their interpretive sensibilities and skilled practice (see also Star 1992, 262). As noted in the previous section, in order to achieve this level of skill the taxidermist is required to have not only an intimate understanding of the material, corporeal and anatomical compositions of the bird in death (in order to make mimetic replacement parts) but must also have a keen awareness of the behavioural and corporal embodiments and affective intensities of the bird in life, if they are to capture something of this when mounting the specimen.

In Lesson 3: Becoming-Bird,[6] Peter is first discussing, in reference to the Eagle Owl balsa wood body, how his favourite part of the process is inter-preting the 'jizz' of the bird, and second illustrating his 'becoming-bird' in order to impute a sense of jizz into his mount of a White-Crested Laughing Thrush. In the video Peter communicates that his favourite part of the craft practice is when the technical part (which he considers to be skinning and making replacement parts) is out of the way and he can concentrate on the composition of the mount, as this allows him to express his interpretive sensibilities. In the video Peter has nearly finished carving the replacement body for the Eagle Owl and has started to think about how he is going to position and compose the mount. He uses one of his own hands to mimic

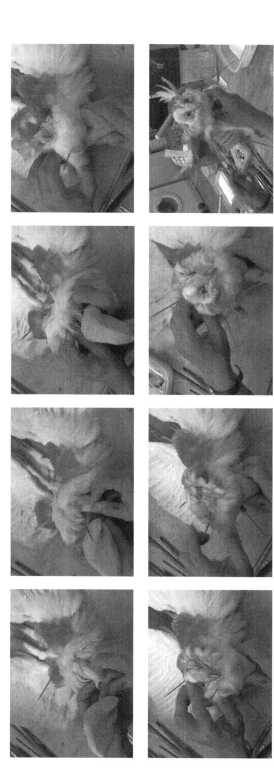

Figure 4.3 Barn Owl stills. Image: Merle Patchett/NMS.

the head and neck of the bird to demonstrate how he intends to position the neck and the anatomical and behavioural characteristics that need to be taken into account when doing so. On beginning to discuss the behavioural motivations behind such positionings he begins to imitate the bird's movements using his own head: "is it looking left [mimics movement with his own head] . . . is it looking right [tilts head right] . . . or is it looking up [tilts head upwards]". Peter then articulates that the most satisfying part of the creative process for him is interpreting the 'jizz' of the bird. Jizz is an interesting concept (and choice of word!), demanding elaboration.

During co-discovery Peter expressed that when deciding how to position a mount and interpret its 'jizz' he would refer to his experience of observing bird behaviour in the wild. Peter, an experienced 'birder', began observing birds as a young boy and it was through this practice that he developed a keen understanding of the corporal and behavioural embodiments and affective intensities of birds in life, what 'birders' term 'jizz'. Jizz, as Helen Macdonald's (2002) study of the concept explains, is used by birders to describe the 'essence' of a particular bird species:

> As a rule, it is characteristics, the tout ensemble of the subject . . . something definite yet indescribable, something which instantly registers recognition in the brain, yet how or what is seen remains unspecified. It is its jizz.
>
> (Macdonald 2002, 71)

Jamie Lorimer's study of 'non-human charisma' further elaborates that a birder's ability to recognise birds by their jizz is understood as a sign of expertise and is built up through "ecological proximity with and corporeal understanding of his or her target organism" (J. Lorimer 2007, 917). Lorimer also outlines how jizz-recognition demands identifying birds more immediately through their performative and affective intensities rather than relying upon the use of any defining representational/physical features. This form of knowing is achieved, according to Lorimer, through the birder's "tuning in", or 'learning to be affected' by their quarry. Latham and McCormack would also argue this type of knowing or "pre-signifying affective materiality" is "felt in bodies" (2009, 252–262) and Peter explained to me during co-discovery that this type of feeling is vitally important for the bird-taxidermist, as they must attempt to impute this felt experience into their mounts, and thus effectively 'become-bird'.

Peter displays this ability in the video when he is working on the mounting of a White-Crested Laughing Thrush (WCLT). In the clip Peter conveys that in attempting to capture the attitude or 'jizz' of the bird in his mount he is not only working from his reference photograph, he is calling forth his felt understanding of the corporeal embodiments and affective intensities of live birds, a process I would like to conceive of as 'becoming-bird'. This resonates with Deleuze and Guattari's move away from species-centred thinking to a mode of thought and material engagement predicated on what a body can do[7] and draws on the concept of 'becoming-animal' they put forward in *A Thousand Plateaus* (1980), which could be thought of as a sort of becoming-other of the human subject. For example, Alan Beaulieu argues we should conceive of becoming-animal "in terms of an immanent exchange of capacities of affectability (potentia), since what matters in becomings-animal is to unlearn physical and emotional habits in order to expand the world's experience" (Beaulieu 2011, 85–86). This contributes to a rethinking of the human subject's perception of their relationships with themselves, with other bodies, and with their environment. It can also contribute to a rethinking of the human subject as becoming-bird, or at least 'more-than-human', during taxidermy craftwork.

I would argue that Peter, throughout his taxidermy training and practice, has unlearned, or at least learned to dispense with or extend, his human subjectivities and sensibilities to the point where he is able to exchange capacities of affectability with birds (live and dead) to in effect 'become-bird'. Now this is more than simply saying that Peter is mimicking a bird—by imitating the movement of its head or body using his own body—as this implies a type of becoming that can only be metaphorical. In the metaphorical case a distinct identity pretends to be able to replace another without considering, according to Beaulieu, "what happens 'in between' or in the 'midst' (au milieu) of things which is precisely what Deleuze and Guattari are interested in" and what I am interested in getting at through the notion of 'becoming-bird' (Beaulieu 2011, 74). It could be argued that the type of mimetic reproduction discussed in Lesson 2: Mimetic Reproduction is a type of metaphorical mimesis. However, here too we witness more than a simple replacement of the dead bird body with a mimetic model as the midst of practice created an exchange of "capacities of affectability" (Ibid, 84) between the dead bird matter, Peter's body and emerging balsa wood body.

As such, becoming-bird in taxidermy practice is not related to resemblance, metaphor or mimesis, rather, becoming-bird is an immanent exchange of capacities of affectability between taxidermist body and bird bodies (both real and manufactured). Moreover, the bird-mount evolves in this setting without the taxidermist attempting mastery or possession but, rather, through what I would like to term as more-than-human craft assemblages. Of course, these anti-humanistic positions go against much of our current understandings of craftwork in the human sciences and humanities, which traditionally emphasise the hierarchic distinction between the human craftsperson and their non-human craft tools and materials. Yet if we embrace the notion of a 'zone of affectability' between practitioner, tools and materials in what I would like to call 'craft assemblages', it is possible to acknowledge the distinctive more-than-human craft techniques and non-human material agencies involved in taxidermy craftwork, and to emphasise their importance for understanding human intentionality during craftwork.

However it is important to caution that the 'immanent exchange of capacities of affectability' only happens during event, or 'in the midst', of practice. Steve Baker (2000) rightly reminds us, in his writings on the becomings-animal in the creative practice of certain contemporary artists, that the dissolution of identities in the experience of becoming is not complete for Deleuze and Guattari. Indeed, assemblages only partially eliminate the identities of each of the becomings' parts: "Separate bodies enter into alliances in order to do things, but are not undone by it. The wasp and orchid, after their becoming, are still wasp and orchid" (Baker 2000, 133). We see this at work in the video when Peter is making some final adjustments to the WCLT mount. Here Peter articulates that he can "see lots of things wrong with the mount", whilst later cautioning "you can tweak them for forever and a day and then you get to the point where you can start spoiling it". Here we start to witness the dissolution of the alliance or immanent exchange of capacities of affectability between taxidermist body and bird-mount. Deleuze and Guatarri's becomings, as Beaulieu reminds us, always imply the risk of the machinic assemblages, or in our case the craft assemblages, becoming "botched" (Beaulieu 2011, 76).

For example, Peter's concern about the potential loss of jizz through 'over-tweaking' highlights how becoming-bird in taxidermy practice can be botched and that the exchange of capacities for affectability begins to break down as we reach the end of the process. Moreover, when the practice does come to a halt, and even though this decision is still a negotiation between Peter and the affective materiality of the mount, Peter is not 'undone' by the process. Peter and the WCLT may have entered into an alliance or assemblage during the process, but at the end of it they go their separate ways; Peter as taxidermist with other bird skins awaiting his attentions and the WCLT as more-than-human made craft-assemblage. I would also like to acknowledge at this point that this 'exchange of capacities of affectability' between Peter and the WCLT says very little about how this works from the bird's perspective, which, with it being dead, remains necessarily elusive.

Before offering some final reflections in this paper it is again worth reflecting on the camera process and presentation. Becoming-bird in taxidermy practice is a subtle, complex and difficult process to witness, capture and present. For example, the becoming-bird of the Barn Owl mount was easier to show through the breakdown of still frames rather than through the use of a clip of the moving images. To 'capture' Peter's becoming-bird and thus the exchange of capacities of affectability between him, bird bodies and craft matter it again required me as 'apprentice camera-person' to be responsive not only to the practice as it unfolded but also to partake in the immanent exchange of capacities for affectability and indeed to allow these capacities to infuse my embodied camerawork. By doing so I was seeking, in turn, to create a zone of proximity or affectability between the more-than-human craft-assemblages and the audience.

This touches again on the idea of creating corporeal and affective exposures through the use of images (still or moving). As Latham and McCormack argue:

> The force of images is not just representational. Images are also blocks of sensation with an affective intensity: they make sense not just because we take time to figure out what they signify, but also because their pre-signifying affective materiality is felt in bodies.
>
> (Latham and McCormack 2009, 252–262)

In this way the video clips and stills made use of in the three lessons not only exist as a series of testimonies to taxidermy practice but also hold the potential to work as corporeal and affective ethnographic exposures to that practice. In this way they more broadly contribute to a rethinking of moving images less in terms of a representational logic of 'image-capture' and more through a material and affective logics of 'exposure-witnessing'.

CRAFT CONCLUSIONS

The aim of this chapter has been to highlight video ethnography as an effective and affective tool for witnessing and evoking the more-than-human craft practices and non-human materialities of taxidermy. Moreover, the analysis opens up new spaces of more-than-human enquiry into the geographies, materialities and embodiments of craft and craftwork, which in turn helps to counter the overly humanistic understandings of craftwork that dominate in the social sciences and humanities. The three lessons Rehabilitation, Mimetic Reproduction and Becoming-Bird are not only testimonies to the skilful embodiments it takes to separate a skin from a body and rearrange it in life-like form, but are also supposed to work as corporeal and affective ethnographic exposures to the more-than-human craft assemblages of taxidermy craftwork. For example, Rehabilitation witnesses an aspect of taxidermy practice not well documented—that of rehabilitating dead matter—and demonstrates the potential of video ethnography to acknowledge and explore the complex corporeal, sensory and material affordances of taxidermy practice. Mimetic Reproduction went further to show how Peter works from and with the dead matter of birds to create mimetic replacement body parts and to argue that craftwork should be thought of as a co-fabrication of practitioner, tools and materials, encompassing distributed and relational socio-technical and corporeal agencies. Finally Becoming-Bird embraces the notion of a 'zone of affectability' between practitioner, tools and materials in the 'craft assemblages' of taxidermy practice to remain open to the becoming-animal of bodies through this process. In particular, this section witnesses the becoming-bird, or 'more-than-human', of the taxidermist through their learning to be affected by and working with bird bodies. By doing so, it becomes possible to acknowledge the distinctive more-than-human craft techniques and non-human material and technical agencies involved in taxidermy craftwork, and to emphasise their impetus for rethinking human intentionality during craftwork more broadly.

These lessons have also highlighted the importance of making and employing video ethnographies to enquire into the distinctive more-than-human assemblages involved in craftwork. Jamie Lorimer has argued the aim in employing videographic methods for the more-than-human geographer is to "open up thinking spaces for an affective micropolitics of curiosity in which we can remain unsure as to what bodies and images might yet become" (J. Lorimer 2010, 252). The aim in employing a video ethnography of taxidermy practice was to produce 'corporeal exposures' that stayed attentive to the complex becomings of bodies and materials involved in the craft assemblages. To expand on this, and by way of conclusion, I would like to offer two interrelated points of reflection about video ethnography, which are timely contributions to the emerging field of video methods more broadly.

First, in reframing my role here as 'apprentice camera-person' I wanted to emphasise how I was learning to be affected by and thus responsive to not only the tasks as they unfolded but also to the distributed and relational agencies of taxidermy craft work that permeated into and animated my positioning and embodied camerawork. This highlights my attempts at learning to be affected and thus led by the practical, sensual and affective dimensions and agencies at play in taxidermy craftwork. This said, Paul Harrison argues that researchers will inevitably "fall short" in their attempts to describe and re-present the "eventful, creative, excessive and distinctly uncertain realms of action" (Harrison 2002, 487). Just as the craft assemblages in taxidermy practice can become 'botched', so too can the immanent exchange of capacities of affectability between a researcher or an audience and the video clips as 'corporeal exposures'. For example, some may find it ironic that the video clips depended a lot on co-discovery and therefore on Peter's words to disclose what was happening in the analysis. However, the crux here is not to be paralysed by the thought of reaching aporias, rather it is to accept the limitations of what can be presented and thus get as close as one can to what is being attempted.

This leads on to my second point of reflection, and contention, about video ethnography: video is still difficult to incorporate into academic research papers and chapters. While live links can be embedded into online papers[8], it is very difficult to enable the same ease of access in book chapters like this one. While it is possible to use still shots for witnessing and interpreting the corporeal and affective registers of taxidermy craftwork, as the Barn Owl sequence exemplifies, on balance moving images are preferable for this purpose. However, the question becomes will readers make the effort to fully immerse themselves in the corporeal exposures of the video ethnography? Furthermore, even if they do so we must be acutely aware at all times that these re-presented events will, as Peggy Phelan reminds us, "'sound differently' in the new presentations of them than in the 'experiencing of them'" (Phelan 1997, 8). For example although the aim here was to develop a video ethnography which would enable both the researcher and an audience to re-experience the sensate aspects of taxidermy practice, the video inevitably falls short of disclosing important aspects of this experience such as smell. However, as Dewsbury asserts, in attempting to attend to the sensate aspects of bodily practices "it is worth remembering as we set about this task that it is not a transparent representation that we are after, nor is it about the representation being a true reflection of the empirical experience or event" rather, "it is the attempt at articulation rather than its success that counts." (Dewsbury 2010, 332).

The aim, then, is to follow an explicitly experimental ethos and develop the best methods of articulation to suit the aims of the project. This emphasises the craftwork demanded of the academic as "a means of composition and channelling which involves bringing together discipline and concentration, understanding and inspiration, in order to bring out potential" (Thrift 2007, 15). The videographic techniques developed and discussed in this chapter underline the serious empirical involvements required of researchers when engaging with the practices, embodiments and materialities associated with craftwork. Thus while taxidermy practice is a complex sensory experience to witness and disclose, my aim here has been to emphasise the potential of video ethnography for not only witnessing but exposing the sensory, affective and more-than-human registers of taxidermy craft practice. In conclusion, and to return to the opening quote, to learn what is necessary when studying craftwork it requires not just the personal instruction of a good teacher and thus placing ourselves in the position of apprentice (though it is a good place to start!), it requires working with an ethic of the apprenticeship—an ethic that recognises that we need to be prepared to experiment and put ourselves and our theories 'at risk' in order to produce methods that openly and creatively respond to our more-than-human, more-than-textual, multi-sensual worlds.

ACKNOWLEDGMENTS

I would like to sincerely thank Peter Summers for allowing me to watch and record his exceptionally skilled taxidermy practice. Taxidermy is often cast as macabre or gruesome, however, in Peter's hands it becomes a wondrous process to witness and I consider myself extremely lucky to have been in a position to do so. I am also grateful to Peter and the National Museum Scotland for permitting me to use and show the video footage.

NOTES

1. https://vimeo.com/72199573—WARNING! This includes Peter using a needle and syringe to inflate an eye with water to measure it.
2. In my time at the NMS this was the injury most commonly experienced by the bird specimens that the museum receives and highlights the vast numbers

(100 to 900+ million) of birds that are killed in this way annually (see Klem 1990).)
3. The process of skinning is not illustrated in the paper, however, the basic aim of the process is to remove all the 'fleshy parts' of the specimen, including all internal body parts, organs, muscles, tendons, ligaments, connective tissue and bodily fluid (basically anything that would decay), until you are left with just the skin, cleaned out skull and outer appendages such as the claws.
4. https://vimeo.com/72200829
5. 'Igor' was a female Eagle Owl that had been donated by a zoo, and Peter informed me that many animals kept in captivity had a lot of deposited subcutaneous fat as they did not get the same amount of exercise as wild specimens.
6. https://vimeo.com/72203249
7. For example, see in particular his writings on ethology, affects and the animal in the essay 'Spinoza and Us'.
8. However as the Erratum to J. Lorimer's 2010 paper highlights, this is not always effectively managed for online papers either.

REFERENCES

Alberti, S. (ed.) 2011. *The Afterlives of Animals: A Museum Menagerie*. Charlottesville: University of Virginia Press.

Anderson, B. and Harrison, P. (eds.) 2010. *Taking-Place. Non-Representational Theories and Geography*. London: Ashgate.

Baker, S. 2000. *The Postmodern Animal*. London: Reaktion Books.

Beaulieu, A. 2011. The Status of Animality in Deleuze's Thought. *Journal for Critical Animal Studies*, 1/2: 69–88.

Braun, B. 2004. Modalities of posthumanism. *Environment and Planning A*, 36(8): 1341–1363.

Braun, B. 2006. Environmental issues: writing a more-than-human urban geography. *Progress in Human Geography*, 29: 635–650.

Browne, M. 1878. *Practical Taxidermy: A Manual of Instruction to the Amateur in Collecting, Preserving, and Setting Up Natural History Specimens of all Kind*. London: L. Upcott Gill.

Browne, M. 1896. *Artistic and Scientific Taxidermy and Modelling*. London: Adam and Charles Black.

Crawford, M. 2009. *Shop Class as Soulcraft: An Inquiry into the Value of Work*. London: Penguin Books.

Davie, O. 1894. *Methods in the Art of Taxidermy*. Philadelphia: David McKay Publishing.

Deleuze G. and Guattari F. 1980. *A Thousand Plateaus: Capitalism and Schizophrenia*. Minneapolis: University of Minnesota Press.

Desmond, J. 2002. Displaying Death, Animating Life: Changing Fictions of "Liveness" from Taxidermy to Animatronics. In Rothfels, N. (ed.) *Representing Animals*. Indiana: University of Indiana Press, 159–179.

Dewsbury J.-D. 2003. Witnessing space: 'knowledge without contemplation'. *Environment and Planning A*, 35(11): 1907–1932.

Dewsbury, J.-D. 2009. Performative, non-representational and affect-based research: seven injunctions. In DeLyser, D., Atkin, S., Crang, M., Herbert, S. and McDowell, L. (eds.) *The SAGE Handbook of Qualitative Research in Human Geography*. London: Sage, 321–334.

Frayling, C. 2011. *On Craftsmanship Towards a New Bauhaus*. London: Oberon Books.

Gane, N. and Back, L. 2012. C. Wright Mills 50 Years On: The Promise and Craft of Sociology Revisited. *Theory, Culture & Society,* 29: 399–421.

Garrett, B. 2011. Videographic geographies: using digital video for geographic research. *Progress in Human Geography,* 35(4): 521–541.

Greenhough, B. and Roe, E. 2011. Ethics, space, and somatic sensibilities: comparing relationships between scientific researchers and their human and animal experimental subjects. *Environment and Planning D: Society and Space,* 29(1): 47–66.

Haraway, D. 1989. Teddy bear patriarchy: taxidermy in the Garden of Eden New York City, 1908–1936. In Haraway, D. (ed.) *Primate Visions.* London: Verso, 26–58.

Harrison, P. 2000. 'Making sense: embodiment and the sensibilities of the everyday'. *Environment and Planning D: Society and Space,* 18: 497–518.

Harrison, P. 2002. The Caesura: remarks on Wittgenstein's interruption of theory, or, why practices elude explanation. *Geoforum,* 33: 487–503.

Hinchliffe, S. 2008. *Geographies of Nature.* London: Sage.

Hinchliffe S. Kearnes, M. Degen, M. and Whatmore, S. 2005. Urban wild things: a cosmopolitical experiment. *Environment and Planning D: Society and Space,* 23: 643–658.

Ingold, T. 2006. Walking the plank: meditations on a process of skill. In Dakers J. R. (ed.) *Defining Technological Literacy: Towards an Epistemological Framework.* New York: Palgrave Macmillan, 65–80.

Klem, D. Jr. 1990. Collisions between birds and windows: mortality and prevention. *Journal of Field Ornithology* 6(1): 120–128.

Kolnai, A. 2004. *On Disgust.* Chicago: Open Court.

Latham, A. and McCormack, D. P. 2009. Thinking with images in non-representational cities: vignettes from Berlin. *Area,* 41: 252–262.

Laurier, E. and Philo, C. 2006. Natural problems of naturalistic video data. In Knoblauch, H., Raab, J., Soeffner, H. G. and Schnettler, B. (eds.) *Video-Analysis Methodology and Methods, Qualitative Audiovisual Data Analysis in Sociology.* Oxford: Peter Lang, 183–192.

Lorimer, H. 2005. Cultural geography: the busyness of being 'more-than-representational'. *Progress in Human Geography,* 29(1): 83–94.

Lorimer, H. 2006. Herding memories of humans and Animals. *Environment and Planning D: Society and Space,* 24: 497–518.

Lorimer, J. 2007. Non-human Charisma. *Environment and Planning D: Society and Space,* 25(5): 911–932.

Lorimer, J. 2010. Moving image methodologies for more-than-human geographies. *Cultural Geographies,* 17(2): 237–258.

Macdonald, H. 2002. "What makes you a scientist is the way you look at things": ornithology and the observer 1930–1955. *Studies in the History and Philosophy of Biology and Biomedical Sciences,* 33: 53–77.

MacDougall, D. 2006. *The Corporeal Image: Film, Ethnography, and the Senses.* Princeton: Princeton University Press.

Miller, W. 1997. *The Anatomy of Disgust.* Cambridge: Harvard University Press.

Patchett, M. 2012a. On necro-ornithology, monstrosity and botched birds. *Antennae: The Journal of Nature in Visual Culture,* 20: 9–26.

Patchett, M. 2012b. Andrea Roe: revisiting wonder. *Antennae: The Journal of Nature in Visual Culture,* 20: 123–134.

Patchett, M., Foster, K., Gomez, G. and Roe, A. 2012. Ruffling feathers: exhibiting the monstrous geographies of the plumage trade. *Antennae: The Journal of Nature in Visual Culture,* 20: 28–54.

Patchett, M., Foster, K. and Lorimer H. 2011. The 'biogeographies' of a hollowed-eyed harrier. In Alberti, S. (ed.) *The Afterlives of Animals: A Museum Menagerie.* Charlottesville: University of Virginia Press.

Patchett, M. 2010. *Putting Animals on Display: Geographies of Taxidermy Practice*. Unpublished PhD thesis, available from Enlighten: University of Glasgow Thesis Service: http://theses.gla.ac.uk/2348/

Patchett, M. 2008. Tracking tigers: recovering the embodied practices of taxidermy. *Historical Geography*, 36: 17–39.

Patchett, M. and Foster, K. 2008. Repair work: surfacing the geographies of dead animals. *Museum and Society*, 6(2): 98–122.

Plelan, P. 1997. *Mourning Sex: Performing Public Memories*. London: Routledge.

Philo, C. and Wilbert, C. 2000. *Animal Spaces, Beastly Places: New Geographies of Human-Animal Relations*. London: Routledge.

Pink, S. 2007. *Doing Visual Ethnography: Images, Media and Representation in Research*. Manchester: Manchester University Press.

Pink, S. 2006. *The Future of Visual Anthropology: Engaging the Senses*. London: Routledge.

Pink, S. 2009. *Doing Sensory Ethnography*. London: Sage.

Pink, S. and Mackley, K. L. 2012. Video and a sense of the invisible: approaching domestic energy consumption through the sensory home. *Sociological Research Online*, 17(1): 3.

Poliquin, R. 2008. The matter and meaning of museum taxidermy. *Museums and Society*, 6(2): 123–134.

Roe, E., Buller, H. and Bull, J. 2011. The performance of farm animal assessment. *Animal Welfare*, 20(1): 69–78.

Sennett, R. 2008. *The Craftsman*, London: Allen Lane.

Star, S. L. 1992. Craft vs. commodity, mess vs. transcendence: how the right tool became the wrong one in the case of taxidermy and natural history. In Clark, A. E. and Fujimura, J. H. (eds.) *The Right Tools For The Job: At Work In Twentieth-Century Life Sciences*. Princeton: Princeton University Press, 257–286.

Thrift, N. and Dewsbury, J.-D. 2000. Dead geographies and how to make them live. *Environment and Planning D: Society and Space*, 18: 411–432.

Thrift, N. 2000. Afterwords. *Environment and Planning D: Society and Space*, 18: 213–255.

Thrift, N. 2007. *Non-Representational Theory: Space/Politics/Affect*. London: Routledge.

Ward, R. 1880. *The Sportsman's Handbook to Collecting, Preserving, and Setting Up Trophies and Specimens*. London: Ward.

Wonders, K. 1993. *Habitat Dioramas: Illusions of Nature in Museums of Natural History*. Stockholm: Almsqvist and Wiksell.

Whatmore, S. 2002. *Hybrid Geographies*. London: Sage.

Whatmore, S. 2004. Humanism's excess: some thoughts on the 'post-human/ist' agenda. *Environment and Planning A*, 36(8): 1341–1363.

Whatmore, S. 2006. Materialist returns: practicing cultural geography in and for a more-than-human world. *Cultural Geographies*, 13: 600–609.

5 Close Encounters

Using Mobile Video Ethnography to Understand Human-Animal Relations

Katrina M. Brown and Esther Banks

INTRODUCTION

A dog and its owner are out for a walk in the woods. The reciprocal pulling and tugging on the lead of the roadside approach is replaced by a palpable sense of mutual relief as the owner unclips the lead at the forest entrance. As they wind their way along the stony trail, the dog trots his zig-zagging olfactory patrol from one side of the path to the other, pausing sporadically to glance back at his owner, or to backtrack towards them when the distance becomes too great. The owner takes in the scenery and enjoys the various rhythms of their walking body, calling intermittently to the dog to 'wait' or 'come back' when its pace, body position or pricked ears suggest to them the possibility of it moving out of sight, and perhaps even out of control. The dog pauses or returns in response, tail wagging and eyes softened. After about 30 minutes the dog freezes, back tense, legs rigid with a front paw held up, staring into the forest scrub, chest pressed up against a bank of heather, nose twitching furiously. Just as the dog becomes poised to bound forward the owner shouts 'lie down'. The dog takes one stride and then looks round at the owner as if checking whether they really mean it. As the owner scowls back confirmation of the command, the dog drops reluctantly to the ground, eyes on the owner but ears still trained into the forest. The owner clips the lead back on. As the pair resume walking along the path, a female capercaillie[1] flies up between the trees about 50 m away and a shuffling in the undergrowth hints at a brood. The owner breathes a sigh of relief.

* * *

This vignette exemplifies how humans, other animals and broader ecologies become entangled with each other in obvious and less obvious ways, and how ways of articulating across species boundaries can affect how those species co-exist, flourish or otherwise. The need to better understand such more-than-human relations has driven a discernible 'animal turn' in the social sciences (e.g. Bekoff 2002; Philo and Wilbert 2000; Urbanik 2012;

Weil 2012; Wolch and Emel 1998; Wolfe 2003). Key issues deliberated include: how animals become associated and disassociated with particular places, spaces, images, discourses and fleshy presences or absences; how they become caught up with notions such as domestic, wild, rural, agricultural or natural; how humans and other animals communicate and are made sensible to one another, and; how space can be shared across species difference.

Questions of agency, ethics and their spatial dimensions are never far away (Whatmore 2002). It clearly matters which modes of interspecies conduct become possible, acceptable, celebrated or otherwise, where they are (in)visible or considered to be 'in' or 'out of place', and how such normative boundaries are created and resisted through bodily and discursive practice. Particularly knotty problems surround how to take seriously the agency and subjectivity of animals as well as humans in the process of their co-constitution (Wolfe 2003), and how to attend to the capacity of humans and non-humans to be affected by, and to respond to, each other across species boundaries (Greenhough and Roe 2011; Haraway 2008). This leaves us with some weighty methodological challenges concerning how we gain access to, and render knowable, the intimate and intangible spaces of human-animal encounters, their situatedness in particular environments, and how they come into being in mutually transformative ways. According to Haraway, these mutual becomings take place in key 'contact zones', "often within radically asymmetrical relations of power" (Haraway 2008, 216).

We are thus obliged to think expansively about traditional notions of the research subject and the various ways in which animals might become enrolled in the knowledge-making process. Recalling our dogwalking example above, it is clear that established talk- and text-based methods have limitations. Animal actions and interactions are often extremely mobile, and in often unpredictable ways (Lorimer 2010), involving fleeting moments and swift manoeuvres. Their communication is fundamentally centred beyond the realms of the linguistic—or rather based on different registers of 'language'—relying heavily on bodily forms of expression and interpretation. Animals articulate through intricate sequences of movement, gesture and sound involving different sensory hierarchies and complex affective dynamics (Despret 2004; Grandin 2006). How do we humans begin to notice, comprehend, attune and respond to such configurations? Wolch and Emel (1998) note how we can struggle to fully 'see' animals when they are so often enrolled in taken-for-granted ways. This is particularly true of dogwalking; a mundane, habitual practice that must be done every day. Making such animal-human encounters tangible, sensible and knowable is no small task.

Using video as a research tool holds potential in many of these regards, and is increasingly employed to investigate dimensions of everyday life, such as the senses (Pink 2009), affect (Simpson 2011), and mobility (Spinney 2011). Video has long been used to study animals and their behaviour, especially in efforts to make objective observations of them. Yet we are only in the early stages of developing video techniques to understand animal-human relations in social research. Here we will reflect on experiences we have had using mobile video ethnography (MVE) in a multispecies setting, whereby minicam video technology was enrolled into the interbodily encounters of people and animals whilst dogwalking. We discuss how video is recorded, viewed and discussed in MVE to witness and make sense of the cross-species entanglements that occur as recreationists and their canine companions interact with each other, and other people and animals. This draws on our recent research concerning how animals and humans conjointly negotiate normative and legal boundaries, in this case how human-dog pairings accomplish (or not) the state of 'control' and 'responsible' practice upon which their rights of outdoor access rely (Brown 2014; Brown and Dilley 2012). Strengths and weaknesses of the approach are elaborated, as are some of the practical and ethical challenges, which also serves to flag the potential of MVE for researching other more-than-human contexts as well as more established social science fields.

USING VIDEO FOR UNDERSTANDING ANIMAL-HUMAN RELATIONS

Ethological and Ethnographic Approaches

Ethologists and other animal behaviourists have a well-established tradition of using video techniques to study animals, whether in a laboratory or under 'normal' conditions (Wratten 1994). They examine patterns of animal behaviour including movements, orientation, posture, spacing and vocalisations. The camera is typically mounted in a fixed position, with the researcher either absent or as still and quiet as possible, in order to minimise the influence of humans ('observer bias'). Analyses are predominantly quantitative (Nadin et al. 2012), and, although qualitative techniques are sometimes utilised (Napolitano et al. 2008), researchers tend to deploy video in a realistic, unreflexive and uncritical way. The moving images are conferred with the qualities of an objective account evidencing the truth of animal lives. Humans and their practices are usually 'airbrushed' out; not only absent in the video recordings, but obscured in terms of their role in the planning, filming and editing that made them possible.

Ethnographic engagements of video for studying animal-human relations are, by contrast, in their infancy,[2] but are already yielding fascinating insights in the fields of geography (Lorimer 2010), sociology (Konecki 2008) and anthropology (Fijn 2012; Grimshaw 2011). This work departs from ethological video methods in three important ways. First, it aims to understand animal lives as they are intertwined in the lives of humans. This entails intentionally bringing people 'into the picture' along with animals in recognition of the bodily and material interrelations through which humans and other animals constitute each other's worlds (Whatmore 2002). It also means critically interrogating the negotiation of separations and contact zones between them (Haraway 2008), and purposely researching "cross-specifically, across species boundaries as anthropologists do cross-culturally" (Fijn 2012, 73). Of the researchers employing video to examine such more-than-human connections (Bear et al. in press.; Fijn 2007, 2012; Goode 2006; Grasseni 2004; Konecki 2008; Laurier et al. 2006; Lorimer 2010; Nosworthy 2013), all attempt to decentre the human, and likewise distance themselves from treatments of animals as atomised entities, preferring to make space for a relational understanding of how humans and animals come into being together.

Second, this multi-species scholarship is reflexive about how video is mobilised in the research process, acknowledging that visual images cannot be taken as a straightforward evidencing of truth or reality (Rose 2007; Shrum et al. 2005). Rather video technologies are considered part of the more-than-human assemblages through which we seek to create understandings with and about animals. The equipment and the imagery produced has agency, which must be addressed as part of the configuration of bodies, practices, materialities and ecologies making up the research process.[3] Accordingly, such work is less concerned with using video to 'capture' or 'discover' how animals feature in our social worlds, as if animal lives were fixed and external to us, but, as Lorimer (2010) suggests, to 'witness' and 'evoke' human/non-human interactions in ways that facilitate an appreciation of the practical, sensual and affective dimensions of their accomplishment.

Third, and relatedly, this work develops insights from the corporeal, aesthetic and affective turns in social science. It is extremely attentive to the central role of the body, the senses and emotion in animal-human relationships, understood not as 'instances' or 'responses' to 'stimuli' to be correlated statistically, but as dynamically co-created lived experience. This is where video is felt to really shine where traditional methods have struggled; in animating the vitality, movement, energies, and fluidities of more-than-human becoming, and coping with ways of being and knowing that take us beyond cognition and beyond the verbal into realms where bodily and multi-sensory grammars prevail, for which we have little established vocabulary.

Accordingly, video holds promise in attending to the sophisticated emotional lives that are increasing recognised in animals as well as humans (Bekoff 2000). Indeed, as Despret (2004) elaborates, learning to affect and be affected is central to more-than-human encounters. Animals and humans take on new interwoven identities when they become sensitive to the motions and feelings of one another, and are able to articulate to one another. She describes the isopraxis of skilled horse-riding involving a synchronous intermuscular ballet of horse and rider enabled by cross-species anticipation and affective attunement. Video has potential to help us witness the practices through which such attunement and skilful interaction unfold (Lorimer 2010; Nosworthy 2013), as well as those that lead to its rupture and dissonance (Brown 2012; Brown and Dilley 2012). Such an approach, in turn, demands that we consider critically how watching video of animals—and our interactions with them—moves us, touches us and affects us (Lorimer 2010). Questions are raised regarding how moving images and sounds work to generate affect, what logics are evoked and what ends are thus served.

Mobile Multi-species Ethnography with Minicam Video

The footage in the aforementioned work is shot mostly using hand-held or tripod-mounted video, which, despite its many strengths, can have limitations for studying some ways of human-animal relating. This became apparent in our research examining the accomplishment of '(ir)responsible' dogwalking practices in the Cairngorms National Park (CNP or 'the Park'; Brown and Dilley 2012; Brown in press). Contemplating the highly active and interactive movement of dog and human, articulating to each other as they make passage with and through forest and moorland areas of the Park raised important questions, not least: how were we to take seriously the fundamentally mobile nature of animal-human becomings?

It became clear that handheld video would be fraught with difficulties in keeping up with, and being involved in, the more-than-human entanglements and encounters under scrutiny. The approach taken by the ethnomethodologists in their dog studies was not going to be sufficient for addressing our questions, as the camera would have been too distant and too static to make available the continuities and contingencies of canine-human partnerships as they produced the manifold mobile spaces of their walk in the Park. Instead, it was decided to experiment with minicam video, which has been at the centre of the mobile video ethnography (MVE) approach burgeoning within mobilities research (Brown 2012; Brown and Dilley in prep; Brown et al. 2008; Spinney 2009, 2011; Wood 2013).

Minicam refers to a small digital video camera recording device that is small and light enough to be worn on the head, body or auxiliary equipment whilst particular practices are undertaken. Also known as 'POV' (Point Of View) camera, it has to date mostly been used attached to a person's head in order to evoke the perspective of the wearer; as if attempting to as far as possible 'see' the world as another sees it. Minicam pushes the frontier of video technology a bit further in terms of opening up previously inaccessible more-than-human spaces for scrutiny, extending what Lorimer (2010, 242) refers to as "new mediated ecologies for comprehensive surveillance and analysis".

Animals often illustrate compellingly how worlds come into being on the move, through recurrent motion, and the moving of bodies in relation to other bodies and materialities (after Urry 2007). They underscore too how movement can be a central mode of communication; and one that is fundamental to the choreography through which different subjects learn how to share space, or otherwise (Brown 2012). As Cresswell notes, "a mobile subject demands a mobile method" (Cresswell 2012, 647) and in this regard, the crucial quality of minicam bestowed by its ease of physical embodiment is being able to 'go with' the subject as they move, to follow the action, and go with the flow of micro and macro movements as they unfold. Dogwalking, for example, is a highly mobile practice produced through multiple scales of motion, from the twitch of a nose to the traverse of a mountainside. Indeed, dogs are highly mobile creatures and have co-evolved to use expressive bodily movement that humans can understand and be affected by (Haraway 2008). Such collaboration and co-operation amongst particular species is a tentative accomplishment, not fixed, which adds to the imperative to engage with the flow and spaces of its fluid becoming as best as possible.

Animal-related use of minicam has in the last decade become firmly established in the domains of entertainment (e.g. use of Crittercam in TV wildlife documentary[4] and lay people posting their own films made with various forms of petcams[5] on YouTube) and emergency service monitoring and surveillance (e.g. working police dogs). As yet its use in animal-related academic research is still nascent. One example where these fields have come together was in the recent BBC Horizon programme featuring a scientific study of domestic cats trying to find out 'what they really get up to'.[6] However, no published studies could be found of social researchers using minicam to study human-animal encounters. Thus, we have begun experimenting with possible ways of developing this approach. In the research documented here we enrolled minicam only with human rather than with dog bodies, but the authors are currently experimenting with the use of 'dogcam' in a social research context.

MOBILE MULTI-SPECIES VIDEO ETHNOGRAPHY IN PRACTICE

Doing Multi-species MVE with Minicam

Given our interest in the practice and performance of dogwalking, a central aim was to enrol minicam in dogwalking outings to see how it might make these dimensions available and tangible to us. However, for the kinds of research questions we were posing, minicam-recorded outings felt insufficient. We needed to situate such practices of dogwalking in the participants' lives, and explore how they framed and attached meaning to them. We also did not want the initial introductory and rapport-building phase between researcher and participant to divert attention from being 'in the moment' during the outings, which did occur whilst piloting. Thus a prior biographical interview was required. In addition, it was also felt that we needed to give the participant a chance to watch the footage with us post-outing to help us make sense of their experience and serve as a reference point to the assumptions, meanings and associations we were making from our own perusal of the footage. Ultimately the minicam footage made limited sense to us by itself. Certainly it seemed to evoke certain aspects of experience and to help witness certain manoeuvres, yet was wide open to missing or misunderstanding what participants thought they were doing or attempting to do at the time and what they were thinking, sensing and feeling.

Therefore, the approach we developed for minicam MVE has three key stages:

- Biographical and background interview (semi-structured);
- Minicam video recording in situ of practice under scrutiny (can be done either without researcher or as a 'go-along' interview); and
- Video review (researcher and participant view and discuss the video footage produced).

Each stage and the preparatory work will be discussed in turn.

Preparation

It is important to consider carefully who will take part in MVE as the three-stage approach is particularly resource-intensive. In our research we engaged not only with dogwalkers (both residents and visitors) but with others having a stake in responsible outdoor access in the Park, such as other recreationists, local community members, land managers, rangers, policymakers, Park Authority staff, outdoor access officers, members of local and national conservation bodies and experts on the biology of protected species. We only used MVE for those for whom moving outdoors was a key in situ practice relevant to their role, i.e. we did the kind of outing that the participant would make anyway.[7] For the remaining participants we mainly used semi-structured interviews.[8] Our approach to recruitment was to continue to engage participants until data saturation was reached. This has meant that 25 dogwalkers have participated in the research so far (10 doing MVE).[9] Recruiting to saturation is not always an easy task with MVE, as getting people to commit to a three-stage process can be difficult since it is three times as onerous as the more traditional interview or focus group.

The need to be flexible given the required level of commitment meant there was no standardised time interval between the three stages.[10] Our only firm stipulation was that there was a gap of at least a day between Stages II and III to allow the researcher time to review the video footage on their own and do some preliminary analysis. Nevertheless, we made sure that the timing of each stage was taken into account in the analysis, as there is no doubt that the doing of one stage influenced the other. The time elapsed between Stages II and III showed the greatest difference. If it was too long, participants found audiencing the minicam footage particularly strange and less richly evocative of the details of the outing, and would sometimes have little recollection of what they were thinking and feeling (especially with dogwalkers because they had done many similar dogwalks in the intervening period).

Stage I: Biographical Semi-Structured Interview

We conducted a pre-outing interview with each participant, usually in their home, in order to: build rapport; establish some basic information on their socio-economic and cultural background; situate the practices and places of dogwalking in their everyday lives and the meanings they hold for them; and begin to explore how they position themselves in relation to the objectives and practicalities of achieving 'control' of dogs for 'responsible' outdoor access. However, we had to be careful in our probing so our lines of questioning did not serve to load the Stage II Video Outing insofar as participants might think the researchers want to see or know about certain things, or they might try to play down or conceal certain aspects they feel might show them in a negative light (e.g. legally 'irresponsible' practices).

Stage II: Video Outing

Equipment

Over the years we have gained experience with several minicam models, the main ones being Archos AV500,[11] V.I.O. POV.HD,[12] and GoPro2 HD.[13] Whilst other and newer versions are now available, a brief discussion of their relative merits helps us understand characteristics of equipment that are prudent to take into account. For example, the specifications that matter for MVE use relate to questions of: is the camera comfortable to wear? Weight, bulkiness and where the camera is to be distributed on the body are key. Leading models differ in whether there is an all-in-one unit or if there is a separate camera head and recording device connected with a cable. Is the device robust? It is important that the cables stay connected, and the camera is shockproof and waterproof. What battery system is used? Battery life has to easily cover the length of an outing even in cold weather, and there are various pros and cons relating to whether batteries are removable, rechargeable or easily available in village shops. Is there an LCD and how is it positioned? It is crucial that the display allows the researcher to accurately set up the camera on the participant's body by being able to see the framing of the images to be shot (see Figure 5.1). This can be difficult with the all-in-one units. What happens to the clip being recorded if the batteries run out? On some models, a 'power off' can create an 'invalid clip' meaning a lost recording if the batteries expire before you manually press the stop button, which we found to be a real possibility on our outings using a battery with 2.5 hours official life. Is the microphone in a position to get sufficient audio quality of the sounds participants make, or is there an option for an external microphone? We found that the built-in microphones were often positioned in a way where speech and sound were muffled or obscured (e.g. unit with mic was in a pocket, bag or extra housing, not close enough to participant's mouth, or drowned out by the rustle of clothing.[14] [15]

Figure 5.1   Setting up minicam for Mobile Video Ethnography. Image: Liz Dinnie.

Minicams usually have options of where they can be mounted and in this researchers can be creative depending on their research questions and settings. Most models have specific mounts available that allow the camera to be positioned on the head, helmet, chest, pole, bike, pram or vehicle. We used the head-mount most often so the camera could follow the head-movement of the participant, which would help evoke what they were attending to. However, some participants initially feel awkward wearing a minicam—particularly pedestrians who, unlike mountain bikers and others, have no established visual cultures of minicam—and for them a chest-mount was much more acceptable as it was more discrete and easier to forget about.

It is worth warning that researchers using this method have to spend a great deal of time and effort becoming skilled and up-to-date with various kinds of technological hardware and software,[16] [17] and this has to be factored into research planning and budgeting. Practicing using the equipment when it doesn't matter—from shooting through to editing—is vital for the same reasons.

Protocol

We had to decide whether the researcher should 'go-along' with the dogwalkers and the video—to walk and talk as they went—or whether the dogwalker should do an unaccompanied outing with minicam video. We found merit in both protocols. Talking whilst walking allows the researcher to follow up immediately on issues prompted by actions, events or the environment, and to take advantage of the celebrated qualities of the peripatetic mode for generating expansiveness in thoughts, feelings and expression (Kusenbach 2003). However, an unaccompanied outing allowed the practices of the participant to unfold in a way that was less disrupted by the researcher and more akin to their everyday dogwalking socialities. We decided to split each outing half and half, with the researcher accompanying the participant to begin with and then peeling off to allow the participant to continue on.[18] But for a cross-species choreographic practice such as dogwalking, our growing conviction is that unaccompanied is more appropriate. The researcher's presence seems to undermine the dog-owner dynamic and raises issues regarding when and how to interject or ask questions in a way that is fair to what the canine-human partnership is trying to achieve. In these cases the dogwalker wore the camera, although there are circumstances when it can be relevant for the researcher to wear it.[19]

Stage III: Analysis and Review

The audiencing of minicam was felt to be the area with the greatest potential for experimentation. Watching, listening and talking around minicam footage can be done in a vast number of ways, and has few cultural referents or precedents.[20] The most fundamental decision is who gets to see what audiovideo material and when. This incorporates choices about who gets sight of the footage before the Stage III Review interview, whether or not to edit the footage and upon what basis the material will be edited.

In our work, the researcher watched the uncut footage through in real-time between Stage II and III, taking fieldnotes, attending, for example, to the happenings (and non-happenings) being witnessed and any feelings, sensations, thoughts or impressions evoked by the viewing. Care was taken to think critically about aspects of the researcher's background, the framing of the research questions and protocol, and of broader visual cultures and their affective logics, and how they might be shaping the feelings and understandings being generated.

These fieldnotes were made using NVivo 9 qualitative analysis software, which allows written annotations to be made at particular video timecodes. Where some of the outings had been done as a 'go-along', the audio material was fully transcribed verbatim. NVivo 9 was then used to code the video, fieldnotes and transcripts in a way that allowed them to be easily associated in particular thematic ways (e.g. linking the researcher's thoughts and feelings surrounding a particular animal-human encounter to those of the participant, to the animal and human movements and gestures and their spatial and temporal situatedness as witnessed through the moving images, as well as to knowledges gained from the researcher's prior experience of the environment, documents or other participants). Together these materials helped the researcher develop some initial themes and further questions to explore in the Stage III Review.

In the Stage III Review, we had the participants watch the uncut footage.[21] This was because we did not want what the researcher counted as a 'happening' or notable—as inevitably would be foregrounded in the editing—to obscure what was important for (and emerging as interesting about) the participant. This included the mundane and taken-for-granted aspects of dogwalking practice that neither participant nor researcher would necessarily have foreseen as important until they made the space to sit together contemplating it, witnessing it and enabling it to affect them. For example, participants were often at first struck by how much 'nothing happens' on their dogwalks but were then drawn into noticing the not-immediately-noteworthy; presences, absences and articulations of dog and human to each other (the typical and atypical), the visceral and quotidian rhythms of breathing, stepping, stick-throwing, dog on-lead here/dog off-lead there and the opening up of spaces for events and non-events to unfold. The 'boringness' and repetitiveness of much of the footage (see Figure 5.2), such as when little seems to be happening other than one footstep following another,[22] often highlighted to the viewer how much their doings were on a subliminal level. Also these times and spaces of hiatus served as a contrast to obvious 'events' such as encounters with other people, dogs and wildlife, and helped piece together how (usually unintentional) 'irresponsible' happenings were borne of—or avoided through—cascades of conscious and subconscious happenings.

Figure 5.2 Using footage participants often deemed 'boring' actually yielded interesting insights into the thoughts and feelings surrounding their mundane practices.

We found that the video audiencing process required some guidance from the researcher about the role expected from the participant and the possible and favoured ways of watching and talking around the footage. Since minicam viewing is not a widely established cultural practice, and talking around it even less so, participants were usually a bit uncertain and tentative as to how to go about it. When and how should they talk? What should they talk about? A key question in using uncut video to elicit affect and discussion is who is to take the lead in navigating around the footage, since there are many possibilities using pause, rewind, fast-forward, slow-motion or simply allowing sustained real-time play to unfold. We demonstrated these various possibilities to the participant in our preamble, adding that they were welcome to use their own techniques. Control over these functions, and the right to speak that sometimes seems accompany it, can be swapped between researcher and participant in an ad hoc manner or with a designated way of taking turns. We asked participants to lead for the first half of the allotted time, [23] suggesting that if unsure they might begin watching the video in real-time and then navigate to and explore particular sections as they wished. In the second half of the Review the researcher led and navigated to sections of video at pre-identified timecodes that they had found particularly interesting or perplexing in their pre-Stage III analysis and wanted to explore further with the participant. Through the interleaving talk of researcher and participant generated from the screening of the minicam images and sounds, and the affects thus evoked and explored, it was possible to work tentatively towards a conjoint understanding of the practices witnessed. This process is resonant with Pink's (2007) notion of co-discovery and Spinney's use of video together with the participant for developing a "vocabulary for the 'unspeakable'" (Spinney 2011, 172). The talk generated in the audiencing of the minicam video footage was also fully transcribed and added to the NVivo 9 database for another layer of analysis, as were fieldnotes written by the researcher immediately after the Stage III Review.

Presentation

We felt continually aware of pressures to turn all our impressions, experiences, images and sounds of dogwalking into talk and the written word; from using the qualitative analysis software, and reporting to funders, to writing up the work in peer review journals. Publications have so far tended to favour montages of stills abstracted from the video footage over video clips embedded within articles. However, this can be overcome by posting video material online and providing a hyperlink.[24] Yet for presenting the video material to others, a bigger challenge still was that the impressions and insights we had generated were not always easily conveyed through discrete, short clips, but rather came from watching hours and hours of footage that most would find uneventful, dull and even nauseating, and considering it together with particular discourses, narratives and observations, which themselves are not always easy to tame into short, pithy quotations. Thus, as with much research there is a substantial amount of trust placed in the researcher for the integrity of the work they have done of tracing and co-generating the myriad associations and disassociations that make up more-than-human configurations. There is also a question of how watchable minicam footage is. Now and again participant or researcher viewers would experience dizziness or nausea caused by the evocation of motion, or found they were not able to watch it for very long.[25]

INSIGHTS AND POSSIBILITIES

In our experience, minicam MVE can complement and extend the capacities of multi-species video ethnography in five key ways.

Addressing Practices as Spatially Situated

Space and the way practices are spatially situated in relation to particular places, materialities and ecologies have been shown to be central to human-animal becomings (Greenhough and Roe 2011; Whatmore 2002). Indeed, the co-constitution of animals and humans together with specific environments is the part of more-than-human intersubjectivity that does not always receive its analytical due in animal studies. Furthermore, many forms of cross-species relating involve mobile, multi-site, spatial practices that cannot be fully comprehended from one location, nor necessarily from a series of discrete locations. For dogwalking, we found the manoeuvrings of canine-human partnerships to be performed through the fluid linking of places, such as home to car to park to fields to woods. Our understanding was deepened by getting at the continuity, ephemerality and cascading of actions and (micro)events that situated dogwalking as a temporal and spatial practice. Clearly, the multi-species 'contact zones' suggested by Haraway (2008) are not necessarily neatly bounded in time or space.

Makes Available Novel Spaces Closer to Bodies and Practices

Minicam brings the bodies of dogs and their humans more directly and intimately into the filming process, enabling angles, proximities and an immersion in the thick of the action that are difficult to achieve with hand-held video. By becoming a mobile hybrid body-camera, participants make available spaces of particular closeness to their bodily practices and novel perspectives on the physical expression of feelings that circulate in dynamics of mutual affect with others (e.g. conjoint corporeal presences, postures, twitches, exhalations, tensions, facial contortions, muscular firings). It takes in situ research to a new and deeper level, and permits more intimate probing into the 'contact' of Haraway's (2008) contact zones; unpacking what exactly contact entails and how it is experienced. For example, one clip showed a dog expressing nervousness at another dog's approach (tense, tail high, and fallen out of the 'heel' position on the left side of the owner), only reluctantly coming back to heel through a combination of a 'heel' command and the human refusing to walk forward until the dog came back into position.[26] Doors can be opened to the sensuality, tactility and viscerality of animal-human contact, connection and exchange. So too can access be given to personal moments and spaces that may be considered too intimate, too strange or too mundane for probing with handheld video, partially as a product of the embodied minicam already being 'in on the act'. No need to manually *film* i.e. actively direct and hone camera in on phenomena of interest, and press 'record'. The minicam is already there, already rolling. This immersive perspective gave us particularly good scope for witnessing and evoking the taken-for-granted routines and rituals of dogwalking. Many aspects came to light through the audiencing of minicam footage of dogwalks that participants had not thought to mention in the initial interviews (e.g. how much dogwalker did not attend to dog because lost in own thoughts or distracted by other humans), or that they had never really noticed before (e.g. the olfactory centrality of a dog's world in contrast to their own sensory hierarchies; see Figure 5.3[27]). These provided insights for dogwalkers and researchers into how a dog might experience and pay attention.

Understand Ways of Becoming Across Species Boundaries

Being party to bodily spaces that evoke visceral, sensory and emotional dimensions of multi-species experience, allowed the researcher (and participant in the Review phase) to appreciate the more-than-verbal ways in which human and dog articulate to each other, and thus mutually transform one another. From footage showing a human using hand and voice signals to ask the dog to stop and wait, and the dog's ears trained on the human, as well as featuring a dog inviting the human to play with the stick it has found,[28] we could begin to grasp how this woman and her dog made sense of each other as they walked, played, looked at, listened to and touched each other, ignored each other, separated, came together, gave and received praise, punishment and numerous (intentional and unintentional) verbal, paraverbal and bodily signals.

Watching and talking around minicam footage provided a feel for the varying degrees to which human-canine partnerships were attending, attuning and responding to one another. Dogwalking was clearly a continual process of humans and animals learning to affect and be affected in particular ways (after Despret 2004). Some of these affective dynamics aided the coherence of dog and human in a way we might refer to as proper or close 'control' (e.g. human-dog maintaining regular eye-contact[29]). Some of them did not (e.g. dog becoming inured to recall signals). The paraverbal signalling of dog or human could be fleeting or unintentional, which meant the

Figure 5.3 Dogs' regular sniffing sparked an appreciation of the centrality of sense of smell in a dog's landscape experience.

problem was more one species missing or becoming inured to the articulations of the other.

How Space is Shared Across Species Boundaries

The minicam gave us an appreciation of how the choreographing of a dog-walk matters for multi-species flourishing. It helped make palpable the spatial and temporal contingencies of affective relations that matter for dog-human coherence, and the consequent capacity to share space across species difference (e.g. human-dog-capercaillie). Coherence and 'control'—and thus 'responsible' outdoor access—is not simply a case of attunement between animal and human, it is essentially attunement where and when it matters. For example, legally, the dog must come back to its human when requested if there might be capercaillie around. Video used in this way enables the researcher to trace how interspecies coherence is accomplished through breaking down 'the moment(s)' and spaces of action and inaction in which affecting and being affected happens (or not, as when humans lose and then regain 'control' over their dog when they chase another animal[30]). This makes visible the competencies and knowledges needed with regard to timing, anticipation and particular disassociations of dog and (material and semiotic) landscape. For example, dogwalkers had to anticipate the loss of visual and aural contact with their dog *before* the dog rounded a corner or went over a rise, lest it become the crux place and moment enabling the chasing of sheep or deer. Yet sometimes they didn't see the need for such attentions in a landscape they deemed 'wild' and thus suitable for a dog to 'run free'.

ETHICAL ISSUES

How various methodological approaches can help us meet ethical obligations to the non-human is the subject of growing debate (Greenhough and Roe 2011). We are prompted to think critically about which creatures, ways of knowing, and ways of affecting, we privilege, obscure or exclude by employing video methods, and what kinds of effects are produced.

Bringing Animals in as Research Participants

Bringing animals in as research subjects—rather than objects—has been identified as a huge but important challenge for scholarship (Wolch and Emel 1998). This is for two reasons. First, the notion of a clear-cut ontological divide between humans and animals has been called into question (ibid.). Attending to processes whereby humans and animals *become together* in inextricable, mutually constituting ways (Whatmore 2002) is now considered a more imperative line of enquiry. Second, there is a greater appreciation of animals—not just humans—as having subjectivity; their own lived experience, competencies and intelligences, their own ways of being and knowing (Despret 2004; Wolfe 2003). This raises questions of the degree and kinds of agency animals might be able to exert in a video-based research process, and how and to what extent we can engage with animals on their own terms through the creation and audiencing of (in this case mobile) audiovisual material.

Methodological Challenges

Finding appropriate methods are particularly problematic for scholars focussing on "animal experience rather than on the human perspective in the interspecies relationship" (Seymour and Wolch, 2010, 306). The standard, largely discursive toolkit of qualitative techniques "clearly privileges the human side of the human-animal relationship" (ibid.). Further complications emerge when we want to look at both human and animal dimensions. A commonly cited limitation is that humans and animals do not speak the same language. Yet we learn from Despret (2004), Haraway (2008) and others that this is not wholly the case, and that humans and animals do communicate by developing their own bodily and paraverbal ways of affecting each other. Nevertheless, the predominantly verbal and word-based format of research means that humans still tend to speak on behalf of animals, with the danger that animal ways of making sense of the world are made visible in limited and disembodied ways. The issue here is whether minicam video allows us to address the asymmetrical agency that is so typical in animal-related research. Does it give us a chance to redistribute to some extent "what talks and what is talked about" (Despret 2004, 128)?

Ethical Implications of Enrolling Minicam Video

On one hand, enrolling minicam allowed more-than-human ways of being to affect the research process more than is usual with talk-only techniques. The recording and playback of on-the-go video in which everyday dog-on-dogwalk doings were evoked gave these animals a chance to be witnessed by humans and to affect them through and in more-than-verbal ways. This provided a novel chance for dogs to 'speak for themselves' and to articulate their 'dogness' (after Haraway 2008) through their own expressions and vocabularies. Unlike any established modes of witnessing dogs on film, the real-time POV trope of minicam made the familiar practices of dogwalking strange for the dogwalker.

Alternative ways of knowing, such as the profoundly tactile, olfactory and kinaesthetic ways dogs express themselves and make sense of the world—and the highly spatialised ways they were sensitive to human moods and bodily expressions—were made visible in a way that allowed lesser-appreciated aspects of dogwalking to emerge. These included the attentional ebb and flow of the dogwalk, where dog and human attunements had their own rhythm of zoning in and out, depending on where they were and what they were doing. Dogwalkers are notorious amongst land managers and outdoor access professionals for never believing that it is *them* or *their* dog that causes a problem with wildlife, livestock or other people. But minicam can make this possibility tangible for them, though not in a way that necessarily makes them defensive, partly because they can see the complex web of agencies at work. This might be how their actions are co-constituted with materialities (e.g. topographies and their effect on sightlines) or socialities (e.g. distractions of babies or friends).

Dogwalking thus illustrates well how minicam can help practitioners develop a different consciousness of their own mundane, taken-for-granted and habitual bodily practices, and particularly as they affect and are affected by the non-human. Making visible that which is blasé for the dogwalkers also demonstrated the power of rewitnessing one's own (multi-species) practices from something akin to one's own perspective. Here minicam gave a chance to reflect that seemed to differ from that produced by practices of consciously filming or being filmed with handheld video. Some human participants conveyed that they felt like a fly on their own wall in the Stage III Review; identifying with surveillant affective logics but ones in which they could be part of the surveilling.

Nevertheless, minicam is not preordained to make viewers care or empathise more for the creatures depicted, as suggested by commercial developers of Crittercam. An upshot of our witnessing of dog lives with minicam video was dogs being incriminated by certain humans who perceived the dog's actions or intentions to be illegitimate, such as in relation to chasing wildlife or sheep (i.e. people felt they were sometimes witnessing 'bad' behaviour). But nor is minicam destined to be the negative colonising, and thus subjugating, force suggested by Haraway (2008) in her critique of Crittercam. Enrolling minicam in dogwalking also made it possible to trace the agency and culpability of humans in generating the transgressions often ascribed to dogs. Realising that a case of a 'bad dog' might actually be as much a 'bad human' could ultimately engender a more affirmative politics for dogs.

On the other hand, despite having image-making at the heart of our approach, we found it difficult to escape anthropocentrism, especially in the shooting and audiencing of minicam video. Since dogs did not wear a camera or participate in pre- or post-outing interviews, there was asymmetry of agency in that humans had more chance than animals to control how their practices and ways of making sense of the world were made visible. Considerable agency in filming was relinquished by the researcher who did not operate the camera once mounted, but it was to the human participants and the video technologies that the agency passed. The human participants were also uniquely positioned to perceive monitoring or surveillance affective logics from minicam being enrolled in the encounter. For example, the human might try harder to 'behave' on the ethnographic outing—in responsive to perceived normative boundaries—in a way a dog would not know to do.

Neither did dogs have the opportunity and agency to co-constitute further layers of knowledges in Stages I and III of the MVE. Humans had the chance to situate, qualify and explain away practices or roles that might undermine or seem incriminating for them, but, for the want of the verbal modes of articulation, the animals did not.

Nevertheless, we did identify scope for experimenting with minicam that could diminish somewhat the privileging of the human and the discursive; most notably through enrolling the camera with animal bodies, which we are exploring in fieldwork at present. Such research needs to ascertain the practical and ethical implications, and critically assess whether anthropocentrism would indeed be addressed. The prospect of bringing 'animal-cam' more to the fore of methodology also reinforces the need to work on the broader issue of how to mobilise minicam footage beyond the confines of project analysis spaces, in a way that attempts to escape the perennial dilemma of reducing images to verbal representation and the associated potential closing down of political possibilities. In both these regards, experimental documentary films such as *Leviathan* (Paravel and Castaing-Taylor 2013) exemplify and expand immeasurably the horizons of what might be achieved with a more-than-human enrolment of minicam.

CONCLUSION

Recent debate on the more-than-human ways in which our social worlds come into being underlines an acute need to develop methods that allow access to, and deeper understandings of, encounters between people and animals. Minicam offers a novel way of using video in research that shows promise in this regard and beyond. It involves new ways of intermingling video technologies with animal and human bodies as they move in and through environments, which creates fresh possibilities for bringing obscure or puzzling aspects of more-than-human becomings 'into view' or into realms of tangibility and sensibility.

The example of dogwalking illustrates some of the insights that minicam video ethnography can generate. In common with some handheld video methods (see Lorimer 2010), minicam helps to witness, evoke and make sense of animal and human worlds as they are experienced and known through the body; a crucial point when non-verbal, multi-sensory and affective dimensions are at the heart of cross-species intersubjectivity, and often so elusive to traditional talk-based methods. For us, watching, experiencing, reflecting and talking around minicam video enabled an appreciation of how a dog and human articulate to one another and significant others (whether through various forms of eye contact, bodily poise, muscular firing or paraverbal signals), how they become sensitive and attuned to one another (or otherwise), and how they learn to be affected (or not) by each other. This helped make visible particular distributions of agency in the unfolding of multi-species encounters, such as the conjoint performance or rupture of 'control' by dog-human partnerships, with implications for wildlife and livestock.

The particular virtue of minicam is that it takes seriously the movement and mobilities fundamental to the mutual becoming of animal and human, and thus allows an appreciation of the spatialities and temporalities of more-than-human choreographies, which unfold on the move, take place through networks of multiple interwoven sites. Moreover, it foregrounds how species constitute each other in conjunction with particular places and (micro and macro) spaces; allowing attention both to wider landscapes and ecologies and the intimate spaces of the moving, feeling, sensing body.

Nevertheless, the resource-heavy and ethical demands of MVE must be carefully considered before choosing this method. Researchers should be sure that the insights are worth the extra time, effort and cost. There is also a need to consider the particular affects and effects produced by enrolling minicam—camera and images—into the research process and how this sits with the additional ethical obligations to animals impelled by recent scholarship (Greenhough and Roe 2011; Haraway 2008).

We must consider how minicam, as a recent incarnation of 'new mediated ecologies', can be mobilised in ways that do not merely reinforce prevailing asymmetries of power and jeopardise multi-species flourishing. We learned that minicam video techniques could not be claimed to be inherently 'good' or 'bad' in this regard, echoing broader visual methods debates that illustrate that visualities can work to dominate (Rose 1993), and can work to empower (Kindon 2003) depending on how they are mobilised, by whom and for whom.

In our experience, minicam facilitated a significant and innovative accessing of the spaces and times of animal bodies, and the practices through which they co-constitute with other animate and inanimate entities. This provided the opportunity for animals to articulate in their own linguistic currency, and for this expression to be more readily apprehended. This is a form of agency insofar as spaces were opened up for humans to be affected by animals in new ways, and could be considered a way of enabling animals to 'talk' that is precluded by more traditional methods.

However, we were still guilty of privileging human subjects and verbal modes of articulating, since it was the human participants, and not the dogs, that had the chance to shoot and talk around video material. It was thus humans who had greater agency in foregrounding and qualifying particular ways of making sense of the world. How we distribute agency in video research processes between human and animal participants is thus highlighted as an important question for future research. There is certainly clear scope to redistribute agency in the *creation* of video images (e.g. by allowing animals to wear the camera), but seems more problematic in terms of *audiencing* video material when, so far, minicam video ethnography has been reduced largely to the verbal in post-analysis dissemination. Therein lies the challenge of how minicam video might enable animals to articulate to wider audiences in an affirming way that does not require discursive translation.[31]

We therefore call for researchers to be creative and exploratory in addressing asymmetries of more-than-human agency and subjectivity in the video research process. With minicam video we are only in the beginnings of experimenting with how it can generate understandings in social research. Yet, building on Lorimer (2010), particular attention is needed to the precise ways in which interspecies relations and 'problems' of cross-species encounter are made visible, and which remain obscured. This includes considering critically the technologies, techniques, visual cultures, expressions, conventions and grammars that the enrolment of minicam video implies (Brown and Dilley, in prep), and the affective logics infusing the generation and audiencing of the footage produced. The affective dynamics of minicam are shaped by choices made in the research process about how to combine technologies, bodies and movements, such as: where on a body to place a camera; which human or animal bodies we seek to evoke a 'view of' or 'view from'; and if and how recorded images and sounds will become edited and interwoven with words and talk. Such decisions shape the cultivation of capacities for researcher, video, human and non-human participants to be affected by, and respond to, each other, and ultimately what we can learn about how to better share space across species boundaries.

NOTES

1. Capercaillie (*Tetrao urogallus*) is a species of large, woodland, ground-nesting grouse that has become very rare in the UK and is protected under the Natura 2000 European legislation that designates Special Protection Areas.
2. Many ethnographic films produced through anthropological study have featured animals as elements of the cultures being examined, but have rarely centered analytical focus beyond the human, especially in terms of agency, subjectivity and experience, even when studying practices, such as herding, where animals are central (see Fijn, 2012; Grimshaw, 2011).
3. Situating video in such ways is informed by assemblage theory (for an accessible overview, see Anderson & McFarlane, 2011).
4. See http://animals.nationalgeographic.co.uk/animals/crittercam/ and Haraway (2008) for a critique.
5. See, for example, the booming sales of various models of pet-mounted minicams such as http://www.mrpetcam.com/
6. See http://www.bbc.co.uk/mediacentre/latestnews/2013/secret-life-of-the-cat.html
7. Since we were particularly interested in the everydayness of dogwalking, we wanted, as far as possible, to enrol minicam in an outing that the participant would have done anyway, rather than an outing arranged especially for the research. This was straightforward for the dogwalkers, as they walked their dogs in the Park on a daily basis. However, the outings with land managers, rangers and conservationists had to be specifically arranged as they walked in the area much less frequently, and were in any case being enrolled in more of a 'show and tell' (see Grasseni, 2004; Pink, 2007) capacity. A 'fly-on-the-wall' style of filming was less relevant for regarding their roles, as it would not easily enable their experiences and perspectives on dogwalking to come to the fore.

Yet we still wanted to harness the agency of place, the environment in which activities are situated, and hence used minicam.

8. Mobile video ethnography (MVE) is one of a number of qualitative methods we have employed in our research on practices of outdoor access and recreation— with a focus on walking, mountain biking and dogwalking—that we have carried out in the Cairngorms National Park from 2006 to the present. The other methods include semi-structured interviews, observation of community and Local Outdoor Access Forum meetings and a participatory video project focussing on dogwalking in particular.

9. Of the 25 dogwalkers, 10 were doing MVE and 15 were doing Participatory Video, in addition to 24 other recreationists and 14 non-recreationists covering the main stakeholder types.

10. Given that a three-stage process is already an onerous commitment for participants, we had to be rather opportunistic in making use of the time (and timings) offered. To minimise the logistical burden for the participant—and often at their behest—it frequently happened that the biographical interview was immediately before the video outing, but in some cases also occurred on different days, sometimes weeks apart.

11. ftp://support.archos.com/AV500/Data/Manuals/EN_AV500_v25.pdf

12. http://vio-pov.com/

13. http://gopro.com/support/hd-hero2-support

14. The following clip illustrates how the sound of voices and the wider environment are drowned out by a rustly jacket: http://youtu.be/pQwYieTMu0E

15. We came to the conclusion that radio mics are the ideal, shortly followed by a cable external mic. Failing that, carrying a dictaphone can provide worthwhile audio back-up, but can be tricky to retrospectively correspond to the image data.

16. It used to be an issue that the format of HD video files produced were not favoured by major editing packages (including the Final Cut Pro 7 that we were using), but now powerful free video file conversion software such as MPEG Streamclip means this is no longer a problem. We converted our files to MP4 to be played in QuickTime on a laptop during Stage III analysis and review.

17. Georeferencing was not done in our case as researchers preferred to become intimately familiar with the places involved, so when they were audiencing the video they 'knew' in some sense where they were seeing, that way of knowing spatial relations was considered enough for us to address our research questions but for certain circumstances there would certainly be merit in using GPS to add another way of knowing space to the configurations of knowledge being generated.

18. This was in order to experiment with the different images, sounds and understandings generated, and the analysis of this is ongoing.

19. Our original plan was for the participant to wear the camera, primarily because we were thinking mainly of dogwalkers and it was their perspective on their doings we wished to explore, but when it came to the other stakeholders we experimented with the researcher wearing it, because of the 'show and tell' format that seemed to be unfolding. 'Go-along' and 'show and tell' modes of doing video ethnography in some ways seem to privilege the verbal just when there is a chance to redress the usual balance. Yet it does allow the non-verbal to exert agency on the verbal in a way not possible in a traditional interview or focus group setting, and still allows the power of *in situ* movement-in-place to work on the research process.

20. Only short clips of extreme sport on YouTube of particular places, trails or encounters, or clips edited in sparingly with other footage as in Crittercam wildlife documentaries.

21. The participant did not have the opportunity to see the footage beforehand, and in this the researcher was arguably privileged in having two opportunities at viewing and contributing to, analysis. However, when we raised this as an issue with later participants they said they would have had little desire or time to watch the footage themselves beforehand anyway. Yet leaving the participant with a copy of the uncut video outing footage may still be the most ethical thing to do, just in case they would like the opportunity to engage with the footage in their own way, in their own time, before the researcher comes back with their own framings and agenda and with greater familiarity with the recording.

22. Minicam footage of dogwalking often first seems 'boring' or that 'nothing is happening', but if you ask people afterwards what was happening they describe a range of activities, often thinking about things that are nothing directly to do with dogwalking, such as pondering 'what will I have for my tea tonight': http://youtu.be/2awPw17nri4

23. Usually approximately 45 minutes of a total 1.5 hours.

24. However, this is only a solution if participants are happy for the material to be in the wider public domain in such ways.

25. This has to be taken into account in the fieldwork, analysis and presentation phases, e.g. for longer walks it would be safe to say that later in the outings received less audiencing attention, unless the participant had memories evoked of a particular part of the walk and went scrolling through the footage for it.

26. See: http://youtu.be/d-erH8oH0T0

27. The following clip features a dog sniffing its way through the environment, changing course when a new interesting smell is encountered: http://youtu.be/mPpQBniNSZM

28. See the following clip showing the human signalling the dog to wait: http://youtu.be/X_NsTuOLogU; and another showing the dog signalling to have a stick thrown: http://youtu.be/Y64OmpsUmD0

29. See the following clips in which sightlines and eye contact were found to be important to achieving and maintaining human-dog attunement. In one the dog is checking on the human: http://youtu.be/_dCh9TJrDmo; in the other the human is checking on the dog: http://youtu.be/rdtN-4OmHao

30. In the following clip the achievement of 'close control' of dog and human partnership is disrupted as dog senses, then chases, a deer. The human realised later that they missed the dog's ways of signalling that it was going to become unavailable to human commands. Once the deer had gone, the dog allowed himself to be affected by human articulations once again and returns to them: http://youtu.be/OZVLHPtWCQ4

31. At the moment we are caught between the long, unwieldy and sometimes near-unwatchable 'boring' uncut footage that the researcher and human participant watch and talk around, and the decontextualized clips or stills that pepper journal articles and conference presentations.

REFERENCES

Anderson, B. and McFarlane, C. 2011. Assemblage and geography. *Area*, 43(2): 124–127.

Bear, C., Wilkinson, K. and Holloway, L. Forthcoming. Visualising human-animal-technology relations: still photography and digital video on the robotic dairy farm. *Society & Natural Resources*.

Bekoff, M. 2000. Animal emotions: exploring passionate natures. *BioScience*, 50(10): 861–870.

Bekoff, M. 2002. *Minding Animals: Awareness, Emotions and Heart*. Oxford: Oxford University Press.

Brown, K. M. 2012. Sharing public space across difference: attunement and the contested burdens of choreographing encounter. *Social & Cultural Geography*, 13(7): 801–820.

Brown, K. M. 2014. The role of landscape in regulating (ir)responsible conduct: moral geographies of the 'proper control' of dogs. *Landscape Research*, published online 14 February.

Brown, K. M. and Dilley, R. 2012. Ways of knowing for "response-ability" in more-than-human encounters: the role of anticipatory knowledges in outdoor access with dogs. *Area*, 44(1): 37–45.

Brown, K. M. and Dilley, R. Unpublished manuscript. Mobile video methods and the reproduction of gender: lessons for a more critical approach.

Brown, K. M., Dilley, R. and Marshall, K. 2008. Using a head-mounted video camera to understand social worlds and experiences. *Sociological Research Online*, 13(6), http://www.socresonline.org.uk/13/6/1.html

Cresswell, T. 2012. Mobilities II: still. *Progress in Human Geography*, 36(5): 645–653. doi: 10.1177/0309132511423349

Despret, V. 2004. The body we care for: figures of anthropo-zoogenesis. *Body and Society*, 10: 111–134.

Fijn, N. 2007. Filming the significant other: human and non-human. *Asia Pacific Journal of Anthropology*, 8: 297–307.

Fijn, N. 2012. A multispecies etho-ethnographic approach to filmmaking. *The Humanities Research Journal*, 18: 71–88.

Goode, D. 2006. *Playing With My Dog Katie: An Ethnomethodological Study of Dog-Human Interaction*. Lafayette: Purdue University Press.

Grandin, T. 2006. *Thinking in Pictures: My Life With Autism*. New York: Vintage.

Grasseni, C. 2004. Skilled vision. An apprenticeship in breeding aesthetics. *Social Anthropology*, 12(1): 41–55.

Greenhough, B. and Roe, E. 2011. Ethics, space, and somatic sensibilities: comparing relationships between scientific researchers and their human and animal experimental subjects, *Environment and Planning D*, 29: 47–66.

Grimshaw, A. 2011. The bellwether ewe: recent developments in ethnographic filmmaking and the aesthetics of anthropological inquiry. *Cultural Anthropology*, 26(2): 247–262. doi: 10.1111/j.1548–1360.2011.01098.x

Haraway, D. J. 2008. *When Species Meet*. Minneapolis: University of Minnesota Press.

Kindon, S. 2003. Participatory video in geographic research: a feminist practice of looking? *Area*, 35(2): 142–153.

Konecki, K. T. 2008. Touching and gesture exchange as an element of emotional bond construction. Application of visual sociology in the research on interaction between humans and animals. *Qualitative Social Research*, 9(3): 33. http://nbn-resolving.de/urn:nbn:de:0114-fqs0803337

Kusenbach, M. 2003. Street phenomenology: the go-along as ethnographic research tool. *Ethnography*, 4: 455–485.

Laurier, E., Maze, R. and Lundin, J. 2006. Putting the dog back in the park: animal and human mind-in-action. *Mind, Culture & Activity*, 13(1): 2–24.

Lorimer, J. 2010. Moving image methodologies for more-than-human geographies. *Cultural Geographies*, 17(2): 237–258.

Nadin, L. B., Chopa, F. S., Gibb, M. J. and Trindade, J. K. 2012. Comparison of methods to quantify the number of bites in calves grazing winter oats with different sward heights. *Applied Animal Behaviour Science*, 139(1–2): 50–57.

Napolitano, F., De Rosa, G., Braghieri, A., Grasso, F., Bordi, A. and Wemelsfelder, F. 2008. The qualitative assessment of responsiveness to environmental challenge in horses and ponies. *Applied Animal Behaviour Science*, 109(2–4): 342–354.

Nosworthy, C. 2013. *A Geography of Horse-Riding: The Spacing of Affect, Emotion and (Dis)Ability Identity Through Horse-Human Encounters*. Newcastle: Cambridge Scholars Publishing.

Philo, C. and Wilbert, C. 2000. *Animal Spaces, Beastly Places: New Geographies of Human-Animal Relations*. London: Routledge.

Pink, S. 2007. *Doing Visual Ethnography*. London: Sage.

Pink, S. 2009. *Doing Sensory Ethnography*. London: Sage.

Rose, G. 1993. *Feminism and Geography: The Limits of Geographical Knowledge*. Minneapolis: University of Minnesota Press.

Rose, G. 2007. *Visual Methodologies: An Introduction to the Interpretation of Visual Methodologies*. London: Sage.

Seymour, M. and Wolch, J. 2010. "A little bird told me . . .": approaching animals through qualitative methods. In DeLyser, D., Herbert, S., Aitken, S., Crang, M. and McDowell, L. (eds.) *The SAGE Handbook of Qualitative Geography*. London: Sage, 305–321.

Shrum, W., Duque, R., and Brown, T. 2005. Digital video as research practice: Methodology for the millennium. *Journal of Research Practice*, 1(1): Article M4. Retrieved from http://jrp.icaap.org/index.php/jrp/article/view/6/12

Simpson, P. 2011. "So, as you can see . . .": some reflections on the utility of video methodologies in the study of embodied practices. *Area*, 43(3): 343–352.

Spinney, J. 2009. Cycling the city: mobility, meaning and method. *Geography Compass*, 7(2): 817–835.

Spinney, J. 2011. A chance to catch a breath: using mobile video ethnography in cycling research. *Mobilities*, 6(2): 161–182. doi:10.1080/17450101.2011.552771

Urbanik, J. 2012. *Placing Animals: An Introduction to the Geography of Human-Animal Relations*. Plymouth: Rowman & Littlefield.

Urry, J. 2007. *Mobilities*. Cambridge: Polity.

Weil, K. 2012. *Thinking Animals: Why Animal Studies Now?* New York: Columbia University Press.

Whatmore, S. 2002. *Hybrid Geographies: Natures, Cultures, Spaces*. London: Sage.

Wolch J. R. and Emel J. 1998. *Animal Geographies: Place, Politics, and Identity in the Nature-Culture Borderlands*. London: Verso Books.

Wolfe, C. 2003. *Zoontologies: The Question of the Animal*. London: University of Minnesota Press.

Wood, P.R.H. Embodied conversation: how video- and diary-elicitation demonstrate the materialities of bicycling talk. Paper at the Eleventh Annual Cultural Studies Conference, Columbia College Chicago, 23–26 May 2013.

Wratten S. D. 1994. *Video Techniques in Animal Ecology and Behaviour*. New York: Springer-Verlag.

6 Jumps, Stutters, Blurs and Other Failed Images
Using Time-Lapse Video in Cycling Research

Katrina Jungnickel

INTRODUCTION

My computer pauses in protest at the volume of data I am attempting to download. I have just returned home from an hour-long cycle ride. The camera strapped to the handlebars of my bike was set to take photos every two seconds. Although the screen stopped counting at 999, the memory card continued to capture images until the battery ran out. It looks like there are close to 2000 photos of my journey from Central to East London, with each image at around 2 megabytes. I watch as they download, images flickering briefly in and out of view. All are wide-angled. Some are sharp and detailed. Others are blurry and distorted. Frame by frame, hundreds flash past. My front wheel, the road, other cyclists, lorries and buildings quiver in and out of view. The messy imperfect images that I would otherwise delete stutter past and fuse with those before and after, creating unexpected coherencies. Through these failed images I relive the potholes, a quick handlebar turn to avoid a crash and the speed of traffic. Much like my computer, I too feel a little overwhelmed by the volume of data. Yet, I am also struck by the filmic qualities of the download (Figure 6.1). These might be still images but here they embody a dynamic and vivid movement. Cumulatively, they afford more than a visual trace of the ride. Even seated at my desk, watching the download generates sense of 'being there'.

* * *

While I would use some of these images as singular representations of my fieldwork, more often and the subject of this chapter is how I collated hundreds in a series of videos using time-lapse methods. Time-lapse is an animation technique that stitches hundreds (and sometimes thousands) of still photographs together to create a sequential story via the dynamic illusion of moving image. Central to this technique is the compression of time. Images taken at set intervals are combined to produce a version of something that would have taken hours or days in minutes. Unlike streaming video, this method is characterised by jumps and gaps produced by small incremental

Figure 6.1 Time-lapse video images. Image: Katrina Jungnickel.

shifts between individual photo frames (depending on the number and timing of images). Often compared with stop-motion video, a similar technique used to animate inanimate objects, time-lapse is commonly used to produce new descriptive forms of drawn out events, such as changing weather conditions or the construction of a building. A central tenet of conventional time-lapse video is a stationery lens. The drama of the animation plays out from a motionless fixed point. In this chapter I draw on a case study using a mobile lens (a camera affixed to the handlebars of a bicycle) during a series of solo and group cycle rides undertaken as part of a mixed-method Economic and Social Research Council (ESRC) funded study of UK 'Cycling Cultures'.

This chapter has two main aims. First, I discuss the use and value of the time-lapse method, its possibilities and consequences, in cycling research. I focus in particular on productions of 'there-ness' generated as a result of this visual experience. Scholars have established the importance of 'being there' (Geertz 1988; Hannerz 2003; Jungnickel 2013), and more recently of 'seeing there' (Laurier 2010; Pink 2007) and 'feeling there' (Spinney 2011), as a means of gaining in-depth understandings of social worlds—the latter two often discussed in terms of new video methods. Further to addressing practical issues involved in using time-lapse methods, I explore a range of expected as well as unexpected findings. As anticipated, the time-lapse process produced a compressed version of events, which provided a new form of sociological description for use in and for different mediums and audiences. It captured with vivid detail the proximity of other road users, detail of urban contexts and changing light qualities, which operated as a catalyst for remembering the experiential and embodied features of the rides. Less expected was my appreciation of 'failed' images and their prominent and coherent presence in the videos. Visual stutters and distorted and blurred photos were transformed via the momentum of the time-lapse method into further visual evidence of multi-sensory cycling experiences. In an animated context, poor quality images conveyed the drama of late night cycling, the rough road surface and reminders of fast swerves from danger.

Scholars have argued that social worlds move on the whole much quicker than academia (Beer and Burrows 2007). Exploring the use of new video methods contributes to a growing interest in mobilities studies, and in social sciences more broadly, to embrace new forms of 'thick' description that resist flattening or, indeed, stabilising the dynamic social world and take into consideration the constellation of available digital devices (Büscher et al. 2011; Fincham et al. 2010; Orton-Johnson and Prior 2013). What I hope this case study offers, in Orton-Johnson and Prior's words, is a chance "to evaluate new conceptual tools and languages with which we can flex our sociological imaginations" (2013, 3).

Second, and related to this, I critically reflect on time-lapse video as a means through which the ethnographer *makes* knowledge via the interweaving of conceptual development and material practice, producing artefacts that move into new social worlds, entangling with diverse socio-technical actors. This takes two parts. As per the fieldnote I was so moved by the sheer volume of still images that downloaded onto my computer that I began to contemplate time-lapse methods. Lury and Wakeford have called these kinds of emergent practices 'inventive methods' which arise in the process of doing the research. They argue that "methods in the making" are "methods or means by which the social world is not only investigated, but may also be engaged" (2012, 6). In a similar way, in his discussion of 'live methods', Back calls for "a revitalisation of our methodological imagination . . . to develop new kinds of device to both explore and produce the social" (2012a, 257). But this is not easy, and as a result this is also a chapter about mess.

Mess in qualitative research has recently been explored in terms of textures, ideas, objects, artefacts, places, people, methods and emotions that are difficult to deal with within the traditional confines of social science; an indefinable array of complexities that are often conventionally ordered and organised in the pursuit of sociological knowledge (Hine 2007; Law 2004; Lury and Wakeford 2012). Law argues that current "academic methods of inquiry don't really catch" these messy aspects of life (2004, 6). Moreover, this desire to clean up actually contradicts our own understanding of the world and, in turn, limits the possibilities of other forms of knowing. Embracing mess affords a new way to consider sociological methods that embrace "impossible or barely possible, unthinkable or almost unthinkable" versions of reality (ibid). Hine similarly critiques sociology's established approach: "Our methodological instincts are to clean up complexity and tell straightforward linear stories, and thus we tend to exclude descriptions that are faithful to experiences of mess, ambivalence, elusiveness and multiplicity" (2007, 12).

Time-lapse video is a way of 'catching' some of the complexity, resisting the impulse to 'clean up' and deal with the volume of digital research materials. The resulting description is not polished; the final forms retain a multi-vocal character via the inclusion of failed images and the stuttering, flickering nature of the animation. I produced these videos not just for my own purpose but also published them online, making them available to use and users beyond my control. This method adds considerably more work to a research project, demanding time, space, technological competency and equipment. To this end, I discuss how the videos operate as alternate modes of knowledge transmission to conventional talk and text outputs. Reflecting critically on the process of these researcher-made knowledge objects, I suggest time-lapse video in cycling research provides not only a way of 'being', 'seeing' and 'feeling there' but also a way of 'making there'.

The chapter is structured as follows. I start by framing the discussion in relation to mobile and inventive methods literature with a focus on 'there-ness'. I address a range of practical issues relating to how the videos were produced from photos of cycle rides and then discuss expected and unexpected findings, things that worked and also failed and how both were enfolded into my research findings. Throughout I ask: What does time-lapse video add to still photo-images? What is the relationship between the moving image and the mobile experience? How and in what ways is it an inventive method and what does it add to a mixed-method research project? I conclude by arguing that the use of time-lapse video offers insights into less easily represented aspects of the cycling experience.

'BEING', 'SEEING' AND 'FEELING THERE'

The theoretical and methodological impetus for 'being there' first emerged in traditional social science methods (Geertz 1988). Being there, an in-depth qualitative engagement with a social group in a single setting for an extended period of time, was deemed critical to gaining an intimate understanding of another culture. Axiomatic to this kind of ethnographic practice was an initial "thick description" (Geertz 1973) of the central location in which action happens for "the purpose of grounding the ethnography" as well as "showing how peoples' lifeways are constrained and enabled by their environment" (Helmreich 1998, 29). Such locations have included the village (Evans Pritchard 1951), science laboratory (Latour and Woolgar 1979) and technology park (Helmreich 1998). Once a location was defined, action was firmly anchored in place and researchers ostensibly remained within its boundaries.

Ethnographic research has grown ever more geographically and conceptually complex in line with awareness of the mutable and heterogeneous nature of social, mobile and digital worlds and increased mobile experience. Concurrently, new methods have emerged in response to people, groups, objects and ideas that are not spatially fixed (Büscher et al. 2011; Hannerz 2003; Hine 2007; Lynam and Wakeford 1999; Marcus 1998). Where once only a minority of studies necessitated the tracing and piecing together of people, things, places and events in virtual and real world contexts across the world, multi-modal practice is now the norm. A multi-sited approach, most notably promulgated by Marcus (1998), articulates a purchase on the complexities of multiple sites, ideas and things by encouraging the researcher to 'follow the people', 'follow the thing', 'follow the metaphor', 'follow the plot, story or allegory', 'follow the life or biography' or 'follow the conflict' across a range of locations. Marcus argues that multi-sited study is particularly powerful for 'suturing locations of cultural production that had not been obviously connected and consequently, for creating empirically argued new envisionings of social landscapes' (1998, 93). Being part of another culture more often means *moving with them*. One such response is provided by Hannerz (2003), who reflects on the challenges not only for his itinerant respondents, who were foreign correspondents, but also for himself as a researcher in "being there . . . and there . . . and there!" in shorter multi-sited studies. Contributing to this literature, I have explored the benefits and practical realities of 'getting there and back again' or what I suggested could be termed "ethnographic commuting" (Jungnickel 2013). This entails focusing on the boring and mundane everyday movements in and between fieldsites that are a reality for researcher and respondents alike. Broadly speaking, this literature advocates ways of focusing on mobility as both subject and tool of enquiry.

This is the crux of this chapter. While many social groups can be characterised by increasing mobilities, it is perhaps studies of mobile cultures which renders this most visible, drawing acute attention to the theoretical and methodological challenges of 'being there'. The 'new mobilities paradigm' is a relatively recent turn in the social sciences to understand the movement of people, things, ideas and objects and the broader implications these shifts pose for understanding contemporary society (Sheller and Urry 2006). Cycling scholars in particular argue that cycling brings to light a range of assumptions built into the urban mobile landscape and conventional methods alike (Aldred 2010; Aldred and Jungnickel 2012; Fincham 2006; Horton et al. 2007; Jungnickel and Aldred 2014; Spinney 2006, 2011). While this work has addressed a wide variety of topics, all contribute to the idea that the view from the saddle draws attention to normalised and as a result overlooked mobile practices such as motorised transport. Car cultures, and the vast infrastructures that enable them, have been so embedded within industrialised urban landscapes and social practices that the role they play in shaping understandings of urban mobility has until recently escaped sustained attention (Elliot and Urry 2010; Miller 2001). Although motorised transport is a relatively recent western phenomenon, many skills inherent in manoeuvring multi-tonne steel vehicles through the city at speed have become unremarkable and taken for granted. As Bijsterveld has argued: "We forget the skills we have had to learn once we have made them our own" (2010, 205). Riding a bicycle presents a means of apprehending the city in new ways. It draws attention to mass motorised infrastructures, recasting them in a new light whereby it becomes easier to question why they are there, who they are built for who, who is enabled and who is less enabled by their presence. Examining cycling in the context of mass motorised society plays a critical role in drawing attention to ways that things, such as urban planning and technological and social interactions, might have been otherwise (Bijker and Law 1992, 3).

The challenge to capture and make sense of this experience has caught the attention of many within this field of enquiry. While the study of mobilities and transport has produced rich and diverse insights into a range of mobile cultures and practices, scholars have raised concerns about the methodological pattern of attending to more fixed and easily representable socio-mobile constructions of everyday life over those that are more ambiguous, sensory and multiple (Büscher et al. 2011; Jungnickel and Aldred 2014; Pink 2007, 2008; Spinney 2006, 2011). Video, in particular, is technology and practice at the forefront of this desire to capture "fleeting, ephemeral and often embodied and sensory aspects of movement" (Spinney 2011, 162). Employing the use of video for instance, is a means of enabling researchers to 'be there' even when they are not. Laurier (2010) has termed this 'seeing there' in his 'Habitable Cars' research whereby he studied everyday social interactions by installing video cameras inside vehicles. Video in cycling has been enlisted as a means of heightening the experience of 'there' in the form of 'go-alongs', which intertwine talking and videoing with cycling (O'Connor and Brown 2007; Spinney 2006). For Spinney, video in this context provided "a way of apprehending fleeting moments of mobile experience" and "a tool to extend sensory vocabularies" (2011, 117).

While video provides new ways of accessing and describing social worlds, few scholars are under any illusion of its ability to capture reality (Pink 2007; Spinney 2008, 2011; Thrift 2004). However, this does not mean that it does not provide new perspectives and insights such as "the ability to sense the small spaces of the body" and "think of time as minutely segmented frames, able to be speeded up, slowed down, even frozen for a while" (Thift 2004, 67). Yet, most would agree, as Spinney writes, that "representations can only ever be a window into practice" (2011, 173). My work with time-lapse video does not challenge this, but rather draws attention to what is viewed as well as to the window itself. What is often less addressed in this field of enquiry is the hands-on role of the researcher in making these artefacts. Regardless of the method in use, researchers make decisions about the subject under scrutiny, data and final artefact. We are in the process and practice of making knowledge. We deal with visualising devices, files and computers as well as circulatory channels in which these artefacts are published and shared. These are the tasks and techniques involved in making 'there'. Here, 'there' is considered an object just as much as the text that describes the method that is published in journals and books.

MAKING SENSE: INVENTIVE METHODS AND MODES OF TRANSMISSION

> It is not possible to apply a method as if it were indifferent or external to the problem it seeks to address, but that method must rather be made specific or relevant to the problem. . . . Inventive methods are ways to introduce answerability into a problem . . . if methods are to be inventive, they should not leave that problem untouched.
>
> (Lury and Wakeford 2012, 3)

This chapter also responds to a growing desire in the social sciences to resist the flattening of live, dynamic processes via a renewed interest in sociological description in relation to digital research methods. As Lury and Wakeford argue, this brings to light a dynamic inter-relationship; neither the subject nor method is untouched by the other. The popularity of digital technologies has transformed not only the subject matter for many researchers but greatly expanded the possibilities of making, communicating and circulating findings to new audiences. On the whole, however, debate and discussion about the tactics and techniques of knowledge translation and transmission has lagged behind their widespread use (Back 2012a; Lury and Wakeford 2013; Orton-Johnson and Prior 2013).

For cycling scholars, video often fits well with the visual practices and culture of social groups under study. Cyclists' videos on blogs, websites and forums are a growing phenomenon. Brown and Spinney recount Spinney's experience of asking permission to film a group of BMX riders: "Somewhat to his surprise, rather than be seen as invasive this turned out to have been one of the best things he could have asked" (2010, 136). Not only did video turn out to be a valuable tool in gaining access to the group but it also provided "insight into the particular aspects of the culture that participants chose to emphasise, and a culturally congruent vehicle through which this could be done" (2010, 136–137).

Yet, despite the ubiquity of video in the social worlds that form the focus of much research, visual representations in sociological contexts have conventionally been narrowly defined in terms of the role they take in the construction of knowledge and the form they are recognised. Innovative findings are predominantly transformed back into conventional presentational formats (text, talk and PowerPoint), with less attention focused on the possibilities of other forms of knowledge translation. Traditional social science has been accused of tidying up the 'mess' left behind by the complexity of the world as it is formed into, for example, sociological categories, analyses and theoretical frameworks (Hine 2007; Law 2004). We might think that for knowledge to be transmitted to those outside our discipline, it is essential that complexity is reduced because we associate this with a clear and direct message. We tend to keep mess for the presentation of process. I am interested in ways in which keeping *in* the complexity in multiple and overlapping forms can be a productive way of representing research findings.

In this article I enfold messiness into cycling research via the use of time-lapse video methods; as both inventive method and knowledge transmission. In doing so I enact a shift from viewing digital technologies as subject matter and method to critical transmission tools and sites of knowledge. Here, mess is not bracketed in the ethnographic immersion period or as an end in itself. Rather, it is considered a vehicle for methodological development and learning. Adopting this approach involves going beyond simply including visuals or materials *in* research outputs, to consider them central *to* new forms of knowledge.

This chapter also recognises the challenges borne of a seemingly inexhaustible volume of documentation produced by contemporary digital 'tools of the trade' and explores what this means for research and researchers. Critically, thinking about 'making there' brings to light the *stuff* of research, a familiar subject to most researchers. As Back writes: "There is something deeply poignant about those cassette boxes full of auditory life" (2012b, 251). Similarly, Laurier notes how he "generated over one hundred hours of video . . . archived into six hundred and sixty indexed clips" which meant that "more than three quarters of the footage disappears at this stage, edited away to the virtual cutting room floor" (2010, 111). While the materiality of research is pointed to, I am particularly interested in what gets edited out and what, if anything, 'failed' data might have contributed to the analysis.

In an analysis of hill-walking, Vergunst (2008) writes about the routine happenstance of 'trips', 'mishaps' and 'slips' which provides insights into analogous 'failed' data. The experience of walking is not always about successfully reaching the destination but often about the dramatic scenery, unexpected weather conditions and all the other challenges that arise along the way. Although an integral aspect of walking, no one ever plans to slip or trip, yet it regularly happens, and because it is so mundane it is often overlooked. This has the effect of distancing the walker from the character of the environment and their place within it. He writes, "by a tiny movement or disjuncture, a slip between a boot and the shale, and the character of the walk changes radically" (2008, 105). Focusing on these aspects of walking draws attention to the way the body accommodates changing conditions and affords a new way of thinking about and understanding an otherwise taken for granted experience. Here, an awareness and inclusion of mishaps serves to bring the walker closer to 'being there'.

BIKE EYE VIEW

The fieldnote and images come from my work as a post-doctoral research fellow on the ESRC-funded 'Cycling Cultures'[1] research project (2010–2011), led by Rachel Aldred at the University of East London which focused on four relatively high-cycling areas in depth in order to try to find out why cycling thrives in some areas. The four areas (Hull, Hackney, Bristol, Cambridge) all had differing social structures, economic histories, spatial characteristics and political environments. The project investigated different ways in which people think about and practise cycling within each locality, and used a range of methods to seek to explain how cycling provides particular ways of experiencing different places. The fieldnote describes an account of returning from a field trip, in this case a cycle ride around East London, and the effort to download and deal with, in both computing and analytic senses, an immense volume of visual data.

I made 10 time-lapse videos during the research that averaged between two and ten minutes in length. Each comprised 300 to 3000 images and were staged without transitions apart from the titles. Videos open and close

Figure 6.2 Digital stills camera fixed to my bicycle handlebars. Image: Katrina Jungnickel.

with uniform credits; a black screen featuring the title of the ride, location and date, my name, project website and reference to the music used with Creative Common License agreement. Soundtracks were chosen to reflect my experience of the ride—the speed, sociality, landscape, etc. Length of images was timed to match the beat of the sonic backdrop creating a pendulum quality, reminiscent of the rhythm of cycling. Videos were published on the Cycling Cultures Vimeo channel, posted on the project website and used in presentations and talks. Each depicts a different landscape, weather condition and cycling practice: off and on road, group and solo, during the day, at dusk and evening.

There are several key features universal in each video. First, in terms of device and framing I fixed a digital stills and video camera on the centre my handlebars (Figure 6.2). The locked-off nature of the frame is similar in each video. The wide-angle lens captures the brake and gear lever hoods on the handlebars. Occasionally my hands are in view as I brake, change gear or clutch a printed map. Things move within this frame. However, it is not a stationery frame as per conventional uses of time-lapse methods; it moves and feels in relation to the bike. The camera was set to take photos at two, five or ten second intervals and the bicycle is constantly on the move. As a result, multiple forms of mobility are at play in the images.

Second, the time-lapse method condenses the length of ride. In some cases it concentrates a four-hour cycle to less than four minutes. Although this is partially to do with the fact that I often stopped the camera at refreshment points, it is also related to the editing process. As Spinney notes: "When using video, the researcher is essentially creating a reduction; a text, in much the same way they would if taking photographs or diarising events" (2011, 173). Time-lapse stresses this feature by eliminating the space and time between photos.

Third, it entails a different editing experience to conventional video. I did not chose clips like other video researchers such as Laurier (2010), who was left with hundreds of hours of footage left on the cutting room floor. Nothing in the time-lapse videos was removed. Rather, the camera could be set to take photos at intervals and the volume of images depended on the length of ride, battery capacity and memory card. The files were collated in a simple video editing software programme. As mentioned, there are no transitions between images; they replace one another in time to the beat of the selected music. Although the camera setting determines which photos are taken, I make no claims about objectivity. I have chosen the device, its location, where I point my handlebars, route taken, how images are used and nature of their publication. I also, as I will discuss, personally feature in these videos.

Finally, I deliberately resisted the desire to remove the blurred, distorted or otherwise 'failed' images in each video. Pragmatically, there were so many of them such an act would have drastically reduced the length of each video. Yet, as I will illustrate, in the context of time-lapse, they unexpectedly provide vivid evidence of the sensory experience and urban environment; the rough/smooth road or path, movement of other road users, shifts in direction of handlebars, speed of travel and shifting qualities of light/darkness.

Like other scholars I agree that it is important not to uncritically accept all new mobile and visual methods for their promise of affording new insights into everyday experiences. Yet, I also keep in mind Back's compelling argument that we need "to rethink the way we work because of the unprecedented opportunities available in a digital age to change the nature of the craft of research" (2012a, 246). In the next sections I discuss the benefits and consequences of using time-lapse as a method for expanding the mobile sociological imagination. To talk more specifically about the practical making issues and expected and unexpected findings of time-lapse animation as a research method I focus specifically on two videos; a group ride and solo ride. Initially, I planned to use the camera fixed to the handlebars as a means of capturing a visual record of the journey in still images; it being easier to set the timer on the camera to take regular shots than for me to attempt to simultaneously cycle and take photos or to stop regularly. I had broken several cameras from attempting the former and missed many good shots from the latter. However, the transformation of the still images into a time-lapse video provided unexpected insights into and representations of the experience.

1.   GROUP RIDE: BEVERLEY ROAD TO BARTON UPON-HUMBER, HULL

This 2.48-minute video is made up of 376 images and documents a 30-mile ride from Beverley Road to Barton-Upon Humber and back with the Beech Holme Tandem club, a long running tandem club for visually impaired cyclists in Hull.[2] For over 60 years the Tandem club in Hull has provided a social event as well as an opportunity to exercise, develop new skills and experience the freedom of cycling for its 30 members. The group meets at the residential centre for assisted living in central Hull on Wednesday nights at 7.30 pm throughout the year. A 'ride list' is distributed at the beginning of the year that documents the lengths and destinations of each excursion and rides vary from 20–40 miles, taking in the nearby Wolds, the coast or local villages and always includes a pub stop at the halfway point. While some members cycled before they lost their sight, many have not or have been blind from birth. As Mike, the treasurer of the club and member for 24 years explains: "it is the only way I can cycle out on the road—there is no way I can jump on a bike on my own. It's brilliant". A mini-bus accompanies the peloton, providing transport for those unable to cycle and support for any mechanical issues and cyclists who needed a rest. Anywhere between five and ten tandem teams take to the road every week and although we travelled in single file in busy areas, it was possible to cycle two-abreast in country lanes. These experiences gave us many opportunities to talk to riders about their experiences in the group and broader cycling biographies.

The video starts at dusk, on a late summer's eve. Nine tandems, two single bikes and a support bus head out from the residential centre, along busy main roads and into less populated residential lanes. The sun lowers, piercing through trees and buildings to catch the camera lens. Needles of light burn the photos, a path of brilliant flares impeding the view for several frames. In others, the sun catches the riders from behind, stretching their shadows along the road and up over the verge into the hedges and trees. The route takes us over relatively smooth roads and some heavily pocked by motorised traffic until we traverse paved cycle paths up onto the Humber Bridge. The texture of road surface is reflected in poor quality images. In some, everything shakes. In others, the camera is jolted just enough to distort the curve of the road or the edge of a building. Sometimes, the entire image is blurred, such as when we hit a series of grids embedded in the road (Figure 6.3).

Eleven bicycles traverse the road in a loose peloton. Conversations are created by our proximity to one another, which is in turn shaped by the nature of the road. Wider streets with bus lanes or cycle ways enable conversational two-abreast cycling. Narrow roads with dense traffic conditions force the peloton into singe file. The time-lapse video captures the fluidity of the group. Riders move next to, in front and behind the camera. Images also capture riders' heads turning to one another to talk. In the context of the animation, the sociality of riders' movements is evident in ways less visible in single photos.

The light continues to drop as we cycle the quiet streets to the pub in Humber. The second half of the video, now in full darkness, indicates we have left the pub and commenced the return journey. At times, the streets appear clear and detailed; the sky a rich blue with the string of urban street lights and shimmer of retail shops illuminating the road with an orange glow. At other times, the photos are almost completely opaque except for a painterly splash from the headlights of an oncoming car or streak from someone's high visibility jacket caught in a cyclist lamp. Occasionally, it is possible to see the trailing dots of cat eyes embedded in the road surface, the painted stripes of a pedestrian crossing or the red lights on passing cyclists. The only consistency in the images, apart from the blanket of darkness, is the circular white spotlight cast by my front light; a marking made coherent only by the repetitive structure of the time-lapse method.

Unlike the first half of the video, few of the images comprising the return journey make sense on their own. They are too dark and blurred. It is only collectively that they produce and reveal a coherent dynamic movement. Arguably, while the contrasting quality of images says as much about the camera lens, the story they also convey is of the ability of cyclists to manoeuvre a vehicle in contrasting conditions. It is striking when compared, for example, with the use of car headlights for a driver, which maintain a consistent light quality regardless of urban infrastructure. Cyclists also need to contend with the blinding high-beam lights of lone drivers who fail to

Figure 6.3 An example of a blurred image caused by the jolt to the camera from uneven road surface. Image: Katrina Jungnickel.

recognise cyclists as fellow road users. An experience so familiar to many, that despite it happening several times during the ride, it was not raised as an issue at the pub. These experiences point to the ways in which urban infra-structures shape, favour and produce particular kinds of mobile citizens. The video ends back at the residential centre car park where once again the sharp streetlights cast a warm glow on riders as they dismount from their tandems.

2.   SOLO RIDE: JESUS GREEN TO NEWMARKET
ROAD PARK & RIDE, CAMBRIDGE

This 3.53 minute video features 545 images and documents a three-mile cycle solo ride from Jesus Green in the centre of Cambridge to Newmar-ket Road Park & Ride.[3] Park & Rides are Council-run car parks with direct public transport links into the city. In Cambridgeshire, these con-sist of bus and cycle links. Several of our interviewees had talked about utilising this path as a means of avoiding congested peak hour roads; the route being mostly off-road, along the river, edges of fields and through public parks. I was interested not only in the links between the city and the car park but also the various cycle-specific infrastructure along the way; new bridges, riverside paths and solar-powered lights. I was curi-ous to learn more about how cyclists wayfind when they venture off the main roads. It is easy to lose your sense of direction when the route takes a winding course. Would there be signs and maps? Would the path be clearly marked? I was similarly keen to experience how different path users interacted; this was a popular area for canal boat owners whose domestic traces spill out of their crafts, walkers, runners, and dog owners, as well as cyclists.

The video starts in Jesus Green, a popular park for many. Several paved paths crisscross the green and the images reveal clusters of people enjoying themselves on this warm August weekend. Shifts in the angle of the frames indicate moves made on the bike to weave in and around people, potholes and dogs on leads. Unlike road traffic, pedestrians and other path users are not required by law to navigate each other in set ways. As per the group ride, which brought to life the contrasting light qualities cyclists deal with, what is evident here is how they are required to adjust to different rules in different places; modal flexibility is required depending on place. While this finding is not distinct to time-lapse, the jumps between images renders it all the more visible.

Similarly, photos tell of curves in the path or when it was necessary to lean into or around corners. Much like the video above, many photos are characterised by blurred and distorted features. The canal path is disrupted in places by tree roots, the occasional branch or stone, which made the bike, and in turn the camera, jump. Similarly, the images bear witness to the textures of rickety wooden bridge planks and the slipperiness of piles of leaves. More significant visual stutters arise from the vibration of cattle grids at the edges of the parklands.

Although not as dramatic as a night ride, differing light qualities are also features of the Cambridge ride. The route passes under the coverage of shady trees, thick hedges and bridges. Cumulus clouds float across the sky in jumps and starts with glimpses of sun reflected in flares of light in the lens. (It would be useful to compare this video to one shot along the same route at night.) More interesting is how the time-lapse method captures shifts in speed. Conventional time-lapse from a stationery lens presents a relatively measured and sequential animation. The mobile lens, on the front of a moving bicycle, does not. Here, the images bring to life multiple forms of movement; sudden acceleration and reductions in speed, otherwise indiscernible in single shots. A concentrated number of images indicate a slowing down for fellow path users, spatial negotiation with dogs or a pause to read maps at junctions. Conversely, the sparseness of images at certain points such as clear, wide portions of path illustrate accelera-tion in speed. The former are the crisp, sharp images redolent of a stable camera, the latter are characterised by blurs and shakes. Again, as before, these shifts in speed, eclectic palette of surface textures and spectrum of path users all point to the cyclists' ability to adapt to constantly changing conditions and how embedded these skills are in the mundane experience of everyday cycling.

The video finishes in the car park at Newmarket Road. The last shot is of the author turning off the camera, which results in an upside down self-portrait. Setting up the camera, checking it was on and turning it off often resulted in photos that included a part of me (my hands, head or feet). Left in the videos, they operate to maintain my presence, reminding the viewer that these are not objective representations of a cycling culture but rather are personal, partial and hand-made. Drawing on Laurier (2010, 11), Spinney reminds that "video appears to offer the possibility that events will disclose themselves without any effort on the part of the ethnographer" (2011, 172). The concern here is that while the video operates to effectively capture an event, it does not divulge the (multi-vocal) meaning or the nuance of the experience. Leaving parts of myself in photos and adding music are ways I sought to offset this issue.

EMERGING INSIGHTS

Spinney has argued that "video data embodies the movement which the fixity of photographs and written texts so often fail to evoke" and "opens up movement for analysis in a way which would be impossible with a static image" (2011, 167). In time-lapse, the images remain fixed. Fluidity hap-pens between the images, in the stutters and gaps. What I hope to illustrate is how time-lapse makes possible dynamic links between fixed images. Photos are no longer single representations but part of a larger choreographed piece that interweaves the movement between visuals via gaps and stutters. Still images do not freeze movement but rather exacerbate different features of the mobile experience. Thinking about the videos in terms of choreography is productive as it evokes a rhythm between what is seen and not seen; jumps in action, place and time serve to trigger the imagination. The camera slices a journey into a series of images, and time-lapse method pieces it back together again in a new form that requires the viewers to fill the gaps. Time-lapse tricks us by making movement through still images. While many of the images on their own were poor quality photos, in this context they told new stories; of speed, light, road texture, urban infrastructures, relationships between riders, and negotiations with other path users. Essentially, these videos do not attempt to clean up or simplify journeys. They retain a messiness from which reconfigured narratives offer new perspectives into fieldwork.

While the chapter has mostly discussed what is caught with video methods, the whole premise of the time-lapse is that it does not catch everything; there are gaps and risks. Any representation is only ever partial and the time-lapse method through its very nature reminds the viewer of this critical point. It brings to mind Back's point: "Many researchers are experimenting with ambulant techniques of doing social research on the move, that do not simply try and reflect movement but which also embody and bring it to life" (2012a, 29). With time-lapse, as viewers we do not attempt to relive the cycle ride exactly how it happened. Rather, we make sense of sequential images by making links between them. The gaps between images are just as important, visually and conceptually, because they narrate not only the journey, but also convey to some extent the feeling of the ride. This method also carries an element of risk. While video researchers such as Laurier (2010) and Pink (2007) set up or carry around cameras to capture non-stop footage, time-lapse captures stills at set points on a temporal scale. As a result there is a risk that it misses things in the gaps between images. Sound is also missing from time-lapse video. The clicks and whir of the bicycle, drone of traffic and streetscape, the wind over the bridge and snippets of conversations with fellow cyclists are all absent. The nature of the still images and method of compression produces a silent visual artefact. Adding a soundtrack to the videos goes some way to offset this absence, re-inserting the rhythm of the experience, but it also adds another level of conceptual complexity.

Brown and Spinney have argued that the strength of video in their research is the "visibility it gave to the taken-for-granted, such as the mundane and ordinary rhythms, details and practices of cycling" (2010, 141). Time-lapse methods share similar strengths. The videos capture things that may not appear important at the time, or are easily overlooked due to the mundane and ordinary nature of everyday experiences but which become critical to developing in-depth understanding afterwards. The diversity of perils that cyclists regularly face and avoid such as pocked road surfaces and blinding high-beam headlights are brought to life in the video, not only in terms of what is captured in the photos but also through the nature of their failure. Blurs, shakes and smudges 'catch' the jumps and shudders translated through the frame of the bike reminding the viewer of tacit experiences. The challenge and opportunity of this method lies in its potential to expand the sociological imagination.

Finally, time-lapse methods require technical competencies. Practically, it provides a useful way of using a volume of data. As mentioned, some of these videos make use of up to 3000 images, and many of them of poor quality. This has its consequences. The digital equivalent of Back's office full of hundreds of "cassette boxes full of auditory life" (2012a, 251) is a computer that pauses and hangs with the weight of data. To use time-lapse methods requires a combination of technology and skills; a computer with ample processing power, relevant software, skills and time need to be taken into consideration. While access to and ease of use of these kinds of technologies has accelerated, the same cannot be said of academia's embrace. "[M]ethods texts have not kept pace with these changes" (Lury and Wakeford 2012). While I hope I have brought to life some of the advantages of making time-lapse videos, the reality is such that many researchers operate within conventional academic systems that value talk and text over other forms of knowledge representation and transmission. However, things are changing. As Back writes: "More than at any point before we have the potential now to do the craft of research differently" and "the future holds out the possibility to animate social research through the use of other kinds of devices" (2012a, 28).

DISCUSSION: MAKING 'THERE'

Recently there has been a claim that sociologists have become complacent in understanding and interpreting the social world (Savage and Burrows 2007). Back argues that one way of addressing this is by expanding our understanding of C. Wright Mills' 'sociological imagination'. He writes: "If we stop listening only to 'voices', then we can reanimate the idea of description and attention" (2012b, 253). In this chapter I set out to experiment with how we might expand our repertoire of methodological practice and sociological description by considering a collection of still images, complete with the spaces in between, failed photos and hands-on messy material practice.

This was one of the core aims—to contribute to a recent shift in mobilities and social sciences more broadly in finding ways of "apprehending fleeting moments of mobile experience" (Spinney 2011, 161). Brown and Spinney argue that the use of video methods "allow richer and more nuanced accounts of the mobile, embodied practices of participants than would otherwise be possible" (2010, 149). Just like the use of conventional video in mobile methods, I argued that time-lapse video offers insights into less easily fixable aspects—more ephemeral intersection of experiences, movement and place in the cycling experience. Focusing on two cycle rides, I illustrated how time-lapse video can be used to reflect less easily represented aspects of the cycling experience. The time-lapse process produced a compressed version of events, and a form of sociological description that differed from ethno-graphic notes, interview transcripts and still photos. As per its moniker, time is central to the videos. The method captures and then re-constructs time, enabling the viewer to watch a four-hour cycle in just three minutes. This produces a heightened way of seeing—in absence of the need to balance and manoeuvre the bicycle we cannot help but see things differently. In this lapsed experience, gaps operate to trigger the imagination. However, it can only ever be a partial experience and I pointed to how the technique is itself a critique of representational forms. Overall, however, critical engagement with tools and techniques like time-lapse enable us to "develop a different kind of attentiveness to the embodied social world in motion" (Back 2012a, 29). In this context, blurred, distorted and other bad quality images, can be interpreted not as failures but rather rich examples of the vivid experience of the urban cycling experience. In bulk, these images disrupt and re-orientate conventional understandings of successful photos. They invite messiness back into the experience which is invariably cleaned up, removed or other-wise distanced from the initial experience via the translation process.

The second aim was to examine the concept and practice of 'making there' with time-lapse methods for cycling research. I explored how meth-ods emerge in the process of doing the research and how they touch and are touched by the subject under study (Lury and Wakeford 2012). Time-lapse video is one way of responding to both the visual culture of the subject at hand while simultaneously dealing with the stuff of digital research. I drew on a recent methodologically led interest in the social sciences and particu-larly in mobilities research to take seriously the challenge of capturing a sense of 'there-ness'. This is where scholars interweave new digital methods into research to enliven the potential of 'being', 'seeing' and 'feeling there'. Building on this, I proposed that time-lapse video opens up a way to criti-cally reflect on the process of 'making there', both as an innovative method and alternate mode of knowledge transmission.

A key challenge in writing this chapter has been to describe in words the visualisation of noise and feeling captured in the time-lapse videos. How to describe a description? This is just another act of translation. But these are our choices. We can be like the downloading computer, which hangs in protest at the extra work. We can resist new digital tools, ignore the poten-tial of voluminous data and new circulatory publishing platforms or we can think differently about methods, enfolding them and their messiness into our practice and like cyclists keep moving, adapting and adjusting to new ways of being in response to constantly changing conditions.

NOTES

1. See www.cyclingcultures.org.uk
2. Video 1—Group ride: Beverley Road to Barton Upon-Humber, Hull, available at: https://vimeo.com/12824630
3. Video 2—Solo ride: Jesus Green to Newmarket Road Park & Ride, Cambridge, available at: https://vimeo.com/27350261

REFERENCES

Aldred, R. 2010. 'On the outside': constructing cycling citizenship. *Social & Cultural Geography,* 11(1): 35–52.

Aldred, R. and Jungnickel, K. 2012. Negotiating mobile spaces between 'leisure' and 'transport': a case study of two group cycle rides. *Sociology,* 46(3): 523–539.

Back, L. 2012a. Live sociology: social research and its futures. In Back, L. and Puwar, N. (eds.) *Live Methods.* Oxford: Blackwell Publishing, 18–39.

Back, L. 2012b. Tape recorder. In Lury, C. and Wakeford, N. (eds.) *Inventive Methods: Happenings of the Social.* London: Routledge, 245–260.

Beer, D. and Burrows, R. 2007. Sociology and, of and in Web 2.0: some initial considerations. *Sociological Research Online,* 12(5): 17.

Bijker, W. E. and Law, J. 1992. *Shaping Technology/Building Society: Studies in Sociotechnical Change.* Cambridge: MIT Press.

Bijsterveld, K. 2010. Acoustic cocooning: how the car became a place to unwind. *The Senses and Society,* 5(2): 189–211.

Brown, K. and Spinney, J. 2010. Catching a glimpse: The value of video in evoking, understanding and representing the practice of cycling. In Fincham, B., McGuinness, M. and Murray, L. (eds.) *Mobile Methodologies.* Aldershot: Ashgate, 130–151.

Büscher, M., Urry, J. and Witchger, K. (eds.). 2011. *Mobile Methods.* Abingdon: Routledge.

Elliott, A and Urry, J. 2010. *Mobile Lives.* New York: Routledge.

Evans Pritchard, E. 1951. *Kinship and Marriage Among the Nuer.* Oxford: Oxford University Press.

Fincham, B. 2006. Back to the 'old school': bicycle messengers, employment and ethnography. *Qualitative Research,* 6(2): 187–205.

Fincham, B., McGuinness, M. and Murray, L. (eds.). 2010. *Mobile Methodologies.* Aldershot: Ashgate.

Geertz, C. 1973. *The Interpretation of Cultures.* New York: Basic Books.

Geertz, C. 1988. *Works and Lives.* Stanford: Stanford University Press.

Hannerz, U. 2003. Being there . . . and there . . . and there! Reflections on multi-sited ethnography. *Ethnography,* 4(2): 201–216.

Helmreich, S. 1998. *Silicon Second Nature.* Berkeley: University of California Press.

Hine, C. 2007. Multi-sited ethnography as a middle range methodology for contemporary STS. *Science, Technology & Human Values,* 32(6): 652–671.

Horton, D., Rosen, P. and Cox, P. (eds.) 2007. *Cycling and Society.* Aldershot: Ashgate Publishing Limited.

Jungnickel, K. 2013. Getting there and back: how ethnographic commuting (by bicycle) shaped a study of Australian backyard technologists. *Qualitative Research,* published online 4 April.

Jungnickel, K. and Aldred, R. 2014. Sensory strategies: how cyclists mediate their exposure to the urban environment. *Mobilities,* 9(2): 238–255.

Latour, B. and Woolgar, S. 1979. *Laboratory Life, the Social Construction of Scientific Facts.* London: Sage.

Laurier, E. 2010. Being there/seeing there: recording and analyzing life in the car., In Fincham, B., McGuinness, M. and Murray, L. (eds.) *Mobile Methodologies.* Aldershot: Ashgate, 103–117.

Law, J. 2004. *After Method: Mess in Social Science Research.* London: Routledge.

Lury, C. and Wakeford, N. (eds.) 2012. *Inventive Methods: Happenings of the social.* London: Routledge.

Lyman, P. and Wakeford, N. (eds.) 1999. Analysing virtual societies: new directions in methodology. *American Behavioural Scientist*, 43(3): 409–421.

Marcus, G. E. 1998. *Ethnography Through Thick and Thin.* Princeton: Princeton University Press.

Miller, D. (ed.) 2001. *Car Cultures.* Oxford: Berg.

O'Connor, J. and Brown, T. 2007. Real cyclists don't race: informal affiliations of the weekend warrior. *International Review for the Sociology of Sport,* 42(1): 83–97.

Orton-Johnson, K. and Prior, N. (eds.) 2013. *Digital Sociology: Critical perspectives.* New York: Palgrave.

Pink, S. 2007. Walking with video. *Visual Studies*, 22(3): 240–252.

Pink, S. 2008. An urban tour: the sensory sociality of ethnographic place-making. *Ethnography*, 9(2): 175–196.

Savage, M. and Burrows, R. 2007. The coming crisis of empirical sociology. *Sociology*, 41(5): 885–889.

Sheller, M. and Urry J. 2006. The new mobilities paradigm. *Environment and Planning A*, 38(2): 207–226.

Spinney, J. 2006. A place of sense: a kinaesthetic ethnography of cyclists on Mont Ventoux. *Environment and Planning D: Society and Space,* 24:709–732.

Spinney, J. 2008. *Cycling the City: Movement, Meaning and Practice.* Unpublished Ph.D. thesis, Royal Holloway, University of London.

Spinney, J. 2011. A chance to catch a breath: using mobile video ethnography in cycling research. *Mobilities*, 6(2): 161–182.

Thrift, N. 2004. Intensities of feeling: towards a spatial politics of affect. *Geografisker Annaler*, 86b(1): 57–78.

Vergunst, J. L. 2008. Taking a trip and taking care in everyday life. In Ingold, T. and Vergunst, L. (eds.) *Ways of Walking: Ethnography and Practice on Foot.* Hampshire: Ashgate, 105–123.

7 Creative Video Ethnographies
Video Methodologies of Urban Exploration

Bradley L. Garrett and Harriet Hawkins

Five of us are standing under the Forth Rail Bridge. We're in North Queens-ferry, a quiet little town near Edinburgh, looking up from the parking lot at the northern tower foundation holding the gorgeous steel monstrosity aloft. Our mission tonight is to climb the bridge, crossing it from north to south, over the three towers and the Firth of Forth. The weather doesn't look promising, but we've driven over 400 miles from London to get here and no one wants to turn around.

Helen, James, Marc, Moses and I are collecting footage for *Crack the Surface III*, the final instalment of a collaborative video triptych we started in 2010. We're shooting on Digital Single Lens Reflex (DSLR) cameras and using two lenses, a 35 mm lens and a 24 mm. Each lens gives us a different frame, different depth-of-field and a different feel. Additionally, we are wearing head- and chest-mounted cameras for Point of View (POV) shots. Keeping in mind that video is as much about sound as visuals, we also have high quality audio recorders in our bags and are strapped up with lapel microphones threaded through our jackets. We are also wearing headphones to monitor the audio. I feel like a cyborg.

Moses turns to us and says, "Okay, everyone ready?" I don't feel ready at all, I feel overburdened with equipment and scared something is going to go wrong after driving all this way, be it rain, the police turning up or worse.

Helen and I sneak in first. I film her hopping the fence. Then I throw the camera over and she films me negotiating it. Once inside, we hide. James films the second group as they sneak in. Then, all together, we run across the construction yard and jam ourselves into the hollow leg of a tower support. Inside, James and I get held up trying to adjust the cameras for the new light situation. I have the camera strapped around my neck as I begin to climb the ladders inside the leg support and the strap is choking me. I'm really hot. As I'm yelling at people to let me climb past them so I can film them climbing up, a pigeon slams into me and flaps feverishly, ripping out my headphones. I climb down to retrieve them and realise the video camera is still recording. That will all be wasted footage. When I plug the headphones back in, the batteries have died on the audio recorder and I can no longer hear anyone climbing. I'm sweating, exhausted and I feel like I want to cry.

Figure 7.1 Garrett climbing the Forth Rail Bridge. Image: Marc Explo.

By the time we reach the top of the ladders, 100 meters above the spraying surface of the water and pop a hatch on top of the tower, I've given up trying to record anything. I have only a moment to take in the view because James, who is clearly a more diligent cameraman, asks me to go back in the hatch and come out again so he can film it. Still sticky with sweat, I climb back in the hatch and close it for a re-enactment.

We take a bit of time to resituate ourselves, changing batteries, tucking wires back in, checking sound. Cooled down, I adjust the camera settings for the night sky and start recording conversations again. Then the climb begins.

It's treacherous. We end up scooting down the steel beams of the bridge like slugs. I try to get people to talk about what they're feeling and it doesn't work—we're simply too overwhelmed by the experience to articulate it. Resting on the top of the second tower, one-third of the way across, I turn off the camera, keeping the voice recorder running, and try to prompt a discussion that goes beyond description by asking everyone if they think they are creating chaos. Moses dryly responds, "Dude, we're not on camera anymore . . ." and looks away, deflating my attempt to record more than embodied, exerted grunting.

Two-thirds of the way across the bridge, just past the last tower, it starts to rain. I realise I'm losing my grip, trying to film with one hand and climb with the other. James, filming us from the other side of the bridge, suddenly yells, "If we don't start crawling really fast right fucking now we are going to die on this bridge!" The cameras are turned off and stowed. The final shots depict a state of panic as the group runs down the train tracks with the morning light beaming in. We're covered in the famous paint of the Forth Rail Bridge as we drive home, replaying the footage in the car, already nostalgic.

* * *

INTRODUCTION: CREATIVE INTERSECTIONS

Our opening vignette is drawn from the ethnographic filmmaking practice of one of our authorial pairing, Bradley Garrett. Over the course of three years, Brad produced 12 videos whilst working on a research project about urban exploration—a not-uncontroversial practice of sneaking into, and often photographing, urban spaces closed to public access (Bennett 2011; Garrett 2010, 2011a, 2013a, b; Mott and Roberts 2014). During the same period Harriet's research focused on 'creative geographies', experimenting with a range of creative visual art and curatorial practices—exploring their value with respect to researching and presenting key geographical questions around senses of place and the sensing of space (Hawkins 2010, 2013a, 2013b). In this chapter we have two aims. Primarily, we narrate the processes of producing a video ethnography of urban exploration, from Brad's experience in the field (described in the first vignette above) to our collaborative editing process (described in a second vignette below). Second, we address the conceptual, political and ethical questions thrown up in the course of producing this video ethnography, and we propose the idea of 'creative video ethnographies' as a way of necessarily complicating potentially reductive accounts of these methods.

The place and value of filmmaking as part of ethnographic research, in one sense, needs no introduction. If geographers have tended to focus on cinematic analyses (Aitken and Zonn 1994; Cresswell and Dixon 2002), wherein film is taken as an empirical object, filmmaking has, for over a century, had a place in ethnographic studies, and played an important role in researchers' ongoing querying of the politics and ethics of these practices (Banks 1992; Ruby 2005). Recently, geographers have begun to embrace the possibilities of filmic production, in, for example, fields of participatory geographies (Kindon 2003; Parr 2007), and in relation to embodied, often auto-ethnographic working (Laurier and Philo 2006; Simpson 2011). With the addition of Pink's (2007, 2009) recent work on video making as part of multi-modal, multi-sensuous ethnographies of place and community, video ethnography has been firmly established as a research method. Yet, as we want to explore in this chapter, there are a series of important questions that geographers, as filmmakers, have yet to address in regard to the production of video, especially as part of ethnographic research.

The pivot of our concern is the need to appreciate the creative possibilities and affective force of filmmaking. We channel this into four strands of inquiry. First, there are important (missing) lines of questioning, we think, around how, and for what purposes, geographers are finding increasing value in filmmaking. Second, we want to encourage grounding these interests not just in a discussion of the practicalities of equipment and the development of technique, but also in the philosophy and politics of these practices. Third, we are concerned with the role of creativity during the editing process. Finally, we want to foreground how, as filmmakers, we need to appreciate how our materials go to work on audiences—how the productive force of these creations exceeds the intentions, desires and capacities of the filmmaker. In sum, and as with other creative (sometimes called artful or experimental) methods, valorisation is based in the possibilities these practices offer to more-than-representational modes of enquiry, and an increasing recognition of the need to understand and appreciate the manifold productive forces of creative practices in the world (Dwyer and Davies 2010; Hawkins 2013b; Last 2012). To elaborate on key questions and chapter structure, we want briefly to return to our opening vignette.

Viewing the still frame with which the chapter opened (Figure 7.1), we are reminded of the trite adage that a picture is worth a thousand words. This image, one still frame from amongst thousands collected that night, contains a sense of the informational concentration that can be packed into a frame, revealing a pace and complexity of social backstory and embodied action that outstrips the possibilities of empirical observation (Brown et al. 2008; Büscher

2005). As we explore via Brad's films, one key driver for geographical video-making specifically is the medium's recognised value for moving us beyond the textual and representational (Lorimer 2010; Merchant 2011; Straughan 2011). Video enables the study of a range of 'bodyworks' that rework the record. As such, it can open out of iterations of the non/more-than-representational through the affective, the atmospheric, the material and the relational. Advancing video technologies enable researchers to go to places and see things that are beyond the capacity of the human sensory system.[1] In the process, they draw to the fore configurations of body-space-technology/equipment relations. These relations go to work on the research subject, as long acknowledged by anthropologists and sociologists, but they also produce the researcher-subject. Being a researcher-subject is never a simple question of the deployment of technology. It involves manifold considerations of the technical and the aesthetic, but also a querying of the role of habit, action and contingency. Considering creativity throughout these discussions, is, we argue, to press at the edges of extant literatures, practices and techniques, spurring us on to build new modes of enquiry and to inhabit our technologies creatively. In so doing, these technologies not only enable extensions of capacities and affordances as embodied researcher-subjects, but also allow us, in turn, to stretch and expand the apparent limits of technology itself through creative, skilful praxis. This discussion of equipment and skilling forms the first part of our chapter.

In the second part of this chapter, following Rose (2007), we extend our collective methodological lens in two directions: bringing into focus the process of editing, and enlarging considerations of audiencing. Video is valuable for its production of an ethnographic archive (Pink 2008) that, as Brad writes elsewhere, researchers can "graze" at times and spaces beyond the field experience (Garrett 2011b, 526). Here, however, we assert other values and spaces of ethnographic video making during editing and post-production. Building on the limited geographical literature on editing (Bauch 2010; Laurier 2009; Parr 2007) we conceptualise it as a creative-analytic process, combining the aesthetic and informational in a suite of digital-material processes that are as much about research and analysis as they are oriented toward the production of outputs.

Editing is of course a question of audiencing. Considerations of audiencing require that we foreground the productive force of films on the multiple audiences of the work, from the filmmaker as first field-based viewer, to myriad 'secondary' audiences who encounter the film as it circulates. Moving through the world, video-ethnographic creations go to work in a range of ways. As researchers, we have a political and ethical responsibility to be aware of the effects of our ethnographic films, effects that might be informational, affective, co-creative, aesthetic, symbolic, political or all of these at once (Hawkins 2013a). We emphasise the need to be vigilant regarding the possibilities of our ethnographic productions being mobilised by others, redeployed in ways that can cut across their creative-aesthetic sensibilities, assert scientism and objectivity where none was claimed and change meanings in ways thoroughly incongruent with situated ethnographic intent.

KIT THAT WORKS: CONCEPTUALISING EQUIPMENT

Equipment choices are often a function of the progress of research and emerging social situations, rather than predictable in advance (Laurier et al. 2008). In making an ethnography of urban exploration, quick adaptation was needed to the physicality of the practice, and to the community's socialities, including its ecologies of visuality (Garrett 2010, 2013a, b). Conforming to a style of traditional ethnographic filmmaking, footage was initially shot on a large, shoulder-mounted High-Definition Video (HDV) camera. The shoulder-mounted HDV camera was valued for material, aesthetic and social reasons. Its physical ruggedness and simple manual controls, combined with the ability to attach external microphones, attracts researchers. Furthermore, the technology produces a particular aesthetic sensibility, with small sensors and deep depth-of-field enabling everything in the frame to be easily kept in focus.[2] This is considered ideal for strenuous, unscripted field shooting where losing the focus means missing a moment (Ruby 2005). Finally, there is a social element. A large camera lends social credibility to the researcher, making them appear more 'professional', which can have important implications for issues of access, especially when dealing with authority figures.

Quickly, however, this equipment was found to be ill-suited to the active nature of urban exploration. Rather than abandoning video as a method, however, a choice was made to work with project participants to address the issue. Collaborative decisions were agreed upon about where and when to shoot, what equipment to shoot with and footage was often pooled for editing.[3] Experimenting with shooting films on a lower-quality handheld camcorder allowed for greater mobility and ease of shooting, but the camera did not perform well in low light situations and restricted manual control. Proficiency with still cameras is normative in the urban exploration community, meaning that it was often necessary for researchers to switch cameras in the course of action, and video footage was only collected until a good photo opportunity arose. DSLR cameras, the still cameras explorers often shoot on, have the capacity for interchangeable lenses (and therefore framing), and a large (full-frame) sensor that approximates a 35 mm shallow depth-of-field paired with a fast lens. Though harder to achieve focus 'correctly', a shallow depth-of-field more closely mimics human optics. Midway throughout the research, a single camera was released that allowed for proficient (indeed professional) production of both still and moving images.[4] Beyond technical detailing, we would emphasise the situated nature of the evolution of an individual maker's tool kit, and the need both to plan, but also to be willing and able to experiment and respond creatively in the field.

Currently, some of the most experimental and creative methods are being developed by scholars interested in embodied ethnographies (e.g. Pink 2008). In this context, video is cast as a tool of multi-sensory and affective discovery *par excellence,* with kit like POV cameras, waterproof casings and increasingly advanced automated settings enabling experimental developments in mobile and sensory ethnographies (Spinney 2009; Straughan 2011). In such studies video ethnographies stand as research artefacts with manifold possibilities. These include: enabling an exploration of events that might otherwise be missed in the course of 'action' (important when focused on climbing a bridge, for example); the presentation of a fine-grained exploration of sensory experiences through the production of a multi-sensory 'feeling there'; or a 'doing something' or 'being someone' that might otherwise not be physically possible or accessible to the researcher.

To explore these ideas further, we turn to the *Hobohemia* travelogue triptych, a series of ethnographic videos made by Brad as part of his urban exploration fieldwork.[5] Through urban camping and ruin exploration, the films raise questions about the interactions between bodies and the forces and materialities of derelict architecture. In the films we 'see' the forces and tensions of explorers' bodies bent on action, as they balance, crawl, wriggle, slither and slide their ways through gaps and spaces. Viewers are reminded of the multi-sensuous possibilities of film beyond the visual and aural, as textures in particular become pictured and sounded (Marks 2002). Frames focused on balanced feet, gripping hands and contorted limbs, render visible the forces of material interaction, physical tensions written in muscles, sinew and across faces.

What is made visible in these shots is the interplay of the five external senses with the internal senses engaged by bodies-in-action. Playing out before our eyes is the thinking-feeling—the in-the-moment decision-making—of bodies, as a ledge is tested for weight-bearing, a rope is swung and reswung to cover distance, the trained-body is honed, its capacities and limitations tested, apprehended and overcome. In their replaying, we can appreciate these shots as a rendering visible of the invisible; both those things which the physiology of the human eye may not normally enable us to bring into focus, and those things—forces and affects for example—that have no visible presence, located in the audio, the inference, the layering and in the imagination of what lay outside the frame.

Different technologies—the shoulder-mounted camera, the DSLR and tripod, the head-mounted POV camera—produce different fields of vision (Daniels 1993). The varying modalities of seeing that inhere within these different "views on the world" (Rose 2007) produce different aesthetic sensibilities that find form in the final films. The headcam, for example—used in both the Forth Rail Bridge vignette above and also visible in the clip *Our Own Private Island* (Figure 7.2)—is celebrated for its first-person viewpoint.[6] Despite acknowledged issues with missing synaesthesia, it is valued for providing "dynamic, in-situ, insider perspective[s]" (Brown et al. 2008, 8) offering a gateway to accessing embodied, sensory, kinaesthetic and emotional knowledge and experiences. Furthermore, the hands-free auto-settings of POV cameras, while reducing the 'quality' of the footage (according to those valorising the technical processes and capacities of filmmaking), is seen as a more objective, less selective mode of recording. As a result, it is fetishised in a different

Figure 7.2 A still shot from the headcam in *Our Own Private Island*. Image: Bradley L. Garrett.

way, as offering a fuller picture of social life by virtue of its "capacity to record comprehensive, real-time activities, which capture the dramatic alongside the mundane without privileging either" (Brown et al. 2008, 7).

For us, what is especially noteworthy are the possibilities body-mounted POV equipment offer for experimentation with new modes and sites of enquiry, as the hands-free mode enables researchers to become more meaningfully engaged in practices. As Brown et al. (2008, 7) state, the 'doing' of research should not eclipse the 'doing' of the activity under research. There are compromises too, though, for footage depends completely on internal technology to deal with things like changing light situations, it presents an inability to do more than crude or rudimentary shot framings, and offers mediocre sound recording capability amidst shaky shots and repeated instances of accidental and failed recordings. We will return to these issues below, but to close this discussion of equipment we want to signal some of the more conceptual questions at stake here. For, as our experiences of filmmaking and other media projects have repeatedly demonstrated, the choice of equipment is as much philosophical and political as it is driven by the practical and aesthetic challenges of the task at hand (Garrett et al. 2011; Hawkins 2013a).

We want to signal the need to recognise the manifold productive agencies of our bits of kit. Gregory Bateson and Margaret Mead famously noted the 'observer effect', a form of reactivity in which a researcher's cognitive bias causes them to unconsciously influence the participants of an experiment (Mead 2001). Building on this, we are concerned here to note the agencies of equipment in the production of the researcher-subject, and the development of researcher-field relations. Thinking back to shouldered HDV cameras, and their perceived professionalisation of the researcher, we can reflect on the effect of other researcher-technology configurations on the researcher as a social, embodied and skilled subject. For urban explorers, the camera is an important prop in a number of regards, lending social legitimacy to them as artists, researchers or journalists (Bourdieu and Lamaison 1986, 113). The ubiquity of visual practices within the urban exploration community means that being an image-maker does not dichotomise researcher-community relations as it might in other research situations. What may mark out the researcher's difference is, however, what they choose to shoot: focusing, for example, on action shots and 'doings' rather than goals.

There are other ways, too, that equipment produces, and perhaps even transforms, the researcher as an embodied and cognisant subject. We might think, for example, of how modes of visuality are shaped by looking through a viewfinder, developing, in aesthetic terms, a 'good eye' through experience. But this is an eye that also, over time, undergoes physiological changes, coming to focus in a different way as lens and muscle are honed by the repeated actions. Continuing with the theme of the visual, and returning to a point raised above, what tends to be overlooked in literatures on embodied ethnographies are the possibilities of video to render visible those things normally invisible to the human eye. As such, the camera works as a prosthesis, with the latter understood less as making up for a lack and more for its opening up of possibilities for knowing and being in the world differently (Massumi 1992; Rouch and Feld 2003). This is to suggest the camera can extend the sensory capacities and affordances of the researcher's body: whether it be picturing more detail than the human eye can process, or making visible things that move at speeds beyond human perception.[7]

A range of critical social theories offer fertile ground for taking forward these ideas of the technological-researcher-subject, for example Haraway's (1991) cyborgs, or Simondon's (2011) technological unconscious. Further resources can be found at the intersections of ethnographic and avant-garde filmmakers. We can think, for example, of the creative-informational cross-breeding that saw ethnographic filmmaker Jean Rouch celebrate the writings, films and manifestos of early 20th century experimental film maker Dziga Vertov, in particular his 'cine-eye' (Rouch and Feld 2003). Rouch's ethnographic films were canonical works not only for visual anthropology but also in New Wave Cinema, influencing Jean-Luc Godard amongst others. Rouch writes of the shoulder-mounted camera as an appendage, an imaginary he develops into a figuration of an experienced-habituated cameraperson's body:

> Thus instead of using the zoom, the cameraman-director can really get into the subject. Leading or following a dancer, priest, or craftsman, he is no longer himself, but a mechanical eye accompanied by an electronic ear.
>
> (Rouch 2003, 90)

Such graftings of bodies and technologies, monstrous couplings, presage the Cyclops eye of the POV camera, and the cranial transplant that its footage provides: figuratively placing the head of the viewer onto the body of the researcher-participant. Such imaginaries enable further thinking on how these technologies remap researchers' bodies and retool their senses, extending their corporeal affordances and capacities. To continue to develop these ideas, we want to turn now to consider the place of skill and creativity in the video-making process.

AUTOMATIC EXPOSURE: CREATIVE RESKILLING

Writings on videographic methods often laud the benefits of contemporary technology; it is affordable (to those doing the writing) and accessible in terms of being both ubiquitous and increasingly easy to use. Features such as auto-focus and in-camera editing capabilities enable, to borrow the language from geospatial scholarship, the amateurisation of video methods (Sui 2008). Keep in mind it was only a few years ago that Crang and Cook (2007) were noting the cost and complexity of video-making. While we would not want to suggest that such accessibility is in any way a bad thing, we do want to caution against the assumed deskilling of the filmmaking process that often accompanies these ideas. Indeed, we would hazard the contrary, that such accessibility makes a consideration of skill sets, including the possibilities for creative experiments to push the limits of these pre-set technologies, all the more important.

Acquisition of skills facilitates and shapes the researcher's relationship with both footage and field. Learning to take good photos and to shoot good footage—with the definition of 'good' up for grabs—involves learning the capacities, affordances and limitations of your camera as intimately as those of your body, as well as learning to become attuned to fieldsites in new ways. The visual literacy associated with image-making folds together the technical with the aesthetic, knowing, for example, how to compose a shot, sensing what might best relay the feel of the moment. It also involves a sensing of site too, an entrainment of bodily capacities as senses become attuned to light levels, and an envisioning of framing through the lens before the shutter is even pressed.

The skills involved in filmmaking are those of building a cognitive and sensory relationship with technology (and site). The ideal version of this technological relationship is often cast, as Rouch above suggests, in terms of habituation. In other words, as Sontag (1977) implores us, we should work with an awareness of what is outside of the frame, labouring to prevent our attention being impeded by the technology. With this is mind, it seems that to be appropriately skilled is to be in possession of a level of comfort and familiarity with equipment that enables a working by feel. The result is an unconscious inhabitation of the frame of the viewfinder and the audio 'bubble' that the camera produces, such that the technical demands of the equipment do not pull the video-maker away from presence in place and moment.

The nature of skill and the human-technology relationship is thrown into sharp relief in the consideration of the contrast between tripod, hand-held and body-mounted cameras, which are all mobilised in the course of making video ethnographies of urban exploration. The process of carrying a tripod, pausing and carefully, even artfully, composing shots can be interruptive to the flow of social life, calling out the researcher *as researcher,* marking them out from the subject under scrutiny or disrupting their experiences. Furthermore, accrued aesthetic knowledge often informs the choice of visual device guiding the framing of the shot. We can compare, for example, the aesthetics of filmmaker Patrick Keiller's triptych of geographical films, *London, Robinson in Space* and *Robinson in Ruins,* with those of the urban exploration films being discussed here. In his deliberate choice of ponderous still shots, Keiller's films proffer a particular pacing of contemporary landscape and life that resonates with both the topographic tradition and the longer history of landscape aesthetics (Cosgrove and Daniels 1988). By contrast, the choice to compose shot sequences as cinematic montage, to intersperse music with dialogue, and to vary camera angle and shot pace within the urban exploration videos has more in common with contemporary imaginaries of mobility and urban space (Adey 2009).

The audiovisualities of the headcam, and its situation of skills, are rather different. The clip *Our Own Private Island* reinforces the common argument that when using a head-mounted camera, "the participant's role as film director becomes blurred with the life roles they are performing in the film, as there is no need to make conscious decisions about where to position and point the camera, or when to start and stop recording" (Brown et al. 2008, 5). The presence of the camera can indeed go relatively unnoticed by the user and the community, less by virtue of habituated use and rather as a result of the automated workings of these devices. Focus, light levels and shot are all determined in advance, either fixed, or only able to be manipulated in a minor way before the camera is body-mounted. For us, this is less evidence of a perceived deskilling, and suggests rather a relocation of key skills to other points in the filmic process, such as creative attachment to the body and editing.

The release of the need to be a skilful camera operator with POV cameras resituates skill as a form of experimentalism based in learning the capacities and affordances of technologies such that we might push at them, developing impromptu alternatives (Laurier et al. 2008). This might include deploying kit in new ways, or noodling with buttons and settings, stretching the limits of technologies and even hacking the procedural orders of firmware.[8] This is precisely the opposite of enabling oneself to become habituated in the use of these technologies, or to become disempowered in the face of the continually 'designed', automated and controlled elements of the process. We want to encourage video ethnographers to experiment; indeed we would suggest that situated experimentalism is one of the key skill sets of video ethnographers. Of course, not all of the skills involved concern the ability to hone authorial control, and we should also acknowledge those forces that exceed intentionality, such as luck, serendipity and chance. We urge researcher-filmmakers, therefore, towards the recognition that the socio-technological formations we are working within are never static, and, as such, we can, and indeed should, work to stretch, extend and mould this formation. Our experiments might fail, but that is the nature of experiments (Davies 2010).

* * *

On the computer screen, in small partitioned windows inside Final Cut Pro, we are fast-forwarding and rewinding through images of an intervention at the *Angel of the North*.[9] Editorial work, all consuming, proceeds slowly, especially at first, as we get to know the footage, labelling the individual sequences with descriptive titles for ease of identification, sorting the material, mentally consigning some as 'B roll'. These clips are not deemed visually or aurally robust enough to stand alone and must be parsed and layered with other material to be made sense of. As we review the material repeatedly and feel our way around the footage, getting to know what is there, visually and sonically, the process becomes easier, more creative. We fix on a place to start, a strong clean studio shot and spoken description by the artist of her project's sensibilities. It is an alluring piece of footage for us, drawing the audience in with an enigmatic description of the piece, and creating the conceptual backdrop for the story we are editing the film to tell. As we drop visual and sonic fragments into the timeline, the story of the project unfolds, almost telling itself. The concern in these later stages of the edit is with retaining an arc that is enticing, which doesn't lose the thread of the story as we work for our future imagined audience. We restart the footage we have edited, watching through until a scene where someone begins to climb the statue on a rope. The action is jerky. Much from the footage produced by the POV camera strapped to the head of the climber is too dark, too shaky. Some of the sequences are too long. The levels of wind noise don't match from one scene to the next. We view, edit, review and edit again, making decisions about what dialogue and visual material is superfluous to the narrative. We smooth wind noise, tinker with light levels, trying one treatment, then another, rolling the audio and video back and forth.

As we work, narrative direction, technical experience and creative/aesthetic sensibilities merge with contingency and luck. Resonances reveal themselves, we are affected by the footage; we consider how we might engage with the non-representational in the film to generate affects in collaboration with it—whether that is even possible. The process becomes one of viewing and reviewing the same two or three seconds over and over again, listening to the levels of wind noise change with the direction of the microphone, trying to blend them so that they're not abrasive. In some places, we overwrite wind noises with ones from different clips. The light levels of the shots dance around, fine-fingered control of keys is trialled over and over again. Often voice intonation stymies the fineness of our editorial control, suggesting a conversation cut short or knowledge out of frame. Reviewing pulls us to the keyboard, screen and speakers, ears bent and eyes focused, fingers rhythmically tapping, moving frame by frame, 25 recorded frames per second. Voices are slowed down to unintelligibility.

Eventually the reviewing process is of sections of longer film, rather than bursts. We review the whole piece, make notes on what doesn't work, stopping the film to discuss. We go back and smooth, chop sequences too long for our imagined audience's attention span, play with shortening quotes, reject the changes, start again, undo. Eventually we have something that does the work we want it to do and we export the chopped, layered, mutilated audiovisual timeline into a slickly-packaged and compressed video file, 5% of its original form retained. The cutting room floor is a battlefield strewn with the dead and we are elated and exhausted.

* * *

Figure 7.3 *Cold Angel.* Image: Lucy Sparrow.

EDITING EXPERIENCE: SIFTING DIGITAL MATERIAL

The redistribution of skills throughout the image-making process sees editing becoming an increasingly important part of that practice. Our second vignette depicts us collaboratively editing footage of an ethnographic account of a public art intervention: *Cold Angel* led by artist Lucy Sparrow (Figure 7.3).[10] The project was technically and physically complex, and the weather conditions far from ideal. This not only caused problems during the intervention's execution, but also presented editorial challenges. While many accounts of visual analysis have focused on the finished product, bringing to bear specific regimes of analysis, we want to engage with editing as itself a mode of analysis in the context of urban exploration. Emerging work on the editorial process has noted: the embodied experiences of editing (Laurier 2009); the technicalities and socialities of the process (Bauch 2010); and editing as a process of social empowerment in participatory research politics (Parr 2007). These examples show us that the editing process is an analytic and creative one; a process of sifting, sorting and composing that is a goal in and of itself.

Let us consider the practicalities of software and what it enables. We used Final Cut Pro, as did Bauch (2010), who highlights the effectiveness of a non-linear approach to editing, wherein the visual and sonic elements selected for inclusion are not delinked from the larger clips from which they are drawn until the final piece is exported. For Bauch, editing is a structured process, ordered from the outset by storyboarding, by the production of a 'script' for the voiceover, and the collecting and commissioning of specific footage. Even here, however, the editorial process emerges as a flexible, creative one, one that encourages experimentation. While easy to use, the setup of the clips and their coding in Final Cut Pro affords the user, we would argue, an experimental licence, cuts are not definitive, they are contingent, and the possibilities for playing are endless, enabled by the flexibility of the software's non-linearity. In short, like the move from typewriters to computers, the move to digital video has allowed for a different type of reskilling that is as much about working through as making record.[11]

Backstopping the ability to creatively, yet critically, play with footage in the technical editing process are a number of other operations, not least of which is the culling process, wherein hours of footage are reduced to a more manageable quantity before finer-grained work can begin on individual scenes. The process of reduction of footage (only 5% used in the case of *Cold Angel*) was, it seemed, less one of cutting and more one of thematic excavation, the concentration of concepts, the intensification of ideas, and the refinement of trajectories. Key to the success of this process seemed to be the intimacy we built with our material (Laurier 2008). Practically, this process of becoming intimate might begin in the field, but it continues through the initial sorting and labelling of material and on into the repeated processes of viewing, reviewing and clipping.

Returning to the vignette, we want to acknowledge how the technical operations of the process, its more mechanical elements—smoothing over wind noise, regulating light levels, removing traffic sound—come together with aesthetic decisions to compose a story which moves past informational documentary evidence. Viewing *Cold Angel,* it should be clear how conventional grammars of film were deployed consciously or unconsciously. We see, for example, switches between view *of* and view *from* shots, e.g. the climber climbing the rope and the switch to the POV footage on the rope. These aesthetic decisions come together with a sense of the content of the footage, the narrative elements each clip contains, and how they slot into an overall narrative to present the story for an imagined audience. We experimented with classic aesthetic framings, shots of the *Angel of the North* silhouetted against the sunrise, for example, or sequences that make use of the operations of the sublime, drawing visual contrasts between the huge, hulking body and the small but animate climber scaling the stationary steel form.

These composed shots and edited sequences come together with other elements of the film. We experiment with framing the animation of the rope's flick and hollow thwack as it smacks against the metal body, the dynamic swish of the arrow as it leaves the bow, the repeated clunks as arrow after arrow hit the wing, the exuberant celebrations when persistence pays off. The aim is to form a shifting imagination that pushes at the edges of the visual and discursive content of the footage, creating a film that works on the body, making its way into the pulse. As such, the editorial decisions that define the final form of the film bring together aesthetic choices and judgements with technical abilities and limitations of the footage; what the software-operator-footage assemblages enables.[12] But there is also something else at work here, too. For reflecting on the process of becoming intimate with the footage, it was clear there were points where we moved beyond 'knowing' the multi-dimensional content of the footage, and into the flow of editing wherein the material seemed to take control, such is the affective force of footage and material interaction.

The vignette above enables us to begin to unpick editing as a complex and technical process, but also as an embodied and affective one, aimed at telling a story for an imagined future audience. While editing has been contained as a post-shoot process—a leaving "behind of the practices of recording and collection to create a filmic object"—such biographical narratives belie the interpenetration of sites of shooting, editing and presenting (Laurier 2009, 16). We can think, for example, of the reshoot of the opening of the hatch in the first vignette, a sort of in-the-field editing, with the composition and refinement of shots, deleting and reshooting, comprising an initial edit of sorts. It is not only editing than can be dislocated from its normative post-shoot position, but also viewing. Indeed, editing becomes a form of audiencing, constituted through multiple moments of viewing and reviewing. In the next section, we take these, and other audience events, seriously.

AUDIENCING: THE CREATIVE FORCE OF MEDIA

"Pics or it did not happen" is an oft-repeated refrain in the urban exploration community. It signals the key epistemological roles that images play
within the community, sometimes to explorers' detriment, as when the
images are used to prosecute 'trespassers' as proof of presence (Garrett
2013a). Such an interpretation of images as bearers of empirical truths
reflects a scientised heritage of the pictorial that is by no means restricted
to the urban exploration community. Its presence there, however, tends to
deny the productive tensions surrounding the informational and the aesthetic that this chapter has been working with. To that end, we want to
raise awareness of the need to be attentive to how our filmic outputs go to
work in the world (Hawkins 2013a). Here we align video-making alongside
geographical writings on the world-making capacities of creative productions, taking forward their replacement of creativity as a form of singular,
human, authorial poesis, with a more distributed sense of creativity (Hawkins
2013a; Kanngieser 2013).

Writing on the process of ethnographic video-making, Laurier describes the
filmmaker 'generously assembling' footage with respect to their audience(s).
We take this point; its ramifications for filmmaking processes are clear in our
account of editing *Cold Angel*. We were concerned to ensure our audiences
learnt about the project, its motivations, processes and effects. Our assemblage of footage was conducted with an awareness that there was more than
narrative at stake here. In other words, in our editorial processes we were
attuned to how images and audio do work via discursive, informational and
representational pathways, but also through a political forcefulness built
through the sensory and affective.

To stay with the latter, geographers, especially those engaged with non-
representational theories, are preoccupied with the possibilities of forms of
knowledge that are about more-than-representational, more-than-discursive
communication. As Latham and McCormack write, "images are also blocks
of sensation with an affective intensity: they make sense not just because we
take time to figure out what they signify, but also because their pre-signifying
affective materiality is felt in bodies" (Latham and McCormack 2009, 253).
Elaborating, they suggest images have the capacity to "produc[e] a certain
affective resonance between somatic, visual, sonic and semantic rhythms,
without necessarily reducing these to the terms of an interpretive narrative"
(Latham and McCormack 2009, 260). The authors are referring to cinema
in this passage, but we would contend the same is true of other filmmaking
processes, "understood as an assemblage of technologies and techniques for
the amplification of the cultural and corporeal logics of affect" (Carter and
McCormack 2006, 230). In other words, configured as bodies of affective
intensity, images have the capacity to affect other kinds of bodies, specifically
here, human bodies. Returning to our opening vignette, we relayed the facts
of that climb across the bridge, but we also wanted to push at words, sounds

and images to generate sensations and feelings, to place you in the midst of the exploration, to generate viscerality.

The urban exploration video ethnographies that we examine in this chapter have been viewed hundreds of thousands of times online, at festivals, in theatres and in academic presentations. Reactions ranged from the critical, where scholars labelled them "music videos devoid of ethnographic content"; to the visceral, where online commentators emphasised their "sweaty hands"; to the excited and inquisitive, as the films appeared to open out imaginative spaces, enticing people to push their own boundaries, resulting in constant requests to join the explorations. As filmmakers, and especially as makers of video ethnographies, geographers need to remain aware of this contagious quality of composing associative sensation and mobilising affect. We must not lose sight of how the work our productions do will remain beyond our authorial control. For, affect and multi-sensuous experience are felt and interpreted in situated ways, based on experiences combined with ingrained memories and culturally codified viewing/listening conventions. As Dewsbury writes,

> non-representational theories provide an important and ongoing cautionary note about how images—like words—are always failing: about how they do not provide dependable techniques of capturing and accounting for the moment. . . . Yet the upshot of this is not the dismissal of practices such as writing, drawing, photographing and filming, but a rethinking of the terms of their use.
>
> (Dewsbury 2009, 324)

The 'rethinking' we wish to foreground concerns the possibilities of creative productions, but also an awareness of those dimensions beyond our control. As units of information and mechanic blocks of sensation thrust into the world, images are possessive of their own forcefulness, but can also be mobilised by others. The films and photographs of the urban exploration community have a wide circulation resulting in the creative experimental reuses of these images and films as they are posted and reposted, blogged about, shared, collaged, remixed and generally hacked to produce new work.

One of the drivers of this chapter has been a framing of tensions between, and possible re-combinations of, the informational and the aesthetic; the captured and the created. As our creative productions circulate and go to work in the world, their manifold aesthetic and experimental intents can become stripped back. The images are made to bear the burden of proof, their perceived mimetic force overriding any ficto-critical and aesthetic intent, potentially recasting ethnographic footage and filmic creations as incriminating, condemning 'evidence'. As such, while we talk about the creative-critical-technical processes of creation, and the imaginative and political work we envision, we should remain aware of the ethics and responsibilities that inhere within image-making when these forms become mobilised to ends beyond authorial control.

CONCLUSION: TOWARDS CREATIVE VIDEO ETHNOGRAPHIES

> Ethnographic places are not simply made in the moments that they are lived. Rather they are crafted over longer periods of interaction and intellectual activity.
>
> (Pink 2008, 190)

This chapter has taken seriously Pink's suggestion of the extended times and spaces for creation in ethnographic accounts. We have integrated an exploration of field-based phenomenological moments with multiple sites of video-making, viewing and editing. In so doing, we have advanced the critical frame of what Garrett has explored as "glass geographies," referencing both the nature of the medium and the various under-articulated fragilities of these methodologies (Garrett 2013c). Our intent was to develop an account of video ethnographies that is perhaps both more critical and more creative than many more practically-oriented accounts allow for. Where Rancière wrote of photography that it is "not merely mechanical reproduction, but rather an interpretation of the world" (Rancière 2009, 8), we have embraced and extended this notion to suggest not only "an interpretation of the world," but also an appreciation of the creative makings of worlds, subjects and knowledge (Hawkins 2013a).

Akin to the figuration of the artist, developed by Simmel and others, the work of the researcher and ethnographic filmmaker is often understood as slicing out pieces from "endlessly continuous sequences of perceived experience", capturing something, making it digestible, portable, sellable (Simmel 1971, 189). This is clear in the formulations of video footage as naturalistic data, understood to provide a scientised, objective account, privileged for its production of better—read more accurate—'pictures' of life. Where more recent work has appreciated the created-constructed nature of the film as research artefact, we have worked to expand this perspective to make claims for the creative force of video ethnographies. We would argue that the researcher who uses video methods merely to capture and slice out a section of social life is at best missing some of the potentials and possibilities of these methods, and at worst is doing them a violence and a disservice. What we have sought to do here is to begin to develop a sense of what an alternative— a critical creative videography—might look like, weaving this sense of creativity throughout an expanded field of film-making.

Questions of creativity and criticality within the ethnographic video-making process guided our discussion of this urban exploration research project, whether this be creatively experimenting with technologies, or appreciating a range of different points of skilling within the filmic process. Examining editing as a creative-analytic process we also draw out, as we did with our discussions of equipment, how these negotiations form intimate relationships between the researcher, technology and footage. Finally, and most clearly in our discussion of the audience of these ethnographic films, we emphasised the need for further attention to the variety of 'work' films do, but also that the filmmaking process can do, noting how these films go to work in the world, and how researcher-subjects are produced in their making.

We have argued that to develop and appreciate creative video ethnographies is to push at the edges of the technologies and procedures of filmmaking. This is to move beyond the perception of video as fieldnotes and video as interpretation, to give consideration to the creative process, to viewers, and to the socio-technical formations that constitute multimedia geographies (Richardson-Ngwenya 2014). These are creative practices, forces and objects that, we would emphasise, have the ability to make, and potentially to remake, subjects, knowledge and worlds in imaginative, critical and politically forceful ways.

NOTES

1. We might think here of an obvious example—Simon Faithfull's *Escape Vehicle No. 6 (chair in space)*, a project which he describes as a "journey of a domestic chair from the earth to the edge of space". Faithfull goes on to suggest that "the chilling nature of the film is that the empty chair invites the audience to imagine taking a journey to an uninhabitable realm where it is impossible to breath, the temperature is minus 60 below and the sky now resembles the blackness of space": http://www.youtube.com/watch?v=_wnyp3Nrp0w
2. Depth-of-field is the distance between the nearest and farthest objects in a scene that appear in focus in an image.
3. Such collaborative working resonates with a range of ways ethnographic research subjects can and have been mobilised in the co-creation of ethnographic data; a process that gives agency to participants through collaboration rather than "giving the camera away" (Ramella and Olmos 2006) in a participatory video model.
4. The camera was a Canon 5D Mark III for those interested. The Canon 5D Mark II and Nikon D800 are also great pieces of 'all-in-one' full-frame photography/videography kits.
5. The *Hobohemia* travelogue triptych is a series of ethnographic videos about travelling through, and sleeping in, ruins in eight different European countries. The videos can be found on the Place Hacking channel on Vimeo: https://vimeo.com/channels/placehacking
6. *Our Own Private Island*, a short video about camping overnight on an abandoned military river fortification as the tide traps us, can be viewed at: https://vimeo.com/64600820
7. For example, the *Slow Mo Guys* have recorded a gun being fired underwater at 27,000 frames-per-second and then slowed the footage down to open up new realms of aural/visual perception: http://youtu.be/OubvTOHWTms?t=2m52s
8. In one particularly artful non-human deployment, a seagull snatches a POV camera and places it on a ledge out of reach with a satisfied squawk. The viewer is left wondering how the camera, and therefore footage, was located and recovered: http://www.youtube.com/watch?v = rIu5B3Fsstg
9. *Angel of the North* is Anthony Gormley's 20-meter tall steel Angel sculpture, with a wing span of 55 meters that overlooks Gateshead, UK.
10. *Cold Angel* is artist Lucy Sparrow's playful engagement with Antony Gormley's *Angel of the North*. Sparrow writes, "myself and three others embarked on a project of epic knitted proportions to create a scarf that would fit the Angel

of the North sculpture in Gateshead": http://sewyoursoul.co.uk/2013/07/23/
cold-angel-short-film-documentary/
11. We can think, for example, of how the editorial process can itself be played
with. In *Jute,* an experimental film produced about Dundee, Scotland, a role-
reversing experimental editing of sight to sound played with ways of knowing
place (Garrett et al. 2011).
12. If effective editing, and certainly if experimental editing is to take place, it is
also perhaps useful to appreciate something of the materialities of digital
images and their composition, apprehending them as intersections of movement, rhythm, speed, flow, refraction, sensor capacity, glass dynamics, light
sources, processing power, weight, intensity, strength, software rendering
capabilities, imagination and interaction.

REFERENCES

Adey, P. 2009. *Mobilities.* London: Routledge.
Aitken, S.C. and Zonn, L. 1994. *Place, Power, Situation, and Spectacle: A Geogra-
phy of Film.* Lanham: Rowman & Littlefield.
Banks, M. 1992. Which films are the ethnographic films? In Crawford, P.I. and
Turton, D. (eds.) *Film as Ethnography.* Manchester: Manchester University
Press.
Bauch, N. 2010. The academic geography video genre: a methodological examina-
tion. *Geography Compass,* May: 475–484.
Bennett, L. 2011. Bunkerology—a case study in the theory and practice of urban
exploration. *Environment and Planning D: Society and Space,* 29: 421–434.
Bourdieu, P. and Lamaison, P. 1986. From rules to strategies: an interview with
Pierre Bourdieu. *Cultural Anthropology,* 1: 110–120.
Brown, K.M., Dilley, R. and Marshall, K. 2008. Using a head-mounted video
camera to understand social worlds and experiences. *Sociological Research
Online,* 16.
Büscher, M. 2005. Social life under the microscope? *Sociological Research Online,* 10.
Carter, S. and McCormack, D.P. 2006. Film, geopolitics and the affective logics of
intervention. *Political Geography,* 25: 228–245.
Cosgrove, D.E. and Daniels, S. 1988. *The Iconography of Landscape: Essays on the
Symbolic Representation, Design, and Use of Past Environments.* Cambridge:
Cambridge University Press.
Crang, M. and Cook, I. 2007. *Doing Ethnographies.* London: Sage.
Cresswell, T. and Dixon, D. 2002. *Engaging Film: Geographies of Mobility and
Identity.* Lanham: Oxford, Rowman & Littlefield.
Daniels, S. 1993. *Fields of Vision: Landscape and National Identity in England and
the United States.* Princeton: Princeton University Press.
Davies, G. 2010. Where experiments end. *Geoforum,* 41(5): 667–690.
Dewsbury, J.D. 2009. Performative, non-representational and affect-based
research: seven injunctions. In Delyser, D., Atkin, S., Crang, M., Herber, S. and
McDowell, L. (eds.) *The SAGE Handbook of Qualitative Research in Human
Geography.* London: Sage.
Dwyer, C. and Davies, G. 2010. Qualitative methods III: animating archives, artful inter-
ventions and online environments. *Progress in Human Geography,* 34(1): 88–97.
Garrett, B.L. 2010. Urban explorers: quests for myth, mystery and meaning. *Geography Compass,* 4: 1448–1461.
Garrett, B.L. 2011a. Cracking the Paris carrières: corporal terror and illicit encoun-
ter under the City of Light. *Acme: An International E-Journal for Critical Geographies,* 10: 269–277.

Garrett, B. L. 2011b. Videographic geographies: Using digital video for geographic research. *Progress in Human Geography*, 35(4): 521–541.

Garrett, B. L. 2013a. *Explore Everything: Place-Hacking the City*. London: Verso.

Garrett, B. L. 2013b. Undertaking recreational trespass: urban exploration and infiltration. *Transactions of the Institute of British Geographers*, Online First, 1–30.

Garrett, B. L. 2013c. Worlds through glass: photography and video as geographic method. In Ward, K. (ed.) *Researching the City*. London: SAGE.

Garrett, B. L., Rosa, B. and Prior, J. 2011. Jute: excavating material and symbolic surfaces. *Liminalities: A Journal of Performance Studies*, 7: 1–4.

Haraway, D. 1991. *Simians, Cyborgs and Women: The Reinvention of Nature*. New York, Routledge.

Hawkins, H. 2010. The argument of the eye: cultural geographies of installation art. *Cultural Geographies*, 17: 1–19.

Hawkins, H. 2013a. *For Creative Geographies: Geography, Visual Art and the Making of Worlds*. New York: Routledge.

Hawkins, H. 2013b. Geography and art. An expanding field: site, the body and practice. *Progress in Human Geography*, 37(1): 52–71.

Kanngieser, A. 2013. *Experimental Politics and the Making of Worlds*. Aldershot: Ashgate.

Kindon, S. 2003. Participatory video in geographic research: a feminist practice of looking? *Area*, 35: 142–153.

Last, A. 2012. Experimental geographies. *Experimental Geographies*, 6: 706–724.

Latham, A. and McCormack, D. P. 2009. Thinking with images in non-representational cities: vignettes from Berlin. *Area*, 41, 252–262.

Laurier, E. 2009. Editing experience: sharing adventures through home movies. *Assembling the Line*, 1–19.

Laurier, E., Lorimer, H., Brown, B., Jones, O., Juhlin, O., Noble, A., Perry, M., Pica, D., Sormani, P., Strebel, I., Swan, L., Taylor, A. S., Watts, L. and Weilenmann, A. 2008. Driving and passengering: notes on the ordinary organisation of car travel. *Mobilities*, 3: 1–23.

Laurier, E. and Philo, C. 2006. Possible geographies: a passing encounter in a café. *Area*, 38(4): 353–363.

Lorimer, J. 2010. Moving image methodologies for more-than-human geographies. *Cultural Geographies*, 17: 237–258.

Marks, L. 2002. *Touch: Sensuous Theory and Multisensory Media*. Minneapolis: University of Minnesota Press.

Massumi, B. 1992. *A User's Guide to Capitalism and Schizophrenia: Deviations from Deleuze and Guattari*. Cambridge: MIT Press.

Mead, M. 2001. *Letters from the Field, 1925–1975*. New York: Harper Perennial.

Merchant, S. 2011. The body and the senses: visual methods, videography and the submarine sensorium. *Body & Society*, 17: 53–72.

Mott, C. and Roberts, S. 2014. Not everyone has (the) balls: urban exploration and the persistence of masculinist geography. *Antipode*, 46(1): 229–245.

Parr, H. 2007. Collaborative film-making as process, method and text in mental health research. *Cultural Geographies*, 14: 114–138.

Pink, S. 2007. *Doing Visual Ethnography: Images, Media and Representation in Research*. Manchester: Manchester University Press, in association with the Granada Centre for Visual Anthropology.

Pink, S. 2008. An urban tour: The sensory sociality of ethnographic place-making. *Ethnography*, 9: 175–196.

Pink, S. 2009. Walking with video. *Visual Studies*, 22(3): 240–252.

Ramella, M. and Olmos, G. 2006. Giving the camera away or giving the camera away. *Papers in Social Research Methods: Qualitative Series no 10*. London: London School of Economics.

Rancière, J. 2009. Notes on the photographic image. *Radical Philosophy,* 156: 8–15.

Richardson-Ngwenya, P. E. 2014. Performing a more-than-human material imagination during fieldwork: muddy boots, diarizing and putting vitalism on video. *Cultural Geographies,* 21(2): 293–299.

Rose, G. 2007. *Visual Methodologies: An Introduction to the Interpretation of Visual Methods.* London: Sage.

Rouch, J. 2003. The camera and the man. In Hockings, P. (ed.) *Principles of Visual Anthropology,* 3rd ed. Berlin: Mouton de Gruyer.

Rouch, J. and Feld, S. 2003. *Cine-Ethnography (Visible Evidence),* Minneapolis: University of Minnesota Press.

Ruby, J. 2005. The last 20 years of visual anthropology—a critical review. *Visual Studies,* 20: 159–170.

Simmel, G. 1971. The adventurer. In Levine, D. N. (ed.) *On Individuality and Social Forms.* Chicago: Chicago University Press.

Simondon, G. 2011. On the mode of existence of technical objects. *Deleuze Studies,* 5: 407–424.

Simpson, P. 2011. "So, as you can see . . .": some reflections on the utility of video methodologies in the study of embodied practices. *Area,* 43(3): 343–352.

Sontag, S. 1977. *On Photography.* New York: Picador.

Spinney, J. 2009. Cycling the city: movement, meaning and method. *Geography Compass,* 3(2): 817–835.

Straughan, E. R. 2011. Touched by water: The body in scuba diving. *Emotion, Space and Society,* Online First, 1–8.

Sui, D. 2008. The wikification of GIS and its consequences: or Angelina Jolie's new tattoo and the future of GIS. *Computers, environment and urban systems,* 32: 1–5.

8 Working with Sound in Video

Producing an Experimental Documentary about School Spaces

Michael Gallagher

SOUNDING VIDEO

As someone with a long-standing interest in sound, it has often struck me as odd that uses of video in research should be characterised as visual methods. The entire field of visual methods is already problematic enough since, as Ingold (2007) points out, it tends to reduce the visual—practices of seeing—to a much narrower set of concerns surrounding the production and reception of visible images. But even if we were to reframe visual studies more specifically, as studies of visible images, where would that leave film and video, with their integration of light and sound?

"Offering three decades of silent films as Exhibit A, scholars have for years pursued their arguments in favor of cinema's visual nature" (Altman 2004, 6). But over the last couple of decades, a number of more aurally-attuned film studies writers have argued that cinema is essentially audiovisual (Altman 1992, 2004; Beck and Grajeda 2008; Chion 1994, 2009; Weis and Belton 1985), calling attention to the varied soundings of film, from the incidental noise of "the kids in the front rows, the air conditioner hum, the lobby cash register" (Altman 2004, 6) and the clacking and whirring of projectors, to the lecturers, live pianists, theatre organs and orchestral accompaniments that soundtracked early cinema. The very notion of 'silent film' turns out to be something of a misnomer (Brown and Davison 2013). My own vinyl collection offers up a little evidence of this lively history of cinematic aurality. 'The World of the Cinema Organ' was a classic charity shop find by a friend, a 1971 Decca LP of reissued 78 rpm recordings from leading lights of the UK cinema organ scene such as Reginald Dixon, Sidney Torch and Dudley Beaven. Its faded cover shows a besuited gentleman seated at an enormous white Wurlitzer console with four manuals and raked banks of stop-keys. From the 1930s, this hefty chunk of film audio hardware was in regular use at a luxurious art deco cinema in Tooting, London, now a Grade 1 listed Gala bingo hall.

The emerging audiovisual sensibility in film studies is taking some time to seep into work on video methods. Compare, for example, composer and film sound writer Michel Chion's (1994) conception of cinema as "audio-vision" with, some 15 years later, visual anthropologist Sarah Pink's (2009) more cautious references to "(audio)visual media". Pink's attempt to place visual media in the context of a multi-sensory approach to ethnography is certainly welcome, but her terminology, literally bracketing out the audio, risks perpetuating a sense of sound's subordination to light. Others in visual studies have been more forthright in asserting the audiovisuality of moving image media (e.g. Cubitt 2002). As Pink herself recognises, "[d]igital media frequently unite the visual and the aural" (2009, 107), with audio recording and playback almost ubiquitous capacities of modern video technologies. Video-based research often depends on the recording and replay of both audio and moving images. Recounting the development of conversation analysis, for example, Laurier et al. (2008, unpaginated) note that "[h]aving consistently utilised audio tape recordings and transcripts to access otherwise overlooked, missed or unimaginable details of talking together, video recordings opened up the possibilities of examining the gestural and scenic details otherwise lost on an audio-tape". In other words, video images supplemented audio, not the other way around. Likewise, some of the earliest motion picture film devices were developed in the 1880s at Edison's labs as extensions to the phonograph. "We think of the 20th century as the triumph of the visual, but it is really the triumph of sound that extends itself into the visual. Moving pictures are sounds that have colonized light" (Cubitt 2002, 360). And for all the talk of audiences in visual studies, the etymology of the word originally relates to aurality, to those who are within hearing range. Only later was the term used to refer to those who look, watch or read.

If these arguments are not enough to convince the would-be video researcher to attend more closely to audio, there is also the issue of research quality. Professional film-makers often remark that sound quality is one of the surest ways to distinguish amateur efforts from more serious productions, an observation easily supported by a brief trawl around YouTube. The high definition cameras on modern smartphones can produce some surprisingly beautiful images, but sound is more tricky to 'get right'. Of course, such notions are strongly normative, shaped by particular aesthetic, cultural and technical values, as I will discuss later in this chapter. Researchers may wish to work critically and reflexively with, and sometimes against, these values. Nevertheless, there are obvious pragmatic advantages in taking care over video sound, both for data collection (producing a more detailed record of the sonic aspects of the phenomena being studied) and dissemination (producing research outputs that take into account the expectations and listening situations of audiences). In most cases, leaving audio to take care of itself or hoping for some miraculous post-production quick fix for sloppy sound (if you ever find one, please let me know) is likely to be detrimental to the quality of video research.

Audio recording and playback are therefore intrinsic to video, and as such deserve greater consideration in accounts of video research methods. This is not to advance an essentialising separation of sound from light, but rather to examine the *relationship* between audio and image, recognising video's transsensoriality, "the ways in which the visual and the sonic interact, combine and separate to create the film or video text" (Birtwistle 2010, 20). With this aim in mind, this chapter presents reflections on the making of *Seven Primary School Spaces,* a short experimental documentary film I produced that used soundscape recordings and video to explore some of the sensory and aesthetic qualities of a primary school.[1] As such, it offers a useful example of the possibilities of working closely with audio in video production. I discuss its genesis and the process of production, covering issues of access, ethics and the technologies used. I then broaden out my discussion to consider how sound in *Seven Primary School Spaces,* and audio in video more widely, might be conceptualised, connecting up to literatures on film sound and sound studies. My particular concern is with the functionality of audiovisuality in video research, what it *does*. I will argue that while video clearly lends itself to representation, it also always has non-representational or more-than-representational elements, and both aspects can be used for the purposes of research; the two need not be mutually exclusive. In particular, disrupting the convention of synchronised audio and images can work to amplify video's more-than-representational excess, with potentially interesting results.

For readers unfamiliar with the notion of soundscapes, a little clarification may be helpful. The concept is problematic, partly due to the looseness with which it has been used (Kelman 2010), and also because any sounding environment always involves more than sound, and is therefore experienced multi-sensorially. The world is not "sliced up along the lines of the sensory pathways by which we enter into it" (Ingold 2007, 10). Nevertheless, the term continues to function as a neat shorthand for the totality of audible vibrations in a given location. Soundscape artists, composers and researchers concern themselves with whatever sounds happen to be happening in a particular place, closely attending to and often recording these uncontrolled environmental vibrations. In the soundscape tradition field recordings are used in ways that maintain recognisability, referencing and representing the recorded place, unlike in acousmatic music where such sounds are decontextualised and approached purely for their aesthetic qualities (Levack Drever 2002). *Seven Primary School Spaces,* whilst a film rather than an audio work, nevertheless draws heavily on the tradition of soundscape art and research.

AN IDEA FOR A FILM: *SEVEN PRIMARY SCHOOL SPACES*

Seven Primary School Spaces was a collaborative project, conceived and created with a film-maker friend, Ben Ewart-Dean. Ben directed the film and I took the role of producer and sound designer. The film comprises static video shots of seven empty spaces in a Scottish primary school (classroom,

Figure 8.1   The film's opening shot, showing the playground.

hallway, playground, gym hall and so on), each a minute and a half long. Each shot is accompanied by a soundscape recording made in the same space when the school was occupied. These recordings were designed to document and re-present the full range of sounds happening in the school spaces, and their general ambiences, both foreground and background, rather than isolating specific sounds such as human voices, as is common in film and television sound production.

The images of the empty spaces enable close scrutiny of the physical, material aspects of the school, while the audio evokes the school's social space, a much more dynamic, noisy set of flows. At the start of the film, for example, after the title 'Playground' we see an empty stretch of grey tarmac marked with coloured lines, a basketball net and floodlights, a line of trees moving in the breeze with houses beyond, and a figure in the distance, running along the nearby road. At the same time we hear a multitude of voices chattering and screeching, rapid pattering, scrapes and dull thuds, the sound of footballs being kicked, then a bell ringing followed by a child's voice saying "awww!" with a palpable sense of disappointment. The following shots include: the school entrance with the voices of teachers and sounds of stapling; a gym hall accompanied by the whistles, commands and ball-bouncing noises of a basketball lesson; a quiet open-plan area with library shelves and computers, in which French tuition is barely audible; a music room whose soundscape includes some wildly out-of-tune recorder playing, adding a humorous touch; a classroom with a pre-recorded story being played back to the children; and the gym hall again, this time framed for a school assembly, complete with a mass singalong. The film was distributed through a short run of DVD copies, which we gave away to anyone who expressed an interest. It has also been shown in several research seminars, conference presentations, lectures, as part of an exhibition on school design and at an experimental film festival. It can be viewed online at http://vimeo.com/20931701.

The idea of using video to pursue geographical research on school spaces came from my experience of the limitations of conventional qualitative methods. In 2005, I had completed a PhD in human geography based on ethnographic fieldwork in a Scottish primary school. Throughout the research, I had a persistent sense that there was something important about the school's spaces that I was unable to address through conventional methods of participant observation, written fieldnotes and participatory activities with the children. This 'something' might best be summed up as the sensory vibrancy of the school environment—a constantly changing flow of sights, sounds and smells, often chaotic but also often predictable, sometimes riotous but at other times highly regulated, often startling and bewildering to me as an outsider but seemingly taken for granted by the teachers and pupils. Primary schools, as institutional spaces, are constructed not only through their physical architecture, but also through certain kinds of interior and exterior design: the markings of gym hall floors and playgrounds; small brightly coloured chairs tucked under low tables; pint-sized bookshelves and carefully crafted wall displays; clear signage and demarcated activity areas. They also take shape through particular acoustic qualities, such as the screaming, swirling, surround-sound noise of a playground, the clattering reverberations of corridors and dining halls, a maths lesson hush growing into a gentle babble of conversation, the patter of small feet on hard-wearing flooring, as well as more regulated sounds such as bells, whistles and teachers issuing instructions or reading stories.

I had tried writing fieldnotes about these aspects of primary school space, talking to children about them, drawing maps and diagrams and inviting the children to draw their own maps and take photos. Some of this data has found its way into publications (Gallagher 2010, 2011). But I was left with a nagging sense that these inscriptions conveyed little of the vibrant multisensory flows of the school space, which seemed far removed from the fixity of maps, diagrams and photos, and the steady tempo of my writing, its regular rhythms and single-track linearity. My ethnographic fieldnotes, whilst useful for narrating specific actions and interactions, seemed ill-suited to addressing the school more holistically, as an environment, with its sheer multiplicity of energies, flows and materials. Writing flattened out the lively spatial and temporal dynamics through the uniformity of printed words, the neat sequential logic of sentences and paragraphs, the rendition of all the messy textures and timbres of classroom life into meaningful human language (Gallagher and Prior 2014). The problem was with the more-than-representational or performative aspects of traditional fieldnotes—their rhythms, tempos, dynamics and sensory repertoire worked against any attempt to convey the much more varied rhythms, tempos, dynamics and sensorium of the school. Perhaps a more imaginative writer might have found inventive textual ways to bear witness to these things, but my sense was that any medium based on written words would be inadequate to the multi-sensory, non-discursive, non-linguistic, affective aspects of what I had experienced.

At the time, Ben and I had a number of converging shared interests. Having trained in documentary photography, he had begun to explore experimental and DIY film, particularly using minimal, static framings. Both of us were aficionados of experimental and minimalist music, something that I was pursuing through various creative projects. I had also been making field recordings in a hobbyist fashion, and was becoming fascinated by soundscapes and environmental sound art. I recount these contextual details to illustrate how the film grew out of the confluence of a fairly rich and varied set of influences. Pulling all of these strands together, I began to get a sense that an experimental documentary short film using soundscape recordings might be a way to work with what I felt had been missed out of my fieldnotes, evoking more of the lively aesthetic, affective and sensory qualities of primary school spaces.

James Benning's 2004 film *Ten Skies* was an important point of reference for Ben's film-making. It consists of 10 static 10-minute shots of skies in

Val Verde, California, on 16 mm film, accompanied by sounds from the filming locations, such as traffic and aircraft noise, voices and other incidental sounds. The film has something in common with ethnography, with its close and sustained attention to unremarkable, everyday phenomena. Inspired by *Ten Skies,* Ben and I wanted to make a film that would provide an opportunity to take a really good long look at and listen to school spaces, allowing time to take in all the details, possibly pushing viewers to the point of boredom or distraction.

Ten Skies also sets up an interesting relationship between soundtrack and image:

> *Ten Skies* adheres to Andre Bazin's notion of the frame as a mask, calling attention equally to what remains outside the visual field. Indeed, it is not simply the passage of cloud formations into and out of the frame, but even more the non-sync off-camera soundscapes that transform Benning's spaces from their minimal enframed sections to a maximal combination of on and off camera fields.
>
> (Anderson 2007, unpaginated)

What Anderson means by 'non-sync off-camera' is that, unlike in conventional documentaries, most of the sounds heard in *Ten Skies* do not correspond to anything that can be seen. The soundtrack could have been recorded in an entirely different time and place to the images, but the film is sufficiently open to invite associations; one begins to imagine the scene beyond the frame, based on the sounds heard. In this way, the audio works to ground the image, contextualising it, bringing it down to earth. Through hearing, one almost sees the camera behind the image, sitting amidst life on land, pointed upwards. At the most basic level *Ten Skies* represents 10 skies, but much of its interest lies in its more-than-representational aspects: a minimalist structure and a disjuncture between audio and image which invite boredom, distraction, imagination and reverie.

Like *Ten Skies,* we also wanted to take a deliberately non-didactic, documentary approach to making a film about school spaces. We had no preconceived message to convey. Rather we wanted to see what a particular primary school looked like, listen to what it sounded like, and document and present some of what we saw and heard. In this sense the film was a piece of empirical research, more exploration than exposition. We began with the structure of static shots and soundscape recordings, but no scripts, storyboards, sequences, or any ideas about which spaces we would shoot or how long each shot would last for. These decisions were made as we went along, steered by our encounters with the school—a broadly inductive approach.

It is worth emphasising that we saw the process of making the film as the research method, and the film as the main research output. This practice-led approach was a form of ethnographic film-making, unlike in social science studies which use video to collect data that are then analysed to produce written research outputs, perhaps with illustrative video clips but with most of the content in textual form. Having produced rich textual analyses of school spaces in my PhD research, and having run into the limitations of that approach, I wanted to try something different.

MAKING THE FILM: ACCESS AND ETHICS

Given the relative simplicity of the film's concept, we were surprised by the complexity and challenge of the production process. We explored a couple of different routes to get funding, eventually obtaining a £1500 knowledge transfer grant from the University of Edinburgh where I was working at the time. Finding a school willing to give us access proved a much bigger challenge, causing many months of delay. The first school we tried was through someone we knew who was working there as a teacher, and who thought that his head would be supportive of the project. We met her and obtained permission from the local authority, but she seemed non-committal, almost evasive, and not enthusiastic—perhaps understandably. As we were trying to agree a date for shooting, she emailed to say that the school had to close for repairs due to woodworm, so we would have to find somewhere else. We then approached a second school in a different local authority. This time the head appeared more supportive, but after filling in a lengthy form for permission from the local education department, and waiting many weeks for a decision, we were turned down with no explanation or feedback. By this stage the project was severely behind schedule, so we decided to return to the first local authority (they at least had given us permission) and ask if they could suggest a school with a head who might be open to a somewhat unusual film project. At that point things started to move much more swiftly. In hindsight, this was the key to the whole project: finding a head teacher with the energy and open-mindedness to support a project which, in all honesty, many would have seen as an incomprehensible waste of time.

We had anticipated that the biggest issue would be gaining permission for the audio recording, since this would involve children and teachers, whereas the video would be shot in an empty building. In fact, the shoot also raised issues of access, since the school was normally closed when empty, and getting it opened out of hours was not straightforward. Having a supportive head teacher was invaluable. She negotiated the various bureaucratic hurdles and generously offered to come into the school in her own time, at the weekend, to give us access to shoot the video while she worked in her office. We were extremely grateful. The cameraman and director spent a full day shooting various spaces in the school, including close and wider angles of some spaces, to give us plenty of options when it came to editing. In total there were 22 shots. The director sent me screenshots of each, so I could see where to make the audio recordings.

Figure 8.2 A shot of an open plan area with bookshelves and computers.

Audio recording raised a number of ethical issues. The consensus in childhood studies is that informed consent should be negotiated with children who take part in research, and where possible also their parents (e.g. Alderson and Morrow 2011). The normal rules around ensuring anonymity are also seen as important for protecting children from harm (Tisdall et al. 2009). However, in our project, gaining formal consent for recording from every individual child in the school would have been extremely impractical and probably not very meaningful. It is likely that many would have opted in (or out) due at least in part to contextual factors such as the head teacher's endorsement of the project and the norms of compliance (and associated practices of resistance) that exist in schools (David et al. 2001; Gallagher et al. 2010), rather than an informed understanding of our rather esoteric project. There was also the practical problem of how, if some children did opt out, to avoid recording the sounds made by them. Ensuring anonymity was also tricky. Any viewers who knew the school would be able to identify it easily through the images, and might then conceivably be able to identify individuals by their voices.

Through discussions with the head teacher, we agreed that we would edit out from the audio recordings any identifiable voices of individual children. The aim of the recordings was to document the ambiences of the spaces of the school, the general hubbub, so individual voices were not so important. Removing them would ensure anonymity, and also felt appropriate given that negotiating individual consent with all children and parents was not practical. In the event, a few children were identifiable in the raw recordings. I cut out the individual voices in audio software and used simple cross fades to smooth over the edits.

The day before making the audio recordings, I gave a short presentation in the morning assembly to the whole school, explaining the film, why we were making it, what I would be doing, and pointing out to the children that if for some reason they did not want to be involved, then they could opt out by keeping quiet or keeping their distance when they saw me nearby with my microphone. I invited the children to ask questions and this led to some discussion. This seemed a respectful and practically feasible way to meaningfully inform them about what we were doing.

An information sheet was sent out by the head teacher to all parents. This was a single side of A4 with details about the film, how it would be made and what would be done with it, written in plain language. My office phone number and email address were also provided, and parents were invited to get in touch if they had any questions. None did so.

In the case of teachers, we opted to negotiate informed consent more actively, since this was more feasible, and we wanted to be able to include teachers' identifiable voices as an important part of the school soundscape that we were documenting. A consent form and information sheet were sent to the head teacher for distribution to the school staff, explaining how the recordings would be used, and that the film would be distributed on DVD and might be screened in cinemas, arts centres, film festivals, conferences and other such events. It also explained that staff had the right to listen to the recordings afterwards and to withdraw consent at that stage if they so wished.

I spent a full day in school with my audio gear, making recordings to match up with as many of the shots as possible. My schedule was carefully planned beforehand with the head teacher, to enable me to record when spaces were in use, and to coincide with activities that might be particularly sonically interesting, such as a music lesson, a gym lesson and a whole-school assembly. Some children seemed to enjoy being audio recorded; others appeared indifferent. However, I sensed that some of the staff had not been entirely comfortable with the process, so afterwards I emailed the head teacher, suggesting I send her a CD of recordings to check out with those whose voices were audible. She replied, saying she thought this was "a good idea. Nobody seemed overly concerned about you being here for the day but I'm sure they would feel happier checking out what's on tape". I duly sent over the CD, and further emails were exchanged in which we agreed on some sections to exclude.

After the film was edited, a copy was sent to the head teacher for her to watch and show to the staff, children and parents. Following duplication, another five copies of the finished film with artwork were sent to the school, for lending out to anyone who wanted to watch it.

TECHNOLOGIES, FORMATS AND THEIR FUNCTIONS

In addition to the considerable effort that went into negotiating access, the audio and video systems used to make the film involved deserve some attention. The level of technical detail I want to provide here about resolutions, bit rates, formats and so on is quite exhaustive, perhaps even exhausting. It may leave some readers wondering what the relevance is for video methods. After all, most researchers just want to record material that is 'good enough' for their purposes, so the choice of technologies might seem a merely pragmatic matter.

However, technical decisions always have implications far beyond the technical. Media archaeologist Wolfgang Ernst has argued for a materialist, object-orientated approach to media, as a counter-balance to the current tendency in science and technology studies to emphasise the role of social context and how technologies are used. Ernst argues for a focus on what is most distinctive about media: the media themselves. He suggests taking "the point of view of the machine" (Ernst 2013, 24) through an excavation of the internal processes of media, the very structure of their circuits and systems, since these aspects are of fundamental importance to how media function. Birtwistle has highlighted the importance of this kind of materiality in film sound, arguing that the "sound of film technology is always playing in and through the soundtrack, always there as 'ground' against which other sounds are 'foregrounded'" (2010, 86). For example, the sound of optical crackle, "whether consciously registered by the listener or not, has a powerful affective dimension, overlaying the film with a feeling of 'pastness'" (Birtwistle 2010, 64).

Technologies that reduce this noise, such as Dolby noise reduction, significantly change film's affective qualities (Chion 2003). The choice of technologies and formats therefore shapes what video can do, both its representational and more-than-representational functions.

Reflecting on the technological details of *Seven Primary School Spaces* five years after its completion, I am struck by how quickly things have moved on. The soundscape recordings were made on Minidisc—a format which, back in 2007, was coming to the end of its life, and has since become obsolete, but which offered (and still does) relatively wide audio frequency bandwidth, high signal-to-noise ratio and dynamic range in a small, portable package. Minidisc was used largely because it was what I had available at the time, and it was 'good enough' for the kind of representational, documentary soundscape recordings we wanted. Minidiscs record audio using a form of lossy compression known as ATRAC, with a bit rate of 292 kbps, comparable to a high quality MP3. Like MP3, ATRAC uses perceptual coding, a compression system based on psychoacoustic principles, which removes elements of the audio that are likely to be inaudible to the 'average listener', thereby reducing bandwidth and file size (Sterne 2006, 2012).[2] My portable Minidisc recorder's microphone preamplifiers were noisy, and I wanted to limit inherent system noise as far as possible so as to foreground the sonic representations of the school, so I hired a small professional quality location mixer (a Shure FP24), which allowed me to bypass the Minidisc preamps and feed directly into the recorder's line-in socket. In this respect, I was taking a very conventional approach to filmic illusion, attempting to make the audio technology 'disappear' transparently into the background.

All the indoor recordings were made with a Rode NT4, a stereo condenser microphone, relatively low cost but again with a wide frequency response and low self-noise. Stereo recording is commonly used for soundscape audio, since it enables the effective representation of the spatial qualities of sound whilst also being portable, affordable and simple to use, unlike more complex spatial systems such as ambisonics and surround sound. My aim could be summed up by Birtwistle's (2010, 53) description of 'direct sound' as the recording "of all location sound, resulting in extremely dense recordings that are rich in sonic detail...in contrast to the well-modulated, well-behaved classical soundtrack".[3] The NT4 was useful for this purpose as its capsules, though cardioid (i.e. directional), produce a fairly wide pickup pattern, unlike the much narrower mono shotgun mics conventionally used for location film sound.

The NT4's capsules are fixed in an XY pattern, angled at 90 degrees. An XY pair involves mics that are positioned co-incidently, i.e. one immediately above the other, creating a stereo field based solely on sound level differences between the two capsules. Spaced pairs of microphones (called 'A-B stereo') are thought by some to produce a more immersive sense of space, since they can also represent time differences between the capsules (soundwaves arriving at one capsule slightly before the other), and are thus more similar to the spaced arrangement of human ears. But spaced pairs can produce unpleasant phasing effects when summed to mono, which again would foreground the sound of the technology rather than the sonic representations, something I wanted to avoid. Stereo systems have become the norm for video playback nowadays, but some technologies still sum to mono, such as older televisions, some laptops, portable DVD players and data projectors. The XY pattern, being co-incident, has no phase issues when summed to mono, and this was therefore another advantage of using the NT4 for our project.

At the time, I didn't have effective wind protection for the NT4, so for recording the playground this was another essential item to be hired. Microphone wind protection—the fur covered blimps often seen on television news—helps to avoid wind noise, a distorted bassy rumbling caused by air currents hitting the mic capsules, which can happen even in a light breeze. Again, this would have obscured the sounds of the children and the acoustics of the school, which is what I wanted to document. My local sound hire firm only had wind protection kits with microphones already fixed inside them, so I hired a kit with a Sennheiser 418: a mid-side mic, with a shotgun middle element that is strongly directional and hence good for picking out specific sounds, but not ideal for my purpose of recording ambient soundscapes. However, it was stereo, lightweight, portable, inexpensive to hire for a day, and mono compatible, so it sufficed for our purposes. On paper, one might expect that the Sennheiser, worth around £1500, would far outshine the Rode, which currently retails for around £350. In practice, for soundscape recording, I slightly preferred the NT4, probably due to its pickup pattern being less strongly directional, and thus more suited to recording ambiences.

Thus my recording set-up, on the face of it the outcome of simple decisions about what tools to use, unravels to reveal a multitude of factors: a concern for producing recognisable representations of the school and making the technology less obviously audible, with attendant concerns about minimising noise and maximising frequency bandwidth; psychoacoustic models and assumptions about human hearing; a particular historical juncture in the development of consumer audio technologies and mobile devices and the associated relations of global capital; speculations about what kinds of technologies the film might be played on; geography, location and associated weather conditions; budget limitations, travel arrangements and the need for portability.

For the images, we hired a professional cameraman and a Sony HVR-Z1 camcorder, a semi-professional 3CCD machine (i.e. with separate sensors for red, blue and green light) which recorded in HDV (a highly compressed form of high definition video), at a 1080-line interlaced resolution, 50 frames per second (1080/50i), with a bit rate of around 25 megabits per second. (The salience of all these nerdy technical specifications will become clear shortly). In keeping with our low-budget, DIY approach, Ben edited the film himself in Final Cut Pro, and we enlisted my brother, who at the time was working as a freelance video editor, to do some grading (a process of colour-correction that takes place after editing) and post-processing, again in Final Cut Pro. The film was then downscaled to standard definition and exported

for DVD duplication and upload to Vimeo. We created the artwork ourselves on home computers, and sent all the files to a duplication service we
had found through the Internet.

At the time, given our limited budget for camera hire, the Z1 was the best
we could hope for in terms of image quality. However, the use of static shots
really showed up its flaws, with lots of visible compression artefacts as the
camera crunched the data down to fit on a Mini DV tape. The footage had
a slightly flickery, harsh quality that was further accentuated when scaled
down for DVD. I felt that, as we were expecting people to watch almost
nothing happening, the almost nothing needed to look really 'good'—and to
my eyes the HDV of the Z1 simply didn't look 'good enough'. What I mean
by this is that it had a distinctly 'video-ish' aesthetic rather than looking in
any way 'filmic', due to a combination of the frame rate (we used 50 frames
per second, whereas the cinema standard is 24) and interlacing (splitting the
image between pairs of adjacent frames to enhance the perception of
motion—very different to the way celluloid film works) and data compression artefacts (areas of the image looking pixelated or appearing to 'twitch').
Avoiding downscaling to standard definition might have helped a little, but
at the time high definition distribution channels were limited. Blu-ray technology was not widely available, and online video was much less developed
than at the time of writing, with neither YouTube nor Vimeo offering full
HD support. DVD felt like the most realistic option for distributing the film.

Not long after we finished the film in 2008, Canon released the 5D Mark
II digital SLR camera, which could shoot video as well as stills. Its full-frame
35 mm sensor (the same as the frame size used in 35 mm film) and resulting
shallow depth of field, HD video recording at 38 megabits per second, pro-
gressive rather than interlaced scan, plus a 24 frames per second option all
made for a strongly filmic image, and at a price that was affordable to DIY
film-makers. The result was something of a revolution in independent video
production. Support for HD distribution has also become much more widespread through Blu-ray discs, HD television sets and online channels. Had
these technologies been available, we would probably have used them, and
the film would have ended up looking very different. The situation may
change again soon, with raw (i.e. uncompressed) recording becoming an
option for independent film-makers on limited budgets. Raw footage is particularly suitable for grading without loss of quality, and for cinema screening. Blackmagic's Cinema Camera, released in 2012/2013, has the capacity
to record 2.5 k raw (i.e. 2500 lines of pixels as compared to HD's 1080), and
is comparable in price to semi-professional DSLRs and HD camcorders.
Recent developments from Magic Lantern, an organisation that makes firmware hacks for Canon DSLR cameras, mean that raw recording is now possible on some models. There are major workflow challenges with raw video
(it eats up massive amounts of disk space, bandwidth and processing power),
but the key point is this: as computing continues to increase in efficiency and
decrease in price, DIY film and video projects such as *Seven Primary School*

Figure 8.3   The final shot showing the school hall, used for assemblies.

Spaces will increasingly be able to adopt a 'look' that is very similar to more professional, big-budget productions.

How is all of this geeky detail relevant for video methods? As I argued earlier, the formats and technologies used, with their particular cultural and material aspects, inevitably shape what functions video research performs, whether intentionally or not. Staying at the level of representation, video researchers may be more concerned with content than form, but if we want to address the more-than-representational, material, affective qualities of video—qualities that are surely central to the medium's appeal—then the differences between formats are not trivial. In the case of *Seven Primary School Spaces,* the video-ish, interlaced look of the shots, which I found unsatisfactory, nevertheless had some interesting side effects. After one showing, someone commented that it was reminiscent of CCTV footage, combining with the static shots to hint at a surveillant, panoptic gaze, with all the associated connotations of security, discipline and control (see Simpson, this volume). Such issues are clearly relevant to schools (Gallagher 2010, 2011), but Ben and I had not consciously intended to highlight them. This unexpected interpretation raises provocative questions about the possible similarities between disciplinary surveillance, the ethnographic gaze, and practices of documentary film-making. Indeed, video is arguably a much more relevant medium to use for researching schools than film, since video is often used in modern schools, not only for surveillance but also for teaching and learning activities. In this context, using video technologies that emulate a filmic look, such as full frame DSLRs or raw cinema cameras, might have aestheticised the school in a way that could have felt problematic. Spaces of childhood often elicit nostalgia and sentimentality, so representing such spaces through technologies whose aesthetics hark back to the comforting familiarity of earlier media might have had powerful effects. There is the possibility, for example, for strongly romanticised depictions of children as cute and adorable, of teaching and learning as pastoral, paternalistic care—the French documentary *Être et Avoir* springs to mind. Equally there is the potential for hauntological effects, fusing childhood and old media to amplify a sense of memory, loss and longing, as with the old Super 8 family movies referenced by musicians such as Boards of Canada. There may be good reasons for making use of such affective capacities in some situations. But in our case, it could be argued that the slightly harsh, modern, warts-and-all look of our HDV footage served the affective purposes of school documentary better than a more flattering cinematic image.

CONCEPTUALISING AUDIO IN VIDEO: REPRODUCTION, REPRESENTATION AND BEYOND

In this final section, I want to think through in more detail how sound and image functioned together in *Seven Primary School Spaces,* and more generally how audio in video might be understood. In audio engineering, phonographic media are conventionally thought of as capturing and reproducing sounds. This process tends to be discussed with reference to the aim of fidelity, striving for recordings that recreate the 'original' sounds as faithfully and accurately as possible. For video research, these notions suggest that carefully recorded, high-fidelity audio, using the best available technologies, might help video data to precisely reconstruct the recorded environment, preserving objective knowledge of what happened there-and-then.

There is a certain common-sense logic here, echoing my comments at the start of the chapter that attending to audio can help produce higher quality, more useful video data. However, as I have noted elsewhere (Gallagher and Prior 2014), the notion of audio as reproduction has been subject to long-standing critique. Chion argues that cinema sound is primarily an art of illusion, not of faithful reconstruction, pointing out that film and video involve such a "radical sensory reduction" (1994, 96) that any sense of 'realism' can only be achieved through techniques of hyper-reality, "accommodations and adjustments, taking into account the audiovisual transposition in order to try to conserve a certain sense of realism and truth in [a] new representational context" (ibid). Likewise, in relation to soundscapes, it has been argued that "[t]he carefully recorded, selected, and edited sound environments that we are able to comfortably enjoy in our favourite armchairs offer an enhanced listening experience, one that we would likely not have if we were hearing those sounds in the 'real' world" (Lopez 2004, 84). Thus what is commonly thought of as fidelity may in fact be more accurately described as definition, "acuity and precision in rendering detail" (Chion 1994, 98), rather than faithfulness to how the sounds would have actually sounded if heard in situ. This is obviously true of foley sound, in which exaggerated simulations are used to convey action. But it can also be found built into the processes and technologies of audio recording, which often enhance definition by amplifying some elements and attenuating others. A good example is DPA's 4071 lavalier (tie clip) microphone, designed for television and film production. For example, it was used extensively for recording the live singing in the 2012 film version of *Les Miserables*. Its frequency response is far from flat, designed to exclude certain sounds and accentuate others, as the manufacturer's website explains:

> When recording voices from mic placement on a performer's body, no frequency below 100 Hz is attractive. For this reason, an acoustical low-cut has been incorporated in the 4071 capsule. . . . Furthermore, it removes distant rumbling from cars, trains, airplanes, etc. Another and equally important consideration is that when placing a microphone on the body, especially on the chest, the frequency range of the consonants is damped, resulting in poor intelligibility. The 4071 has a built-in boost [of 5dB at 5 kHz] to compensate for this loss.
>
> (DPA 2013, unpaginated)

All of this aligns with Altman's argument that recordings represent rather than reproduce sound: "according to the choice of recording location, microphone type, recording system, post-production manipulation, storage medium, playback arrangement, and playback locations, each recording proposes an interpretation of the original sound" (Altman 1992, 40). If audio recordings, in their very materiality, already contain interpretation, then in ethnographic terms we might consider them to be thick descriptions (Geertz, 1975)—never purely descriptive, always already laden with technical, cultural, economic and historical meanings. And composer John Levack Drever (1999, 2002) has proposed that soundscape recordings, when used for their referential qualities rather than abstracted for purely acousmatic purposes, are best understood as a form of ethnography, with all the attendant concerns surrounding representation, ethics, positionality, power and the politics of knowledge.

These ideas suggest that audio's main function might be to contribute to the representational aspects of video. In other words, audio and images, brought together in video, can be used to make meaning by showing and telling, re-presenting certain phenomena in a way that highlights certain aspects and overlooks others, framing them for the contemplation of an audience. In making *Seven Primary School Spaces*, this kind of representation was a central concern, using audio and images to convey aspects of school life that I had struggled to represent through more conventional written ethnographic methods. The choices made about technologies and techniques can be understood in relation to this representational aim, the aspiration not being for fidelity per se but for a rendition of the school's spaces that would convey as much as possible of their colours, lighting, design details, frequencies, dynamics and a sense of movement, and make the technologies used 'disappear' into the background. Despite its 'video-ish' look, the film appears to function reasonably well in this regard. Those who have responded positively to the film tend to find it interesting for its representation of the physical and sensory aspects of primary schools. For some these representations evoke memories of their own primary schooling, small details triggering vivid recollections: the benches in the gym hall, the squeak of a trainer on linoleum, the stark fluorescent lighting.

However, there is also always a certain failure of representation in soundscape recordings, perhaps better understood as a more-than-representational excess. Koutsomichalis (2013) suggests that soundscapes are ephemeral and fleeting interactions between environmental sounds and listeners in specific spaces and times, with all the multi-sensorial complexity, perceptual and psychophysical filtering this involves. Environmental phonography, by contrast, decontextualises sound from one environment and recontextualises it in another, thereby giving rise to a radically reconfigured interaction between listener, sound and environment. Recording a soundscape cannot "preserve the original semantics and subliminal significances of someone's encounter with an acoustic environment" since it effectively "isolate[s] physical sounds from a broader scheme . . . radically dismantling the associations they bear" (Koutsomichalis 2013, unpaginated). As

LaBelle (2006, 211) remarks, "as a listener I hear just as much displacement as placement, just as much placelessness as place . . . the extraction of sound from its environment partially wields its power by being boundless, uprooted and distinct".

Such effects may be due as much to the excess of audio technologies as what they miss out. Sound recording registers the entire "messy, asignifying noise of the world" (Cox 2011, 154) without the same discrimination as human hearing. Thus what Birtwistle suggests about direct sound recording in films applies even more so to soundscape audio:

> Background sounds, ambient sounds and sounds without an obvious visual source located within the frame all find a place in direct sound recording. Consequently there is . . . a proliferation of detail that is confusing, "irrelevant" and perhaps unintelligible. While this in itself can stand as a mark of fidelity and immediacy, it can also bring the soundtrack to a point of excess.
>
> (Birtwistle 2010, 57–58)

The audio technologies and formats of *Seven Primary School Spaces*, chosen primarily for their representational abilities, also generated this kind of more-then-representational excess, which was further accentuated by the disjuncture between audio and image. The film does encourage a certain representational alignment between the two aspects—we can see what looks like a playground and hear what sounds like a playground. But there is also an obvious mismatch, a glaring absence in the image. We are clearly *not* seeing what we can hear. The visible frames are empty, still and flat, far exceeded by the sound with its vibrant signs of life, its motion and messiness. This disjuncture has varied effects. Inevitably, quite a few people have been left dissatisfied, bored, confused, irritated or non-plussed. For others the split creates a heightened sense of both hearing and vision, the lack of visible bodies encouraging close scrutiny of physical space, and close listening to social space. Some have found the film ghostly or haunting, the children and teachers an absent presence, heard but not seen. As Toop (2010) has suggested, sound is particularly prone to creating uncanny sensations. In a culture where truth is strongly associated with seeing, sound often seems more uncertain and ambiguous, a fleeting and phantasmal presence disappearing into thin air. The image-audio dislocation also troubles the very notion of documentary film as representation, as truth, since it reveals an obviously constructed artifice. The emptiness of the images makes it clear that the sound must have been added later, which raises questions about its veracity. The audio could have been recorded in a different school, or perhaps even simulated or faked. In this sense, *Seven Primary School Spaces* bears some relation, albeit rather distant, to experimental films which overtly manipulate the relation between sound and image as a way of deconstructing film and its truth claims, such as Luis Bunuel's *Land*

Without Bread (Mauer 2008) and John Smith's *The Girl Chewing Gum, Om* and *Lost Sound.*

Overall, it seems that setting image and audio in an uncanny relationship, partly aligned but partly estranged, can generate effects both through representational functions and through an undermining of representation, a more-than-representational excess or slippage. In *Seven Primary School Spaces,* had we opted for a more conventional representational approach in which sound and image were recorded at the same time and synchronised in post-production, as is common in documentaries, the affective qualities of the film would have been different, and probably less interesting. In conclusion, I want to suggest that there may be much to be gained for video researchers by experimenting with the relationship between audio and image. The convention of synchronous audio and images, taken for granted in most video research, is by no means intrinsic to the medium. Many other configurations of relations between the audible and the visible are possible. As well as documenting pre-existing associations between things seen and things heard, video can be used to unsettle and rework those associations, or to generate wholly new associations. This is surely one of the most intriguing and affectively potent aspects of the medium.

NOTES

1. When referring to *Seven Primary School Spaces* as a 'film' I am referring to film as a broad genre of audiovisual production, rather than as a medium. In this sense it was a short film produced using the medium of digital video. At some points in the chapter I use 'film' to refer to celluloid film as a medium; this meaning should be clear from the context.

2. Of course, encoding by the Minidisc recorder was only the start of the process. The Minidisc recordings were later re-recorded into a computer as uncompressed 16-bit 48 kHz AIFF files, used for editing. When the film was output for DVD duplication and web upload, both audio and images were compressed again using various compression routines, and in the case of the web upload compressed yet again by Vimeo. Digital video (and digital media more generally) can be understood as a process of continual transformation of data, with repeated cycles of encoding, decoding and re-encoding. Purity and simplicity of form are abandoned in favour of mobility, transferability and interoperability. The result is a kind of accretion or sedimentation of multiple layers of encoding, forming a patina of compression artefacts layered into both images and audio, a kind of digital 'grain' that may be virtually unnoticeable or very pronounced depending on the number and type of processes used.

3. This is ironic, since 'direct sound' in film production usually means sound recorded on location while the film was being shot, whereas our film deliberately involved recording on location when the film was not being shot. Birtwistle's description is also somewhat misleading, since direct sound commonly involves technologies designed to focus on the desired sounds and reduce the pickup of ambience, such as shotgun and lavalier (tie clip) mics.

REFERENCES

Alderson, P. and Morrow, V. 2011. *The Ethics of Research With Children and Young People: A Practical Handbook*. London: Sage.

Altman, R. 1992. *Sound Theory, Sound Practice*. New York: Routledge.

Altman, R. 2004. *Silent Film Sound*. New York: Columbia University Press.

Anderson, M. J. 2007. New film: *Ten Skies. Tativille: A Place for Cinema & the Visual Arts*. Blogger, 24 February. Available at: http://tativille.blogspot.co.uk/2007/02/new-film-ten-skies.html

Beck, J. and Grajeda, T. 2008. *Lowering the Boom: Critical Studies in Film Sound*. Urbana: University of Illinois Press.

Birtwistle, A. 2010. *Cinesonica: Sounding Film and Video,* Manchester: Manchester University Press.

Brown, J. and Davison, A. 2013. *The Sounds of the Silents in Britain*. New York: Oxford University Press.

Chion, M. 1994. *Audio-Vision: Sound on Screen*. New York: Columbia University Press.

Chion, M. 2003. The silence of the loudspeakers, or why with dolby sound it is the film that listens to us. In Sider, L., Freeman, D. and Sider, J. (eds.) *Soundscape: the School of Sound Lectures 1998–2001*. London: Wallflower, 150–154.

Chion, M. 2009. *Film, a Sound Art*. New York: Columbia University Press.

Cox, C. 2011. Beyond representation and signification: toward a sonic materialism. *Journal of Visual Culture,* 10: 145–161.

Cubitt, S. 2002. Visual and audiovisual: from image to moving image. *Journal of Visual Culture,* 1: 359–368.

David, M., Edwards, R. and Alldred, P. 2001. Children and school-based research: 'informed consent' or 'educated consent'? *British Educational Research Journal,* 27: 347–365.

DPA. 2013. *4071 Omnidirectional, Low-cut, Presence Boost*. Available at: http://www.dpamicrophones.com/en/products.aspx?c=Item&category=139&item=24057

Ernst, W. 2013. *Digital Memory and the Archive,* Minneapolis: University of Minnesota Press.

Gallagher, M. 2010. Are schools panoptic? *Surveillance and Society,* 7: 262–272.

Gallagher, M. 2011. Sound, space and power in a primary school. *Social & Cultural Geography,* 12: 47–61.

Gallagher, M., Haywood, S. L., Jones, M. W. and Milne, S. 2010. Negotiating informed consent with children in school-based research: A Critical Review. *Children & Society,* 24: 471–482.

Gallagher, M. and Prior, J. 2014. Sonic geographies: exploring phonographic methods. *Progress in Human Geography,* 38(2): 267–284.

Geertz, C. 1975. *The Interpretation of Cultures: Selected Essays*. London: Hutchinson.

Ingold, T. 2007. Against soundscape. In Carlyle, A. (ed.) *Autumn Leaves: Sound and the Environment in Artistic Practice*. Paris: Double Entendre, 10–13.

Kelman, A. Y. 2010. Rethinking the soundscape: a critical genealogy of a key term in sound studies. *The Senses and Society,* 5: 212–234.

Koutsomichalis, M. 2013. On soundscapes, phonograpy, and environmental sound art. *Journal of Sonic Studies,* 4. Available at: http://journal.sonicstudies.org/vol04/nr01/a05

LaBelle, B. 2006. *Background Noise: Perspectives on Sound Art*. London: Continuum.

Laurier, E., Strebel, I. and Brown, B. 2008. Video analysis: lessons from professional video editing practice. *Forum: Qualitative Social Research,* 9(3). Available at: http://www.qualitative-research.net/index.php/fqs/article/view/1168/2579

Levack Drever, J. 1999. The exploitation of 'tangible ghosts': conjectures on sound-scape recording and its reappropriation in sound art. *Organised Sound,* 4: 25–29

Levack Drever, J. 2002. Soundscape composition: the convergence of ethnography and acousmatic music. *Organised Sound,* 7: 21–27.

Lopez, F. 2004. Profound listening and environmental sound matter. In Cox, C. and Warner, D. (eds.) *Audio Culture: Readings in Modern Music.* New York: Continuum, 82–87.

Mauer, B. 2008. Asynchronous documentary: Bunuel's *Land without Bread.* In Beck, J. and Grajeda, T. (eds.) *Lowering the Boom: Critical Studies in Film Sound.* Urbana: University of Illinois Press, 141–151.

Pink, S. 2009. *Doing Sensory Ethnography.* London: SAGE.

Sterne, J. 2006. The mp3 as cultural artifact. *New Media & Society,* 8: 825–842.

Sterne, J. 2012. *Mp3: The Meaning of a Format,* Durham: Duke University Press.

Tisdall, E.K.M., Davis, J. M. and Gallagher, M. 2009. *Researching With Children and Young People: Research Design, Methods, and Analysis.* London: Sage.

Toop, D. 2010. *Sinister Resonance: The Mediumship of the Listener.* London: Continuum.

Weis, E. and Belton, J. 1985. *Film Sound: Theory and Practice.* New York: Columbia University Press.

9 "Everything Is Going On at the Same Time"
The Place of Video in Social Research Installations

Britt Hatzius and Nina Wakeford

We do have a genuine sense of what's happening. You know, things become real to us. We've seen shootings and bombings. We've seen roads taped off. It does put you in touch with your city. . . . You really do get to feel it at a level the other people don't. They go to work. They go to the suburb. Work, the suburb, work, the suburb. And they watch the rest on the local news.

(Cycle courier R. interview, London)

Almost 8000 km separate the cities of London in the UK and Portland, Oregon, in the US. The former was the place we conducted our sociological research about cycling cultures, which included several experimental video works. The latter was the location in which we showed the outcome to corporate researchers, designers and engineers. The many distances between these two locations were of key significance in how the videos that we describe in this chapter were created, presented and viewed. At the most straightforward level, the difference in location (London streets versus Intel Research offices) and context (London cycle couriers and commuters versus mostly car-driving Intel Research employees) became central to this endeavour. For we set ourselves the challenge of not only simply showing empirical data analysis, but finding ways to *create an atmosphere* or environment within which conversations about empirical research and sociological representation could take place. We wanted the conversations to be informed by an encounter with the material that was in some way an experience in itself. What we describe in this chapter are the videos that resulted from an experimental 'installation' inside Intel Research.

The use of video to research and document the social world is now well established in sociology, and its diverse modes of capture and representation are elaborated in other chapters in this volume. Less well rehearsed are the ways in which we might innovate in how we present this time-based media, in particular through attempts to break out of the confines of the conference presentation and the journal article—that is if we want to go beyond videos which are narrated in illustrative mode or offered as screenings, or provide an alternative to moving image data being translated into still images for publication. By using the phrase time-based media here we wish to raise questions about all kinds of moving image and audio work. The videos we captured, recorded and edited were digital. Nevertheless we have also worked with 16 mm celluloid film, and there are many other formats which, although not seen as 'new' are still available, such as VHS tape cameras. The products of some software such as Flash, or other animation applications, can also be seen to unfold in time.[1] Despite the advent of online publications, such as the pioneering *Sociological Research Online* launched by the British Sociological Association, which allows multimedia to be embedded within articles, there is a curious lack of experimentation with the embedding of time-based media within sociological research's sites of presentation, whether on- or offline.

Sociologists, we suggest, rarely consider the spaces in which they communicate as having site-specificity, and yet it is clear that even in the most standard lecture theatre (let alone the worlds-apart space of a corporate 'cube farm' which we encountered at Intel Research) factors such as the size of the screen, the resolution of the projector, the quality of the speakers, and even the way in which people physically inhabit the space will all impact upon the ways in which the presented work unfolds and is experienced. Drawing on the promises of the capacity of installation as it is instantiated within installation art, we offer a description of, and reflection about, what happened when we took up the challenge of collecting and presenting video in an inventive manner. In other words we tried to address it *inventively* to the problem of researching cycling cultures, and suggest in so doing neither the visual method nor the problem remained unchanged (see Lury and Wakeford 2012).

The experiment described here attempted to embed digital video, collected as part of a research project on cycling cultures in London, in the offices of the sponsor of our research project: a high technology company's research organisation which had expressed an interest in knowing more about the co-constitution of mobility and temporality in urban settings. We conceived of this embedding as installation, influenced by the repertoire of installations that populate contemporary art and the capacities that they promise for foregrounding the generation of experience (Reiss 2001; Bishop 2006). We are not alone in beginning to consider installation as a practice that might be fruitful for the enactment of social science. Cultural geographers have begun to think about the capacity of installation art for the development of critical accounts of vision (Enigboken and Patchett 2012; Hawkins 2010). In a theoretical contribution, Harriet Hawkins has drawn on installation as an 'empirical object' which might offer a useful 'twining together of a spatial politics with an embodied visual politics' (Hawkins 2010, 323). A manifestation of an installation by geographers themselves was undertaken by two experimental practitioners who fashioned a mobile video installation that toured New York City in the back of a U-Haul truck (Enigboken and Patchett 2012).

Given that much contemporary artwork might be said to incorporate aspirations towards both a spatial and visual politics, a brief clarification of what we mean by installation art as a specific form of art practice is necessary. We hope that this will allow the reader a foil against which our contribution might be understood. We did not seek to fabricate a piece of installation art, but rather appropriate some of its conventions. Art historian Claire Bishop suggests that, at its most general, the term 'installation' should be used to describe art into which the viewer physically enters (2006). Bishop explains how we might distinguish installation art from previous forms:

> An installation of art is secondary in importance to the individual works it contains, while in a work of installation art, the space, and the ensemble of elements within it, are regarded in their entirety as a singular entity. Installation art creates a situation into which the viewer physically enters, and insists that you regard this as a singular totality.
>
> (Bishop 2006, 6)

We took from such a conception the idea of creating a *situation* through which the human body might move, and the need to pay attention to the precise choreography of objects and other elements, including the existing social and physical infrastructures. One illustration used by Bishop is Olafur Eliasson's work *The Weather Project* shown at Tate Modern in 2003–2004. This piece presented itself as an illusion of a sun setting inside Tate Modern's vast Turbine Hall. Artificial fog and a large backlit semicircular screen mounted along the back wall (and reflected in mirrors covering the entire ceiling) drowned the space in a misty yellow glow. Visitors would stroll aimlessly in this environment or spend time lying on the ground, staring up at themselves reflected in the mirror foil covering the ceiling. The monofrequency yellow light (usually used as street lighting) cancelled out any other colours. It emanated a calming glow on people entering the space. Dispersed as tiny black bodies throughout the space the visitor was confronted with an atmosphere within an otherwise empty space. Although the 'sun' was central to the composition, there was no focus on any particular element of the installation. Instead of looking at the space, visitors were enveloped by it.

The physical encounter with the space in which the work has been constructed is a resource that artists such as Eliasson expertly manipulate. However another way of characterising installation art proposes that it is, by definition, unfinished until entered by the spectator. In her history of installation art Julie Reiss suggests that "the spectator is in some way regarded as integral to the completion of the work" (Reiss 2001). This highlights the issue of the participation of the audience. Our study also hoped for participation, although in our case it was participation in the output of research. What was of particular interest to us was the promise of installation in terms of the phenomenological staging of experience rather than the achievement of completion or totality. We were concerned to create some kind of incitement at Intel Research that took into account the everyday environment of the office, and to stimulate an embodied participation that opened up questions about the research in the minds of the audience.

Art installations often contain a multiplicity of objects, and the video we collected sat alongside other kinds of representational and performative or 'more-than-representational' forms (Lorimer 2005). In art installations this strategy of enacting multiplicity has been associated with a destabilising of the viewer. Hawkins documents the density of objects, and vast array of scenes, sounds and micro-dramas in the installations of Tomoko Takahashi, an installation artist who is known for creating sprawling environments out of thousands of everyday objects (Hawkins 2010). She suggests that the installations made by Takahashi can hold together elements in a way that offer multiple ways of viewing. After encountering Takahashi's installation *Myplaystation2@serpentine2005* at London's Serpentine Gallery, she writes:

> The scale and internal complexity of the installation, thousands of objects laid out, confounds the ability to them in with a gaze, no matter how steady. Overview is disavowed, I do not—or rather cannot—take in this densely detailed world all at once. Instead I consume the work through a succession of movements: the shift of the feet, the flick of an eye, the twist of waist, the shift of weight and the turn of a head. To experience the installation is to become aware of that experience as one of active and drawn out exploration. . . . The position of the stable, sedentary and autonomous subject was not one the installation allowed me to occupy.
>
> (Hawkins 2010, 327)

The emphasis on performance, process, sensation and experience that installation art might offer resonates with the discussions of mess and multiplicity in recent writings about sociological methods (Law and Urry 2004). Even though our installation was far more modest in terms of accumulated 'stuff' than the thousands of objects marshalled by Takahashi, Hawkins reflections of the experience of being 'immersed' in the installation, of being corralled into an 'exploration', and in particular the account of the difficulty of a stable overview resonate with the strategies drawn from installation art which we attempted to use in constructing our intervention at Intel Research. Although we stress the role of video within the wider project, we want to reiterate here what is made evident in Hawkins' account: that installation necessitates a succession of embodied movements in space (rather than just immersion in the content of the moving image) and that participation involves the creation of subjects, which for us included our interaction corporate researchers, engineers and designers, rather than art audiences.

Video in our project was not used to elicit responses from our research participants, nor, as will become clear below, could we keep up with many of the cyclists to document their trips as participant observers. For us video was an element in a larger set of empirical materials and media, used as a tool with which to communicate our research process to those outside and distant from it, as well as a material that provided matter with which to experiment in the fieldwork. The challenge of presenting our research findings as an installation (rather than a written report) was our guide in designing and editing the audiovisual material. In this sense video became a *different sociological material* from video recordings that aim to help participants themselves better articulate their experiences (e.g. Merchant 2011; Spinney 2011). Furthermore we treated this video data as generating different kinds of *material properties*. Our interest was on the moment of 'output' that allowed event-based elements of surprise and unfolding. To do this we conducted a series of video experiments with our research participants to find a way to express specific experiences of temporality and mobility within London urban cycling cultures to an audience at Intel Research, and simultaneously we explored the capacity for empirical research to create and engage a kind of temporary public for sociology.

TEMPORALITIES IN THE CITY: A STUDY OF CYCLISTS IN LONDON

In common with many innovation-focused computer and technology companies, Intel Corporation has a long-standing interest in speed and capacity—not only of the computer chips that they manufacture, but also of the user. Just like other technology-focused organisations, Intel Research, a cluster of research and development projects within the larger Intel Corporation, was involved in fabricating ideas of the 'future user' (c.f. Michael and Wilkie 2009). In 2006, when the themes of this research were being discussed with the company's internal social research team *People And Practices Research* (PAPR)—a group of anthropologists, cultural theorists, psychologists and designers—a dominant narrative within the company involved the need to address the demands of ubiquitous computing, one of which was getting 'live' information to consumers (often discursively constructed as 'businessmen') as they moved around urban locations. The PAPR group from Intel Research approached us with a more provocative proposition. They wondered if a study of cycle couriers would be able to provide an interesting case study of meeting deadlines and an obsession with speed which would address, and perhaps disrupt, the assumptions of ubiquitous computing, while also testing out what might be done with visual sociology, an approach which was not used in their repertoire of research strategies.

The university and corporate researchers negotiated a short pilot project that expanded from this initial focus to investigate both cycle couriers and cycle commuters in central London over a one-month period. Fieldwork was conducted using several visual experiments to attempt to capture the lived experience of both groups. As well as video, these experiments included drawing, still photography and sound. Interviews were carried out with five couriers, five commuters and two 'controllers' (the cycle courier dispatchers). Some of these materials were generated collaboratively with two Intel researchers, and the project was supported by other university-based researchers who brought in perspectives from cultural theory and urban studies to data analysis sessions both at Goldsmiths, University of London, and in a workshop at the corporate headquarters of Intel Research in Portland.[2] Despite the short time span the project generated an extensive set of video experiments which could be integrated alongside other artefacts from the drawings, interviews and sound recordings into an intervention at Intel Research. As might have been expected from the way in which the project was set up—and its modest budget—the most significant implications for sociological work lie with the methodological innovation rather than the capacity to provide an expansive account of these two cycling cultures that could have been expected from an extensive study. Nevertheless before discussing how the video experiments unfolded, it is useful to summarise what we began to see as emerging in our analysis.

The central finding of this small scale investigation was that, far from focusing on deadlines and speed, both couriers and commuters experience the time of their urban mobility as a temporality of flows and unfolding sensory engagements (see also Jungnickel, this volume). This became clear in the very first interviews, and was corroborated as we progressed through the fieldwork. The couriers, whose work lives appeared from the outside to be governed by a series of races against the clock, understood their circulation around the city not in terms of pick-ups and drop-offs but rather as continual flows of sensory juggling. Paying attention to the words of interviewees reveals the extent to which the experience of movement through the city for these cyclists was a practice of alertness and attunement (as well as forms of narrating such practices), and it forced us to consider how we might create experimental video forms and installation strategies that would somehow speak to these experiences. In order to generate our materials, we did not go out and shoot hours of unplanned video footage to come back and then edit it. Instead we created 'frames' or 'frameworks', a set of constraints for the recording of video that was informed by the research (interviews, conversations, observations):

> We are calculating a thousand things, whether it's the angle of the light, the surface of the road, the hatch covers, whether it's raining, wet or dry, how much weight we've got on our back, everything is all going on at the same time.
>
> (Cycle courier R. interview, London)

> Most of us are in tune with the year. We have to be. We know when we're going to earn the most, when the weather is going to be hardest. What

kind of weather is coming. We know what it's like to ride in unspeakable heat. We also know what it's like to ride in unspeakable cold, you know?
(Cycle courier R. interview, London)

As well as this idea of attunement, we had to consider how digital video itself would tackle the investigation of temporality that defined the project. The idea of time which pervaded the accounts given by interviewees was not that of clock time—this would have been neatly translatable to Intel engineers, and relatively easy for the technology-centric design imagination—but one which was responsive in a much more complex way to the urban environment. The experience of speed, even for commuters, could not be captured by clock time, but rather was a tuning in to the body. For example

> You measure your speed not with a stopwatch but by your willingness to push yourself, willingness to accelerate, to invest—it's your own choice.
> (Cycle commuter F. interview, London)

> Some days you feel you are going so slow. You know you are slow but you don't feel like pushing. You get to a junction, you see the lights are turning and you know you are not going to make it through in time.
> (Cycle commuter F. interview, London)

Furthermore the experience of time could not be untangled from the physical infrastructure of streets, cars, traffic lights and pedestrians that had to be negotiated. The urban infrastructure might even be understood as a virtual gaming environment, as in the words of this courier:

> The city is a maze system. We are channelled down these tunnels, like a lab rat and things fly out at you. Different kinds of monsters, things shooting fire. It's like a video game.
> (Cycle courier R. interview, London)

The words of our interviewees are consistent with other recent work that suggests cycling involves multi-sensory work (Jungnickel, this volume; Spinney 2011), but also revealed some specificities tied to the specific cycling cultures we had investigated. For couriers this also involved interactions with their controllers. Even this interaction could be often experienced both as an unfolding flow and as a stop-start set of instructions. For example, during quiet times one controller, himself an ex-courier, regularly read out poetry into the microphone that broadcast to all couriers. The couriers could tune in to a steady soundtrack of his voice rather than a staccato set of instructions and silences.

An experiment in which we asked one of the couriers to take a photograph of his bike every time he left it to deliver a package emerged from the observation that being a courier is not, in fact, necessarily about riding your bike, but about stops and starts within a flow. The daily routine of a courier includes that of waiting: waiting for a call from the controller, waiting for the porter to open the door, for the papers to be signed, for the lift to arrive or for the package to be fetched. The experience of flow, which couriers would speak about—the intensity, the risk—is only one component, broken up by pauses, stops and waiting. With these still images, in succession, we get a sense of the couriers' rhythm.

For commuters, the daily journeys to and from work have a clear beginning and end. One of the commuters we interviewed spoke about two journeys to work, one on a good day and another on a bad day. The first he said felt 'whole' and 'in one go'. Well slept, he enjoyed the ride and guessed it took him 25 minutes (in fact the time was 26 minutes 30 seconds). The second time, he struggled with a hangover and felt as if the ride was 'broken up into many journeys'. This time he guessed 35 minutes (exact time 27 minutes 30 seconds). The difference in these two experiences shows how his sense of time was very much dependent on how he felt, his own fluctuating physical and mental state. Ultimately though it was not important to him whether the journey was a few minutes longer or shorter, what mattered was his personal experience of riding.

> When I don't take the bicycle and I have to take the bus and you just stand there. That is really when I'm bored. It [bike riding] is totally different every time around and it is different than the bus.
>
> (Cycle commuter D. interview, London)

Commuters spoke about the shift in temporal experience when arriving or departing the office, that "everything seemed to be in slow motion" (Commuter F.) when getting off the bike.

> I love the first few minutes when leaving work, or anywhere. It's a way to relax, relieve your brain. From a place where you are sitting in an office, writing reports, solving problems, complex thought patterns, to an activity where you just have to pedal, feel the air.
>
> (Cycle commuter F. interview, London)

It was in the context of these emerging discoveries that we began to experiment with the collection of video materials. However studying mobile actors in such immersive environments, as other sociologists have commented, is not always straightforward.

EXPERIMENTS GENERATING VIDEO MATERIALS

In her attempts to use video to document how scuba divers come to terms with their surroundings, Stephanie Merchant (2011) points out that from early on in her fieldwork it was clear that the pace and place of traditional qualitative methodologies would need to be adapted to her chosen site. As she points out "underwater communication is limited at best". Attempting to follow cyclists through London also posed challenges, albeit that our immersive environment was not water but the city of London. At first we spent days immersed in the courier's daily cycling routines of stopping and starting, a physical rhythm dictated by 'runs' coordinated by the controller and communicated to them via mobile radio devices. Although on bikes ourselves, it became clear after a few attempts that most encounters would be limited to the resting moments, and placing ourselves at the points throughout the city where couriers break, and wait. In these locations we asked couriers to empty their bags and we took still photos of the contents. However in terms of generating moving images which also might enact their sensory sensations of cycling we found it impossible to follow a courier's way of weaving precariously through the city on a bike.

This view from behind, watching cyclists from an increasing distance as we failed to keep up, was clearly insufficient (although it might have provided some material about the incapacities of urban social researchers). We, the observer, the viewer, the camera, had to be there, with them. In common with Justin Spinney, in his study on urban cyclists, we realised that the camera had to travel with the cyclist, finding a way of 'feeling there' without actually being there (Spinney 2011). Our request that cyclists carry a camera on their body was declined on our first few attempts—too heavy, too bulky, too cumbersome for the required freedom to move with flexibility—and we had to develop other strategies.

Video experiment 1: The compromise was to attach the smallest possible video camera to the bicycle itself. We should point out that this was before the widespread availability of the GoPro camera (Brown et al. 2008). Instead, a small homemade polystyrene case fastened with Velcro to the handlebars allowed for safety and ease of attachment and detachment. We deployed this ad-hoc camera-case construction with both couriers and commuters. The resulting video footage included sound, and showed the precarity of cycling that both groups had described in interviews. Statements such as 'everything is going on at the same time' achieved a legibility in the moving image. With a view forward, somewhere between eye- and ground-level, the video footage captured the speed and risk-taking involved in weaving through cars, pedestrians, across humps, curbs and up and down narrow streets. The sound amplified the sense of an intensely visceral experience: exposed to the weather, to the obstacles on the road and to one's own bodily exhilaration and/or exhaustion. Besides the familiar city soundscape of bike wheels on tarmac, cars honking and people shouting, we hear the courier puffing, panting and speaking to his controller via radio, or a commuter occasionally humming, singing or swearing. All of this added up to footage that showed the vividness—the multidimensional sensoriness—of the experience. In choosing this particular camera position the recording resulted in a viewing experience resembling that of a first person video game.

Video experiment 2: Following this initial exercise, we became more ambitious in our use of these devices for the collection of video. What would happen if we attempted to generate moving images that captured the different kinds of temporalities that seemed to occur simultaneously? We asked one of the commuters to ride on his daily trip with an expanded device attached to his bike. In the interview this individual had described how much he appreciated the bodily sensation of being on the bike, and how, after a day at work of writing reports and solving problems, he loves getting on his bike, focusing on the act of cycling and "just pedal, pedal, feel the air, feel one's body". In the interview he spoke of how the concentration required from him in moving across the city would vary. He talked of 'zones', some of which allowed for a fluid, continuous, 'moving through' cycling experience, others demanding more concentration and alertness. Yet he was still having to navigate the infrastructure of London streets—often inhospitable to cyclists. Attempting to capture more than one perspective, we constructed a second polystyrene box with a second camera and pointed it upward from the handlebars at the cyclist himself. The intention was to try and capture the movements and gestures performed by this commuter, movements that are very much embodied. We wanted to allow the video to capture the sensations of cycling as a commuter as well as what might not be expressible in words.

When synchronised using the same timecode, the two moving images generate the uncanny sensation that the time of the footage is both synchronous, and reveals two very different flows of encounters. Watching his face look from left to right, often in a repeated movement, clearly shows the embodied reflexes, his facial expressions revealing the effort and attentiveness required in dealing with the many stimuli around him: traffic, puddles, pavements, junctions and obstacles, including pedestrians. Recording his journey with two cameras simultaneously—one attached to the front handle bars, the other pointing up towards his face—gave us two different perspectives of the same experience. We chose two peripheral perspectives: one at bike-level of the street in front, the other looking up at the cyclist's face. In the resulting footage we hear the wheels of the bike turning, we hear the cyclist's body moving, but we cannot see either. The bodily experience is hence only alluded to, not depicted in its totality. Unlike much of visual sociology's use of the moving image, there was no human behind the camera to reframe or refocus once these experiments had been set up. After the camera was attached, turned on and filming, there was no other intervening in the choice of angle or position. The framing was not guided by a constantly monitoring viewer/filmmaker, but rather it was the result of the movement of the bike to which the camera was attached. There was a sense of automation in how we approached the use of video, in contrast to a classic ethnographic filming of events. The intention was to 'see what the bike sees', and not what the rider or the researcher sees. In focusing on the bicycle as a 'point of view', there was no single subject as author of the footage.

When looking back at the footage, the video became accessible as an object's point of view, rather than a person's single perspective.

Video experiment 3: Our polystyrene cases allowed us to continue a series of experiments that expanded the set of visual materials generated for the installation. As already mentioned, talking to both commuters and couriers it became clear that their sense of time when cycling was often talked about through a language of mood, energy or inner drive. We wanted to try and reflect this distinction between clock and felt time in the material—to try to make it visible through the material that we could configure in the installation. On one commuter's journey to work, we again strapped a camera to the handlebars of his bike and asked him to take a photograph every time he thought one minute had passed. The camera we used was able to record both video footage and photographs. What we ended up with was one continuous video clip and numerous still images. In the edit we then aligned the still images with the video clip, positioning the images within the timeline at their correct points in the video. To juxtapose this 'felt time' with clock-time, we included an indicator showing each 'actual' minute passing—based on the video timecode.

Video experiment 4: Spending time in the controller's office gave us another perspective on the sensory temporalities of urban mobility, and another strategy for creating audiovisual material which would inform both the analysis and the installation. Immediately striking in this office environment was the high noise level, which was just as intense as the courier's sonorous environment out on the street, but of a very different nature: doorbells and phones ringing, people speaking, laughing, joking, shouting, calling, fingers tapping on computer keyboards and couriers' voices dropping in and out of the mix. Equipped with a video camera, the temptation is often to 'film everything', and we could have pointed the camera at all the different activities going on in this small room, in the hope to 'capture' it all. Instead we wanted to make an analytic decision about what the essential connection was between this environment and the couriers riding out in the streets. In the initial data analysis sessions we noted the radical difference between the temporal experience of the cyclist out in the streets, and that of the controller, sat in front of his computer screen, receiving orders by email or phone, giving orders via radio mics to his 'riders'. He, the controller, was in fact the one choreographing the cyclist's time. Back in the controller's office, the task was then to find and focus our attention on where exactly this temporal shift lay between the controller 'in here' who determines the courier's cycling rhythm, and the riding experience 'out there'. We found these to be two specific things: the vocal exchange between controller and courier over the phone—an often humorous, entertaining and motivating speech (including the occasional poem)—and the map which the courier needed in order to fully understand and visualise the courier's 'moves'. As a consequence we recorded the sound of the controller speaking into the phone, and the image of the map. Tracking the moves of the couriers dotted across London, the controller had each courier represented by a small magnet, which he repositioned after each drop off or pick up. This decision of recording only these two elements in the room was a way to filter out all the other activities going on in that space.

INSIDE INTEL

As we undertook these video experiments, we were mindful that the procedure of gathering and displaying information about 'the user' using moving images was not a novel approach for Intel Research. In fact, there already existed representational conventions against which our productions might be measured, often involving the presentation of PowerPoint in meeting rooms. The use of visual images—both moving and still—to invoke the social world has an extended history within technology companies, albeit one which tends to provoke an ambivalent or anxious reaction amongst many anthropologically or social scientifically-trained corporate researchers who are expected to communicate their findings to internal audiences using such representations (Wakeford 2006; Nafus and Anderson 2009). Nevertheless, there is a widespread belief that providing visual materials to designers and engineers is more persuasive than words alone. There is an impulse to persuade the audience to sense that the researcher has really 'been there' (Wakeford 2006). Certain kinds of video recording appear to fulfil this function. Two researchers with the technology industry report:

> Key decision makers who many resist acting on expressed insight if it conflicts with their own perception may be easier to persuade with the aid of such visual accounts.
>
> (Rosenthal and Capper 2006, 235)

Video recording of users, or settings of potential future devices, has been advocated as an ideal method to serve 'design ethnography' due to the generativity and malleability of the representations of the world which result (Buur 2007). Amongst corporate research groups video is regularly used to document in-home interviews or in the process of shadowing participants. Cameras are offered to participants as a means by which they can create their own representations of their behaviour, guided by research questions (Wasson 2000). Yet, when they are finally presented to their audience of designers or engineers, the visual forms which circulate in such settings often end up collapsing into a very narrow set of representational forms, and in this form have often lost any sensation of malleability or contingency. Often video is only experienced by the audience through a set of PowerPoint slides which come to function as the final output, and make much of the ethnographically inspired work undertaken invisibly 'behind the scenes' (Wakeford 2006). PowerPoint in many industry contexts has become the singular object of value, to be redistributed via email through the organisation, although not without the discomfort of researchers who see photos and video clips circulating without the necessary contextualisation of the studies (Nafus and Anderson 2009).

In this context, our attempt to use video as one element of an installation was highly unconventional. We had to try to understand how the space at Intel Research already functioned, as well as the ways in which the installation might operate to reinforce and even accentuate the distances between London and Portland, academic research and industry strategy, user behaviour and engineering imaginaries. Ken Anderson and Dawn Nafus, both Intel researchers involved in our project, have written about what they perceive as the dangers of specific representational conventions within corporate research given the pervasive atmosphere (and décor) of the interior of corporate research labs. Project rooms festooned with photographs of fieldwork can become sites of a problematic form of enchantment rather than reflexive engagement with modes of representing the social.

> To people who spend the majority of their waking hours in uniformly sized gray cubicles, the photographs also enchant in roughly the same way as fleeting glimpses out the window to the outside world do. Viewing them is not so much a replication of some experience "out there" as the promise of new possibilities "in here". The "facts" that they capture, such as the presence of commerce on the street or the practices of putting out the trash, are in a sense less important than how they perform the "outsideness" of the world.
>
> (Nafus and Anderson 2009)

Attempting to highlight the potential problem with the representational conventions (both in corporate research *and* in mainstream visual sociology), we titled our installation *Now You See It, Now You Don't*. Our performance of 'outsideness' was intended to occupy the everyday spaces of the grey cubicles rather than a separate project room. In order to create this site-specific work within what one Intel employee called the 'grey cube farm' office environment of our interlocutors, we sought to understand the existing spatial and temporal atmosphere of the corporate culture, including the architecture, and incorporate this knowledge into how the video was presented using strategies of multiplicity and juxtaposition. We later read the experimental video installation undertaken by Enigboken and Patchett and found their hopes very much in tune with what we had hoped to do, albeit in a corporate office rather than in a mobile truck.

> Creating spaces of encounter with "unseen" elements of urban experience allows for opportunities in which participants might reconsider their own ways of thinking and moving in the city, and thereby become urban researchers themselves
>
> (Enigboken and Patchett 2012, 544).

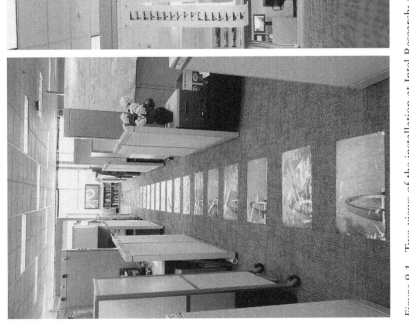

Figure 9.1 Two views of the installation at Intel Research: printed still frames taken from video laid out on the ground (left) and life-size photographic prints of a London bus (right). Image: Britt Hatzius.

Next, we describe the installation as a whole and then focus on the ways in which the videos were intended to function within it. The installation included 12 elements in total, installed within one part (approximately 10 square metres) of an open plan office space. The most obstructive elements were a number of single frames laid out as prints on the ground, and two life-size photographic prints hung adjacent to each other (Figure 9.1). The first were stills taken with a digital camera mounted to a bicycle, partially showing its wheel and the changing texture of the road surface. It was an attempt at creating a sense of rhythm by walking along the corridor, and suggesting that the office cubicles to the left and right might generate similar distractions, obstacles and interruptions to those faced by a cyclist riding in a city such as London. The two large prints depicted the side of a London bus. Hung very close to each other, they echoed a cyclist's experience of squeezing through gaps between cars and buses on busy roads. A third, more subtle but similarly disrupting, element was six life-size laminated photographic prints mounted onto moveable tables. These remained part of the familiar office furniture and continued to be used as work surfaces. The photographs showed contents of courier's bags, giving an insight into courier's daily habits (what kinds of snacks they carried) and individual attitudes towards their mobility (whether they carried rain clothes, maps, phones, passport), independence (bike fixing tools) and revealed other individual interests (books, notebooks or other personal items).

Besides several London maps showing the various different 'zones' commuters spoke about on their journeys to and from work, we installed large white sheets of paper with drawings of social network circles gathered from each interviewee, hung one behind the other. Besides these, we installed two large drawings made by one of the commuters and one of the couriers of their daily bike rides across town. Loosely attached to the ceiling, they were accompanied by a series of small photographs taken of the commuter engaged in the actual process of drawing the map (a number of single frames taken from a video animation). While the courier's map showed lines crisscrossing the page in a complex web of arrows and annotations (reflecting his remark during an interview of "riding as a way of life"), the commuter's map was a single line stretched across the sheet of paper with numerous marks indicating the different 'zones' he had spoken about during our conversations. The most conventional display within the installation consisted of a collection of 18 photographic prints hung at eye height along one of the office cubicle frames. Taken by one of the couriers using a small disposable camera, they showed the various different locations in which he had photographed his bike on every pick-up/drop-off during one day.

It was important to us that all elements of the installation could be easily taken down, fixed temporarily, that nothing might give the impression of any definite conclusion and that everything stood in an open relation to each other. Several quotes, which we had selected from interviews, were mounted onto the windows surrounding the space as delicate letters seemingly hanging in mid-air, underlining the ephemeral quality of the spoken word (Figure 9.2).

"IT'S LIKE A VIDEO GAME. THERE ARE THE MONSTERS THAT JUMP OUT AND THE ONES THAT SHOOT.
[..]
YOU'VE GOT TO OVERCOME THE MONSTERS."
"WHATEVER IS OUT THERE WE SEE IT. THINGS BECOME REAL TO US ON A VERY VIVID LEVE

Figure 9.2 Above: Quotes mounted onto windows. Below: Double screen video of commuter's journey to work on monitor (left) and a section of video recorded of courier's ride across London on monitor (right). Image: Britt Hatzius.

Referring to the central themes of the research, they described the acute awareness, the risk and the sense of flow experienced while navigating London city streets.

For reasons of brevity, the following exposition focuses on the decisions we made in constructing and installing the second and fourth video experiments. The second experiment involved creating the footage from two video cameras simultaneously. The fourth experiment generated video footage of the controllers.

Installing Video Experiment 2

The two video recordings of the commuters' journey into work were presented as a double screen video (Figure 9.2). As in all the footage, the material was shown without 'cuts', which gave the viewer the time to settle into the footage. The act of viewing demanded attention and effort from the viewer. Showing the two different sets of footage alongside each other in a double-screen edit added a sense of space to the flat images, two viewpoints of the same place in time. As an experience, watching the two demanded a constant mental readjustment to include both perspectives. The need to imagine the space in between the two cameras required a different engagement with the footage. What was left unseen required the viewers' own input. With eyes moving from one image to the other in a constant state of distraction, it seemed to be able to reproduce the cyclists' perpetual need for an acute awareness of his/her environment. This selective framing and double-screen edit might also reflect the cyclist's descriptions of peripheral vision or bodily sensations—of cars passing, "noticing a pedestrian out of the corner of your eye", or "thinking about the drops down your back, your shoes, your squinting eyes".

Installing Video Experiment 4

In preparation for the installation, the video and sound material gathered from one of the bike courier's offices went through a second stage of decision making. Instead of showing the video footage itself, as 'raw footage', we chose only stills from the video and presented them alongside the sound recording of the controller's voice (Figure 9.3). We realised that it would not make sense to show the video as a moving image as it would give a false illusion of movement and timing. The small magnets did not in fact move with the couriers' movements in real time, but were repositioned by the controller according to his own sense of timing. Contrasting with the listing of jobs he had to allocate to the individual riders, the map gave him the necessary overview at all times. The single frames (taken every 10 seconds) were printed out and loosely hung in a grid, evoking a sense of animated moving image, but maintaining the physicality of the map. This part of the installation was accompanied by a soundtrack listened to on headphones. A

Figure 9.3 Loosely attached printed video stills of controllers map. The small dots are magnets representing the individual riders that make up the 'fleet' of couriers. Image: Britt Hatzius.

short extract from recordings made at the bike courier company's offices, presented a mixture of the controller communicating with the individual riders via radio signal, bits of conversations amongst controllers in the room, waiting couriers and visitors entering and exiting the office space. Together, the two elements gave an impression of the complex time keeping, calculation and negotiation occurring in this central hub, which allowed for the various flows experienced by the individual couriers.

The emphasis on experimentation in this process of creating an installation (as a crucial 'outcome' of the research project itself) allowed us to try various different forms of presentation and display. It offered an opportunity to really 'try things out' and there was a sense that anything beyond photographic prints would be likely to create a disruption in the space. Besides large whiteboards and a seating area with several large tables there were no walls to hang from or dedicated space to show in. The challenge hence was also to 'make do' with what we found, to integrate and interfere at the same time. In this sense, the more we physically disrupted the space (for example, two life-size prints of a London bus blocking a passage way between two office cubicles), the more effective was the intervention. Using existing windows and tables as display surfaces (quotes on windows and photographic laminates on tables) meant that there was a subtle but persistent interference into the researcher's daily routines. Central to this disruption were the various different elements of the installation, the fact that there was not one, but many forms of display.

However, although the video experiments were effective in their use of editing techniques, we felt they could not hold the necessary impact within the installation itself. We had a limited choice of high-end monitors, and did not manage to negotiate an adequate surface to put them on—not least in terms of the internal arrangements of the space. Framed by large open windows, the space was so bright that the monitors themselves almost attracted more attention than the actual video playing on them. We concluded that the whole installation needed more tools, time and thought put into the viewing set up for it to succeed. A small monitor installed in each office cubicle for example, which would have been visible as one walked up and down the rows of cubes but which was *also* available for private viewing, might have been more interesting. We also regretted not investigating if one of the storage cupboards or corners could have been turned into a small, darkened, cinematic space with a projection and screen.

In terms of thinking through how sociology might be presented through installation, it became evident to us that to present video material within such a site-specific context needs more than simply pressing play on a TV or computer monitor. Would separating sound and image for example (single frames taken from the controllers map and hung alongside an audio recording of controller speaking; Figure 9.3) have had a stronger impact than two monitors stood on a filing cabinet (Figure 9.2)? Or would single frames taken from a video printed and laid out along one of the corridors

(Figure 9.1) have attracted more attention? Or would this simply be taken as a decorative addition to the layout? Was the installation indeed able to contribute to a discussion, beyond being 'a snare or a trap' in the manner suggested by anthropologist Alfred Gell (1999)?

CONCLUSION

An installation approach to video has no more capacity than any other form to stand alone as a 'summing up' of the research project. However we propose that, in combination with other (photographic/sound) elements, it might function as a useful trigger in reflecting on key research questions and resulting arguments.

Nevertheless we should make a final point about its longevity, the fact that this particular installation was always only meant to exist for a few weeks. It was part of a series of discussions and presentations in a workshop-type atmosphere. The focus on process and experimentation was hence built into the set-up itself and informed the way the installation was read. The question remains how effective it was beyond its momentary existence within an actively discursive environment of a four-day intensive workshop. As it was only on display for a short time it was also difficult to gage the reaction from the Intel researchers, designers and engineers who experienced it at the time.

> Sights and sites are memory places that may continue to work on us long after our first—in this case, our only—glimpse of them. And in fact I think that Christo's Gates will continue to resonate for some time to come, if only because their very elusiveness and vagueness will elicit a continued filling in by the imagination, an interpolation of meaning, and a long incubation of images in memory and the photographic record.
>
> (Mitchell 2006, 4)

In February 2005 the artist duo known as Christo and Jeanne-Claude set up over 7,000 'gates' of orange-brown nylon along 23 miles of the paths in New York's Central Park. In his commentary on this site-specific installation, the art historian W. J. T. Mitchell argues that the elusive and vague nature of this work will partly be enacted through the ongoing circulation of the photographic documentation—this extends the time during which we might remember the installation itself.

Mitchell's article speaks to *Now You See It, Now You Don't* in two ways. First, it was an article that we shared amongst collaborators at Intel in the period between the London fieldwork and the Portland installation. Situated in public space, the 'gates' staged an invitation to experience walking through a freshly annotated Central Park. Mitchell's article is a reminder of how we might think through the capacities of an open and ambiguous work that nevertheless had effects on the viewer. Second, Mitchell's article is a reminder about the force of documentation in relation to extending the time of an artwork. This has a more poignant resonance for this project. As far as we know, we were the only ones to take documentation of the installation, suggesting that the installation could not work on our audience at Intel Research without the event of the workshop and analysis session that accompanied its completion.

NOTES

1. The conservation department of the Tate includes under their time-based media remit "artworks that use video, film, audio, 35 mm slide and computer-based technologies". The dependence on technology of many of these artworks is highlighted (see http://www.tate.org.uk/about/our-work/conservation/time-based-media).
2. Dawn Nafus and Ken Anderson from PAPR visited London to participate in the gathering and analysis of the data. At Goldsmiths we thank Celia Lury, Les Back, and Alison Rooke for their contributions to the organisation and realisation of the project.

REFERENCES

Bishop C. (ed.) 2006. *Participation*. London: Whitechapel Art Gallery.

Brown, K. M., Dilley, R. and Marshall, K. 2008. Using a head-mounted video camera to understand social worlds and experiences. *Sociological Research Online*, 13(6). www.socresonline.org.uk/13/6/1/1.pdf

Buur, J. 2007. *Designing with Video: Focusing the User-Centred Design Process*. London: Springer.

Enigboken, E. and Patchett, M. 2012. Speaking with spectres: experimental geographies in practice. *Cultural Geographies*, 19(4): 535–546.

Gell, A. 1999. Vogel's net: traps as artworks and artworks as traps. In Hirsch, E. (ed) *The Art of Anthropology: Essays and Diagrams*. London: Berg Publishers.

Hawkins, H. 2010. 'The argument of the eye'? The cultural geographies of installation art. *Cultural Geographies*, 17(3): 321–340.

Law, J. and Urry, J. 2004. Enacting the social. *Economy and Society*, 33(3): 390–410.

Lorimer, H. 2005. Cultural geography: the busyness of being 'more-than-representational'. *Progress in Human Geography*, 29(1): 83–94.

Lury, C. and Wakeford, N. (eds.) 2012. *Inventive Methods: Happenings of the Social*, London: Routledge.

Merchant, S. 2011. The body and the senses: visual methods, videography and the submarine sensorium. *Body & Society*, 17: 53–72.

Michael, M. and Wilkie, A. 2009. Expectation and mobilisation: enacting future users. *Science, Technology and Human Values*, 34(4): 502–522.

Mitchell, W. J. T. 2006. Christo's Gates and Gilo's Walls. *Critical Inquiry*, 32(4): 587–601.

Nafus, D. and Anderson, K. 2009. Writing on walls: the materiality of social memory in corporate research. In Cefkin, M. (ed.) *Ethnography and the Corporate Encounter: Reflections on Research in and of Corporation*. New York: Berghahn Books.

Reiss, J. 2001. *From Margin to Centre: The Spaces of Installation Art*. Cambridge: MIT Press.

Rosenthal, S.R. and Capper, M. 2006. Ethnographies in the front end: designing for enhanced customer experiences. *The Journal of Product Innovation Management*, 23(3): 215–237.

Spinney, J. 2011. A chance to catch a breath: using mobile video ethnography in cycling research. *Mobilities*, 6(2): 161–182.

Wakeford, N. 2006. PowerPoint and the crafting of social data. *Ethnographic Praxis in Industry Conference Proceedings*, 2006(1): 94–108.

Wasson, C. 2000. Ethnography in the field of design. *Human Organization*, 59(4): 377–388.

10 Life Off Grid

Considerations for a Multi-Sited, Public Ethnographic Film

Jonathan Taggart and Phillip Vannini

GOING OFF GRID: AN INTRODUCTION

The Hawker-Siddeley 748 is far and away my new favourite airplane. Considering that I've never even liked an airplane, this is something of a transition for me. It's a sublimation that, in terms of pre-flight nerves, works in my favour. Sitting on the runway at Whitehorse airport—a necessary stopover between my home in Vancouver and the arctic town of Inuvik, Northwest Territories—peering out of my unshuttered window from my unreclining seat to admire the riveting on the sleek metal cigar that is the port-side Rolls Royce Dart engine, the small turbo-prop puts me in mind of what it must have been like to fly Pan American during the Golden Age of Aviation. I feel like I'm going somewhere important, in comfort that is not excessive, and that no other craft could possibly get me there with such economy and efficiency. I am sitting in the 1930s Volkswagen of 1950s-era airplanes, I conclude, and the cabin's interior completes this pleasing utilitarian image, save for the rear eight seats.

Those are occupied by freight, masked eerily, military-style, in grey-green canvas tied in with webbed straps. "We take on as much cargo as we can when there are empty seats," the flight attendant explains. "Good," I think, as my heels tap the heavy duffel bag of audiovisual gear at my feet. After all, it's expensive to ship to the North, as I would undoubtedly have learned if this small-scale airline had insisted on weighing the cameras in my carry-on. I'm still contemplating my good fortune and my newfound affinity for this aircraft when we lift off, slow and smooth.

And then there's a pause.

A stall.

My heart, expectedly, goes to my throat. Life, of course, flashes before my eyes. My eyes dart to my traveling companion, Phillip: the caramel macchiato-loving, island-dwelling, geocaching ethnographer who got me into this mess. It was his idea to study the lives of Canadians living in these isolated and ice-locked locales, far from continental road systems and even further from runways of familiar suburban length. He probably never said it, but I attribute the words to him now as I sit, motionless, upright, possibly receiving my just deserts: "What could possibly go wrong?"

And then, as if nothing happened, we continue through the air in the general direction of up. The "stall"—and I shall cease to call it that—lasted no more than a half-second, probably the commonplace drag of retracting landing gear or the delayed inertial shifting of several tons of dry goods, Arctic-bound under their drab drapings in the rear seats. The Hawker bounces playfully in Whitehorse's southern wind and soon the Yukon River is visible below, winding its way north of the small city to where it is joined by the Takhini. The milk run circuit between Whitehorse and Inuvik includes stops in the remote communities of Old Crow and Dawson City, and over the course of the week's film-making I become oddly proud of my ability to anticipate the Hawker's characteristic take-off lurch. Indeed, over the course of the next two years I become accustomed to all manner of uncomfortable and often unnerving travel.

* * *

This chapter draws on two years of ethnographic fieldwork in remote locations across Canada—13 provinces and territories in all—to discuss the opportunities and challenges presented by a multi-sited (Coleman and Von Hellerman 2011) visual ethnographic study of the off-grid lifestyle. The expression "off grid" refers to a variety of strategies by way of which individual households and communities disconnect from—or alternatively and strategically connect to—the dominant technological infrastructures that provide energy, water, and communication flows. As we have experienced, such a remove (Vannini 2011; Vannini and Taggart 2013) from electrical infrastructure is often accompanied by varying intensities of disconnection from other infrastructures such as telecommunications, reliable all-season roadways, and municipal/regional provisions for water supply and waste removal, to name just a few such 'grids'. Collectively these infrastructures of light, speed, and power, as well as an array of related consumer technologies (Shove 2003; Thrift 1996) create a world characterised in large part by domestic comfort, connectivity, and convenience. Off-gridders aim to question these values and endeavour to reinvent the very practices of everyday life typical of an advanced consumer society. By disconnecting from grids altogether, or connecting to them in counter-hegemonic ways, off-gridders potentially enact countercultural technological choices that can shape alternative socio-material assemblages and can constitute alternative mobility constellations. Informed by the principles of sensuous scholarship (Stoller 1997) and sensory ethnography (Pink 2009a), our reverberations of the off-grid way of life aim to evoke and animate the lifeworld under examination.

Inspired by Carey's idealist view of cultural studies as a pursuit of a public dialogue (Carey 1992; Hardt 2009), the project has targeted multiple publics since its inception. While the outputs for our off-grid research have been varied—ranging from popular magazine articles accompanied by photographs and online video shorts to peer-reviewed articles and a forthcoming ethnographic monograph—here we present our argument for a public visual ethnography as approached through film. We then move to discuss the more nuanced concerns—logistical, ethical, relational, and technological—that may arise when planning and producing a long-term, multi-sited ethnographic film for popular audiences. It is not our intention to be overly instructive or prescriptive; rather, our aim is to offer further insight to those already familiar with the uses of video for the purposes of gathering and presenting ethnographic data, but a current and comprehensive introduction to the techniques and technologies can be found in Heath, Hindmarsh and Luff (2010).

In this chapter the use of the pronoun 'I' refers to the first author who, for the purposes of the research described, was predominantly in charge of video data collection, editing, and dissemination. 'We' refers to both authors. For additional clarity, while the film project described is still in the editing stages, we refer to the project as we envision it completed: a 90-minute documentary entitled *Life Off Grid*.

ANIMATING THE LIFEWORLD: JUSTIFYING A PUBLIC AND VISUAL ETHNOGRAPHY

"Much too often research in the social sciences and humanities suffers from an ivory tower complex", writes Vannini (2012, 2), the symptoms of which prevent wide audiences from fully enjoying the processes or appreciating the value and utility of research. As a result, research is often destined for and consumed by a small cadre of readers who have access to both the narrowly accessible media in which research is published, and the difficult lexicon that characterises academic writing. As new, experimental, blurred genres of research, as well as new distribution media, new academic imperatives, and new ideas and wills emerge, the need to popularise academic research grows.

In the past decade ethnographers have been gradually moving away from a traditional pursuit of what can be referred to as basic research (Denzin and Lincoln 2005; Pink 2006, 2009a), resulting in the experimental blurring of popular and academic genres and the increased acceptance of creativity, innovation, and multi-disciplinary applications in the academic field. Not satisfied with the monologic flow of dissemination, nor with limited audiences, venues, and modes of representation, the ethnography emerging from this experimentation aims to be both performative and practical, shifting ethnographic product and process towards transformative and relational forms of learning (Pink 2009b; Tedlock 2005). This new public ethnography embodies a synthesis of the arts, humanities, and the sciences, and places equal premium on the aesthetic and the technical. It dismantles and reconfigures the relationship between researchers, the researched, and research audiences, essentially reconstituting knowledge as a manner of relational and cooperative techne. This relational techne is the art and technology of facilitating encounters, establishing mediated relations, and creatively producing conditions for new and transformative exchanges amongst multiple publics, and it is in this spirit that *Life Off Grid* was conceived and executed.

Drawing on relational aesthetics (e.g. Bourriaud 2002; Kwon 2002), the public ethnographer is a mediator, facilitating encounters amongst learners and co-creating research outputs for multiple and non-specialised publics. Ethnography's intimacy, narrativity, performativity, and sociality are powerful attractors that humanise common concerns and make the abstract personal and concrete. Taking inspiration from more-than-representational theory (e.g. Ingold 2000, 2007; Lorimer 2005; Thrift 2008), public ethnography aims to invigorate both the academic and non-academic landscape by imaginatively capturing the flows of everyday life, not for the express intent of symbolic distillation or the sifting-out of deep value systems, but rather to reanimate the power of the sensate (Pink 2009a), the non-cognitive, the affective, the kinesthetic, the material, and the spatiotemporal immediacy of "taskscapes" of "dwelling" and "livelihood" (Ingold 2000).

As a form of qualitative inquiry, public ethnography rejects the realism and the uncommitted objectivism of positivist scholarship (see Denzin and Lincoln 1994, 2000, 2005). According to Denzin—the foremost exponent of the movement—qualitative inquiry offers an empirical alternative to the supposedly apolitical stance of positivism and post-positivism. Mixing a transformative drive for social and environmental justice, an ethos of aesthetic sensibility, and a commitment to public relevance, qualitative inquiry has expanded the definition of ethnography to encompass more or less all forms of research carried out through scholarly reflexive engagement and in-depth participation of people into the research process. These new forms of scholarship succeed in popularising research and scholarship writ large by way of constant experimentation, innovation, genre-blurring, collaboration, and application to multiple social problems and issues. As Vannini argues,

> whether inspired by public sociology, public anthropology, qualitative inquiry, art-based research . . . the popularization of research answers the need to make scholarship relevant to the many, not the few. And whether in communication or education, sociology or anthropology, geography or cultural studies, or whatever other discipline or field, more and more scholars and students are now starting to recognize that a scholarship that wants to be meaningful has to have an audience and has to be consequential to its stakeholders.
>
> (Vannini 2012, 6)

Considering the preceding justification, the impetus for public ethnography shifts the focus away from early and ongoing debates concerning the rigid disciplinary adherence and capabilities of ethnographic film. Within the early traditions of visual ethnography some were adamant in relegating ethnographic film to a supporting role, arguing that the medium "demands an accompanying written ethnography for a more serious use and deeper understanding" (Heider 1976, 7). Others view the potential of film more positively, positing instead that "film must be regarded as a medium of communication with the potential for transmitting anthropological understanding in a manner parallel to, but not necessarily less significant than, the printed word" (Ruby 2000, 22). Public ethnography takes the latter route, and with *Life Off Grid* the outputs of both film and the printed word—once coupled in strict hierarchy—exist separately and equally for diverse audiences. In reaching audiences outside the academy, we believe strongly that ethnography's foci on the personal, the intimate, the particular, and the narrative are key elements for popularisation (Gans 2010), opening the way for a sensuous scholarship (Stoller 1997) capable of appealing to wider publics through visual media (Scheper-Hughes 2009).

Despite slowly easing views towards visual ethnographic products appearing in the popular sphere, process too has been a topic of much debate: interdisciplinary teams have been much maligned, with Ruby arguing that the ethnographic designation "be confined to those works in which the maker had formal training in ethnography" (2000, 6). Early collaboration between ethnographers and those outside the academy was limited, and interdisciplinary teams experienced "very little, mostly accidently success", demonstrating that "the best visual anthropology is by anthropologists, individually or as a team, using the instruments themselves" (El Guindi 2004, 63). But even the team of Mead and Bateson differed in their approach to the application of those instruments, famously (though presumably goodnaturedly) arguing over the implications for art and science found in manipulations of the observational neutrality of the camera (Brand 1986). Public ethnography, conversely but in no way in overt contradiction, exploits the potential of interdisciplinary teams in its enthusiastic pursuit of diverse audiences. Indeed, in its endeavour to reach audiences both within and beyond the academy, public ethnography actively seeks to collaborate across these boundaries in both the pursuit and production of its outputs. *Life Off Grid* serves as a case in point as the collaboration between a trained photographer, film-maker, and student of communication (the first author) and a sociologist and cultural geographer with broad ethnographic experience (the second author). Central to the research and production of *Life Off Grid* were the complimentary skills of film-making and ethnography that may have, in unequal application or emphasis, resulted in the limited success observed by El Guindi (2004). Though developed individually and in differing contexts (the worlds of journalism and academia) our respective approaches to film-making and ethnography share much in common in their reliance on interviews and participant observation, as well as in their attention to the cues and characteristics of the environments of their participants, and over the course of two years of fieldwork we found that film-making had much to learn from ethnography and vice versa. While it is too early to tell, we hope through our equal emphasis on film-making and ethnography—balancing the aesthetic, communicative, and descriptive capacities of our respective disciplines—to arrive at success that is designed rather than "accidental" (El Guindi 2004, 63).

Omori describes two distinct types of ethnographic film, "research footage" and the "monographic documentary," the former functioning rather like a notebook for field observations, the latter taking the form of "long, descriptive films for understanding the entire culture . . . or sometimes describing a particular theme" (2006, 119). MacDougall (1978) makes a similar distinction between raw ethnographic footage and the polished films that are the result of later analysis and assembly, "analogous in this sense to an anthropologist's public writings or to any other creative or scholarly productions" (1978, 406). While we have used our field footage in the former capacity—drawing on unedited sequences to confirm for ourselves details of environment and technology that might have escaped our attention in situ—our intention for *Life Off Grid* is "to tell a story, not just to present a record" (Postma 2006, 323). We find ourselves in partial opposition to Heider when he states that "when we are talking about 'ethnographic film', ethnography must take precedence over cinematography" (1976, 3), advocating instead for a harmony of technological, methodological, and aesthetic considerations, believing that "very often . . . the most complex and influential works function on several levels and defy such strict classification" (MacDougall 1978, 406). While the disciplinary definitions and distinctions of ethnographic film are no doubt important within certain fields, in our efforts to evoke and animate the off-grid lifeworld we lean heavily on film's "unique capacity to evoke human experience, what it feels like to actually be-in-the-world" (Barbash 1997, 74–75).

SKIP TO THE CREDITS: THE MAKING OF *LIFE OFF GRID*

Hurricane Leslie brought surprising devastation to the shores of Newfoundland, I learn from Ian and Meranda over the course of two days and nights spent on their several-acre property on the Avalon Peninsula. The two are in the process of building cabins and other infrastructure for the artist community they one day wish to host on the site, and along with Tenzing, a long-time friend visiting from Tibet, have spent the days clearing wind-blown trees from future building sites and milling logs into lumber suitable for construction. From my cot late in the morning, still feeling a little jet-lagged even after a few days on the east coast, I lift the corner of a makeshift curtain and see the source of the racket that woke me up: Tenzing feeding branches into a gas-powered wood-chipper before disappearing along a wooded trail on an ATV, soon to return with another wagonload of deadfall. The curtain also serves as a baffle against draughts in the unfinished main building I've been sleeping in, and the chilly coastal spring air pushing its way through an invisible gap in the envelope is quickly feeding my reluctance to get out of bed to help with the yard work. But overhead the soaring ceiling of this architectural marvel—hand-hewn beams joined without any metal fastenings—remind me of the day's agenda: I had promised Ian I would lend a hand with the milling of logs on his 18" bandsaw mill. Eager to learn more about this process and its implications for sustainable building in this remote location, I tumble out of bed and towards the coffee promised by the plume of smoke rising from the chimney of Ian and Meranda's cabin across the compound.

Phillip is already up and is doing his own milling around the log sorting site, audio recorder in hand while Ian prepares logs to be cut into slabs by the motorised saw. We sat down in the kitchen last night with our hosts to discuss the more abstract elements of their lifestyle—their motivations, values, challenges, and inspirations—in an on-camera interview, but there are always more questions to be asked and more lessons to be learned. Indeed, for us on these fieldwork trips there is no break from interrogation and reflection: we arrange our own off-grid accommodation whenever possible, immersing ourselves in the experience of disconnection, and helping our hosts with off-grid tasks whenever our competences allow. Milling lumber is not a skill Phillip or I possess, but as I ready the camera on the lightweight tripod that doubles as a steadicam I can see that he has learned a great deal already: I zoom in and follow the whirling dust of the saw as it slides the length of the log, and, pulling back, record as Phillip hammers a wooden wedge into the space left behind to ensure the weight of the offcut doesn't pinch the blade.

This was our last day of fieldwork and after lunch, driving back to St. Johns along the southern shore of the Avalon Peninsula, we park our rental car within sight of the Ferryland lighthouse to scout a suitable site for an on-camera discussion of methods that will serve as a behind-the-scenes explanation of the making of our film and the unfolding of our research process. Descending the cliff from the dirt road leading to the lighthouse, past a historic canon guarding the small harbour and a gigantic rusted Rodgers anchor sitting proud from the hill like a ruddy cetacean fishhook, we find an outcropping of rock and ready our cameras on a couple of tripods. We look perhaps a little under-slept and probably a touch overfed (Newfoundland is renowned for its seafood, after all), but with our single lapel microphone tucked secretly between scruffy sweater and scraggly beard, and with cameras A and B capturing northeast views of Ship and Bois Islands over our tired shoulders, we begin our explanations.

* * *

The project unfolded as a series of 13 case studies, using Canada's division into provinces and territories as an intuitive way to divide the study into manageable chunks, each loosely focused on a particular element of living

Figure 10.1   Phillip and Ian milling lumber in Newfoundland. Image: Jonathan Taggart.

off the grid. Connecting with individuals who choose to be disconnected presents unique challenges, and our methods of recruitment warrant brief mention. We recruited informants largely through the Internet, by email, and we were surprised to discover that many off-gridders maintain prominent online presences, some keeping blogs about their unique lifestyle or running bed-and-breakfasts in their idyllic locations. Despite their relative isolation, there is also a thriving online off-gridder community that utilises blogs and other forms of social media to connect and discuss technologies and tactics, and we discovered that many of our informants had worked with or knew of other off-gridders in their local community or in neighbouring provinces. This community enabled our recruitment to also grow by word-of-mouth. In places where we did encounter a dearth of public off-gridders, emails to local solar panel retailers with requests to share our study information with their clientele were very successful in drumming up participant interest. Once we located a sufficient number of informants in a given destination, we drafted a rough itinerary and booked flights to the most proximate city with a national airport. Wherever possible we booked accommodation in off-grid wilderness cabins to allow for greater reflection on the lifestyle under study—as, following Crang and Cook, "to be a 'participant' in a culture requires a full immersion of the researcher's self into the everyday rhythms and routines of the community" (2007, 37). We travelled considerable distances by rental car to reach off-grid homes and communities, which, with the exception of a handful of urban and suburban households, were generally located in rural areas. Off-gridders, however, are remote almost by definition, and over the course of fieldwork we also travelled by snowmobile, ferry boat, kayak, bicycle, snowshoe, and a chartered Cessna equipped with skis to reach informants where weather and roads precluded automobile access.

Our on-camera interviews generally followed the same format. After introductions and the disclosure and review of our ethical obligations we would set up for the first part of the interview in a location deemed appropriate by the informant, often seated in a kitchen or living room but occasionally outside in yards or gardens. These initial unstructured interviews typically lasted an hour and consisted of questions and conversation about the off-gridder's motivations, challenges, histories, values, and comments on the general adoptability of the lifestyle by society at large. During these interviews about the non-performative aspects of off-grid living two cameras would be recording high-definition video: a tripod-mounted digital SLR recording a mid-shot of the subject and the immediate environment, and a smaller handheld 'point-and-shoot' camera recording details and close-ups. Throughout the interview a pocket-sized high-definition audio recorder would record the informant's voice via a lapel microphone, and a camera-mounted shotgun microphone would record a wider range of voice and ambient sounds. The first author was responsible for audiovisual recording while the second author conducted the interview.

Figure 10.2 Jonathan canoeing in Quebec. Image: Jonathan Taggart.

Following this initial seated interview we would ask for a tour of the home and property. Tours were recorded using a single camera, our digital SLR mounted on the original tripod that now served double-duty as a low-tech steadicam unit. These tours offered the opportunity for further explanation of off-grid technologies and tactics, and for the recording of an off-grid task, generally solicited with the question, "if we weren't visiting today, what would you be doing instead?" This approach yielded a wide variety of descriptive footage of activities over the course of many seasons and in many different climates, from chopping wood and turning compost to gutting fish and forging knife blades.

Travel between interviews also provided many opportunities for gathering footage of landscape and weather, and of contrasting suburban and undeveloped rural settings. In our interviews it was apparent that many off-gridders experience a profound attachment to place—often a piece of land passed down through generations of family, or a remote wilderness visited often as children—and, in endeavouring to live full-time in the places with no electrical infrastructure, were obliged to seek alternative solutions to powering their homes. Others expressed a profound dissatisfaction with the privations, pace, and pollutions of an urban lifestyle, and when not recording seated interviews or demonstrations of practices we would endeavour to record images that we felt represented the affective (and in some cases disaffective) qualities of the places inhabited or eschewed by our informants.

The equipment used for the filming of *Life Off Grid* was chosen based on its accessibility, durability, portability, and adaptability. We used a Canon 5D Mark II digital single lens reflex camera capable of recording both high-quality still images and high-definition (1080p) video—an important consideration given our dual goal of also making photographs for magazine pieces—equipped with a small but versatile assortment of interchangeable lenses. Our primary lens of choice was a 24–105mm f4 lens with optional image stabilization; this was used the majority of the time due to its moderate size, functional zoom range, and ability to record a significant depth of field under most daylight conditions. Lesser used but of great value was a 35mm f1.4 fixed-length lens, used primarily for providing a moderate field of view in low light conditions without the need for supplementary illumination, and a 70–200mm f4 fixed-length lens, which we would mount on a tripod and use primarily for recording environmental detail at greater distance. Each of these lenses was manufactured by Canon Inc. and was used with an optional lens hood to shield the front element from inclement weather and stray light. A second 'point-and-shoot'-style camera, a Fuji x10, was used for secondary high-definition video and as a backup in the unlikely event the primary camera should fail (it didn't).

High-quality audio was recorded both on-camera using a small hotshoe-mounted shotgun microphone and using a portable 'Zoom H2' field recorder capable of recording ambient sound from multiple directions, as well as audio directly from an external microphone. For seated interviews and property tours our field recorder was connected to a small lapel microphone and worn by our informant. We carried an assortment of backup batteries as the ability to charge our equipment was not always guaranteed—especially when camping in Newfoundland's national parks—and occasionally bene-fited from the ability to charge large camera batteries using a DC adapter plugged into our rental car's cigarette lighter. Our field audio recorder was powered by easily-available AA batteries and we carried an adapter capable of powering our primary DSLR on AA batteries as well—albeit with reduced lifespan—in case of an emergency.

With the exception of the tripod used for seated interviews and as a sta-bilizing mount during tours, all of our audiovisual equipment fit in a shoul-der bag capable of passing the size and weight restrictions of most commercial airlines. Although we travelled (carefully) without bulky protective 'Pelican' cases, the modular nature of our camera and lens outfit meant that for short excursions—kayaking across a small bay for an interview on a private island, for example—our gear could be purposefully pared down, allowing us to meet short-term requirements of light and sound without putting all of our equipment at risk of immersion.

AESTHETIC, ETHICAL, AND LOGISTICAL CHALLENGES FOR A MULTI-SITED ETHNOGRAPHIC FILM PROJECT

Film-makers used to working in more traditional documentary contexts may find themselves faced with new constraints and considerations in the produc-tion of a public ethnographic film project. As an ethnographic/cinematic hybrid, *Life Off Grid* presented many challenges in filming, and while the project is still in the early stages of editing at the time of writing, a nuanced approach to post-production is already proving necessary.

As a multi-sited ethnographic project, fieldwork for *Life Off Grid* has included interviews with 175 off-gridders in nearly 100 sites throughout Canada's 10 provinces and three territories. This sheer volume of interviews ensures the study's academic rigour: it enables us to present a thick descrip-tion of the off-grid lifestyle, both on screen and in print, that is based on a broad study base, and guarantees that the statements and inferences made about off-gridders' motivations, techniques, and technologies are ones that are shared across a spectrum of Canadian climates, cultures, and classes. The relatively low density of off-grid communities and dwellings necessi-tated extensive travel in the data-gathering stage of the research in order to achieve this volume of interviews, and the cost of this extensive travel, as well as the concurrent professional and familial duties of the research team, necessitated a relatively short period of time (circa 10 days) in each of the 13 primary fieldsites. This approach emphasised breadth over depth—a rea-sonable compromise given the common academic constraints of time and money, as well as the specific geography of the population under study. In the interests of this breadth, field interviews in homes and communities were necessarily short, averaging two to three hours, and consisting of a seated semi-structured and open-ended interview followed by a short tour of the off-grid home or property. These tours typically included the demonstration of a typical off-grid task—an off-grid "performance of rurality" (Edensor 2009)—ranging from splitting wood and firing up a wood-burning stove to equalizing deep-cycle batteries and sweeping snow from solar panels. Where classical anthropologists like Mead and Bateman had the benefit of years in the field to film the same rituals and interview the same informants time and again (Barbash 1997) in each instance we were generally limited to a single conversation and a single take or camera angle for recording an off-grid demonstration, with little opportunity for repetition. For both ethnographer and film-maker, this limitation comes with the pressure to get it right the first time, as academic and aesthetic demands converge and descend upon a frequently jetlagged research team.

It is important to note that not all of the interviews referred to above were video recorded, and not all of those that *were* video recorded will be used in the final 90-minute film. Indeed, to include all of the on-camera interviews would introduce somewhere in the vicinity of sixty characters to an under-standably overwhelmed audience, and would make for an unwatchable film dozens of hours long. In many instances the decision not to record an inter-view was made when we felt we had reached the point of data saturation in a particular medium and in a particular site: as our ethnographic project has a number of academic and popular outputs, including illustrated magazine articles and peer-reviewed journal articles accompanied by descriptive pho-tographs, there were times when further video footage of wind turbine dem-onstrations on Nova Scotia's blustery coast would have been repetitive and superfluous. In such instances we opted instead to take photographs to bol-ster our thick description in other media.

In some circumstances, however, the decision to leave the cameras off was made by the informant during the process of informed consent. Off-gridders, we have learned, choose to live at a disconnect from prevailing infrastruc-tures and networks for a variety of reasons, many relating to pace of life and the empowerment found in a lifestyle rich in independence, but others for reasons of privacy and solitude. As a result, many off-gridders avoid unneces-sary publicity, understandably preferring not to appear on camera. In many remote communities building codes go unenforced or are non-existent, and many enterprising off-gridders are as guarded of their hand-built and non-code-conforming homes as they are of their personal identities. Similarly, many off-gridders are wary of seeing their isolated paradises overrun with tourists and developers seeking the latest untouched wilderness, and opt to keep their locations private. In consideration of these multiple privacy con-cerns we worked with an informed consent form that allowed participants to opt-out of any visual recording and to specify how (or if) they prefer us to identify them and their location in our various ethnographic outputs.

In seeming contradiction to this propensity towards anonymity, many off-gridders also see great benefit in sharing the messages of their lived experiences with a wider audience, as, for some, being off grid constitutes an extension of values and an experiment in living (Marres 2012), and as such contains valuable critiques of environmental norms, consumer culture, and materiality. We found the result of these often conflicting aims—the general preference for privacy and the willingness to demonstrate—to be a great number of informants who were happy to speak with us in their homes but unwilling to appear on camera—still incredibly useful for the purposes of an ethnographic study, but a significant flat spot for an effort in documentary film-making.

While the recruitment process, conducted primarily through advance email, clearly stated that making a film was part of our ethnographic process, we often didn't know until we arrived at a participant's home whether or not we would be allowed to record video. As many of our interviewees lived at some distance from the urban centres we flew into—and occasionally in seemingly camouflaged homes made of natural building materials in wood and earth tones, difficult to find at the end of dusty dirt roads—we experienced more than a few days of panic, wondering whether a province or territory was going to produce any footage at all for our film, leaving us with potential gaps in our narrative. For a typical film production this uncertainty would constitute an unacceptable risk—a potential waste of both valuable time and money—but film-makers venturing into this interdisciplinary territory need to be prepared to relinquish control and accommodate the often-conflicting ethical and aesthetic requirements of ethnography and cinema.

Keeping within the ethical sphere, control is often also relinquished to—or at least requested by—third parties, particularly media outlets with an interest in the work. As part of our mandate is to make the research leading up to the release of *Life Off Grid* as public and accessible as possible, part of the recruitment efforts prior to any fieldwork trip included reaching out to local print and radio journalists to share information about the project. This outreach also served the purposes of building public interest in the research products, the monograph, and the film, which we will then be able to build on when both are released. Often this outreach would lead to requests for interviews, and it was here that the privacy of our informants came under the most pressure. Radio interviews, in our experience, are fairly self-contained: on-air hosts are typically interested in our personal fieldwork experiences, in our motivations as researchers, and in engaging anecdotes that can be easily presented under a veil of participant anonymity. Although presenting an ethnographic project on radio certainly requires the letting-go of certain academic conventions and the distillation and encapsulation of complex observations (see Ryan 2012), almost never during these radio interviews were we asked to put journalists in direct contact with off-gridders for follow-up pieces. Print media journalists however, especially in smaller communities, were generally keen to follow-up with our informants and to produce their own stories, hoping to reveal some insight themselves into the alternative lifestyles being lived in their own communities.

While we have no objections to these requests on any grounds of intellectual property—after all, public ethnography can claim to be most successful when it exists beyond the research context in continued public discourse—fulfilling them faced us with some complicated mediation. After such a request, we would let our informants know that a local journalist had expressed interest in interviewing an off-gridder, and ask whether they would be willing to share their contact information. If they had no objections we would then share their contact information with the journalist in question. All this seems straightforward enough, but, as Ryan (2012) also discovered regarding media interest in his research on Australian horror movies, sharing these contacts often implicated us in narratives that ran counter to our research findings, as journalists used our names and affiliations in articles that wrongly characterised off-gridders as backwoods hippies and country bumpkins, or focused on radical new building trends to the exclusion of the deeper implications of a lifestyle of increased attention to consumption. While the primary danger here is to the journalistic integrity of third parties, there is certainly the risk that these superficial newspaper characterisations reflect poorly on us as researchers, wrongly accused of unscrupulous association, or at very least, bad public relations. "At the core of popularizing research through the media is finding the right angle", asserts Ryan (2012, 201), and we have learned very quickly in our two-year relationship with both radio and print media to redirect errant or overly-suggestive inquiries back to our core messaging, using easily-relatable analogies and anecdotes to diffuse any sensationalist journalistic tendencies.

Needless to say, 175 informants spread across a hundred fieldsites yield a lot of data, visual or otherwise, and we estimate that over the course of two years we have recorded hundreds of hours of high-definition video footage, as well as dozens of hours of interview audio recordings and hundreds of still photographs. Fortunately for our two-man research team my previous training includes video editing in addition to cinematography, the benefit being that as a film editor I already have an intimate understanding of the footage, the fieldwork process, and the research findings, and am therefore in an appropriate position of understanding and ability to assemble our extensive and diverse visual data into a coherently encapsulated narrative. "Film is a quintessentially phenomenological medium," acknowledges Barbash (1997, 74), and the video editing process—that is, our data analysis and subsequent assembly—is based on established procedures of post-phenomenological research (Moustakas 1994, 118–119). This process entails the horizontalising of data, or "regarding every horizon or statement relevant to the topic and question as having equal value" (1994, 118); clustering units of meaning from the horizontalised data into common themes; developing descriptions of experiences and practices based on clusters of meaning units; and integrating descriptions into the meanings—experiential and theoretical—of the phenomena under investigation.

In a digital editing suite this is achieved with layers of keywords attached to individual video clips and interview fragments: every observation, or clip, is regarded as having equal weight, and each clip is keyworded according to what it describes. A second round of keywords is then applied based on emergent themes, or 'clusters', independent of the purely illustrative qualities of each clip. This thematic and descriptive clustering is sufficient for footage with no interview content. Interview footage is broken down into thematic chunks, typically comprising the response to a single interview question, and these chunks are similarly keyworded. In this way it becomes very easy not just to identify and access key themes in the research—'quality of life', 'independence', etc.—but also to find particular performances and associated technologies (e.g. 'heating', 'powering', 'refrigeration'), as well as less-thematic cues that are used to link locations, activities, and interviews together in ways that make cinematic sense: 'water', 'winter', and so on. These latter clusters are particularly useful in creating an intuitive narrative trajectory using footage taken in widely diverse locations and across two full seasonal cycles: it would be confusing to an audience, to use an extreme example, to jump from an exploration of boat-access communities on the British Columbian coast to a demonstration of underground refrigeration in the Canadian Arctic. Post-phenomenological clustering enables us to avoid this kind of jarring transition, allowing us instead to relate discussions of water transit in British Columbia to similar springtime issues of access in thawed Arctic river deltas, or to connect common themes of food storage across a similar geographic distance, simply by juxtaposing the two in an editing suite timeline.

SUN, SLEET, SEAWATER, SOIL: HOW NOT TO RUIN YOUR EQUIPMENT 1000 KM FROM THE NEAREST BEST BUY

In Nunavut, Canada's largest and northernmost territory, at a remote fishing camp on the frozen shores of Baffin Island, Niviaqsi guides me through the preparations for our trip home—a trip that will take us by snowmobile across 80km of frozen sea ice back to the hamlet of Cape Dorset. His tight features scrutinise my modest skills in lashing (honed to a dull proficiency while working as a tugboat deckhand during my earliest years in graduate school), and we work back and forth as if nailing railroad spikes, alternating exertions on either side of the long plywood sled known as a qamutik as we pass a length of rope between us to secure our load of frozen fish, jerry cans, and hunting rifles. The small high-definition camera around my neck records the task from my perspective. It's April—technically spring despite an average outside temperature of −30° Celsius—and Phillip and I have been camped out with our hosts Timun, Kristiina, and Niviaqsi at their ice fishing camp for the past five days, sharing the intimate 4 m by 4 m plywood cabin in the steamy warmth of a propane stove, eating our fill of raw arctic char and bannock while learning about an off-grid life that was a daily reality for many families in the north only a generation ago. An arctic fox has been making nightly visits to the clearing in the middle of our small compound of

Figure 10.3 Preparing frozen char for transport in Nunavut. Image: Jonathan Taggart.

buildings to drag fish scraps back to a den in the surrounding white hills, and I've taken to hiding behind a snow bank—for as long as I can stand the chill, at least—with my camera, zoom lens, and tripod in an attempt to record these stealthy visits on video. What I've discovered, much to my consternation, is that the glass components of my equipment—lens and eyepiece, in particular—fog heavily when I re-enter the warmth of the cabin, rendering them mostly useless while they acclimatise. Timun is long accustomed to this phenomenon and has a spare pair of eyeglasses inside the cabin that he swaps for his fogged lenses when he returns from working outside; I, unfortunately, do not have the benefit of a complete second set of audiovisual tools, and am confined to at least twenty minutes of forced inactivity between my outdoor-to-indoor transitions.

* * *

As the above vignettes suggest, doing multi-sited ethnography across diverse geographic regions and climates, through two complete changes of seasons and in remote locations, presents unique technological and logistical challenges for the documentary film-maker and cinematic ethnographer. Unlike the early motion film equipment used in the field by the progenitors of visual anthropology—much of which was mechanical, requiring no electronic source of power in order to operate—today's digital recording devices, both audio and visual, are notoriously sensitive to humidity and moisture. In addition to playing havoc with optics through fogging and thawing, water ingress can easily short-circuit cameras and recorders that are not sufficiently weather-sealed, bringing about much more inconvenience than a simple twenty-minute time-out as the ethnographer/film-maker waits for external condensation to dissipate. Inclement weather or surprise immersions can effectively render digital equipment useless, and will probably do so when you are hundreds of rough kilometres from the nearest source of repair or replacement.

Dust has similar powers of invasion, and sand and other fine particulates can work their way through gaps and cracks in camera and lens bodies, damaging circuitry, scratching image sensors (producing the digital and permanent equivalent of a hair in the film gate when viewing the final image), and jamming moving parts. For the comfort of both researchers and their equipment it is of course preferable to conduct field recordings under optimal conditions—in dustless and desiccated environments, for example—but the desire to capture "whole actions" (Heider, 1976) and to participate in the cultures of the observed (Crang and Cook 2007) often demands that we engage with conditions that are far from ideal. While doing fieldwork for *Life Off Grid* my video and audio equipment was subjected to freezing wind and sub-zero temperatures in Nunavut (that, incidentally, can chill an aluminium alloy camera body to the point where it becomes dangerous to touch with exposed fingers); to hail, snow, and sleet in New Brunswick's Bay of Fundy; to airborne dust and dirt in the gardens of a Manitoba ecovillage;

and to sea-spray on the shores of Nova Scotia's Musquodoboit Harbour. Fortunately for researchers and film-makers many professional and advanced amateur-level SLRs and camcorders are equipped with weather seals, rendering them impervious to moderate amounts of dust and water. It is therefore reasonable to expect that with only moderate investment visual ethnographers may be able to provision themselves with recording equipment that will survive all but a complete immersion. It is advisable though, for peace of mind if not for the continued comfort of maintaining dry gear, to have a raincover on hand for especially wet weather, and in Canada's wetter regions I have benefitted from a sleeve-like plastic camera cover with holes for both the lens and eyepiece. Purpose built raincovers like this can be purchased for a few dollars at most camera shops and come with a drawstring at one end to cinch securely around lenses, but a slapdash solution can be quickly and easily fashioned out of almost any plastic bag and an elastic band—a solution any consumption-savvy off-gridder would readily approve.

CONCLUSION

In presenting our experiences in producing a long-term, multi-sited, and public ethnographic film, our aim has been to bring visual ethnography out of the rigid disciplinary and methodological debate following its inception by outlining its potential to reach multiple publics and inspire dialogue among audiences beyond the academy. We agree with Barbash (1997), in that

> there's no precise distinction between ethnographic and documentary films. All films, fiction films too, contain ethnographic information, both about the people they depict and about the culture of the film-maker. . . . Though ethnographic films have characteristics of their own, they can't be weeded out from the broader documentary traditions from which they have borrowed, and to which, in part, they belong.
>
> (Barbash 1997, 3)

In advocating an approach to ethnographic film that aspires to be more-than-academic, we maintain that the result of such an approach will be the broad spread of research findings, interest in projects, increased institutional approval, and the continued participation of research subjects in documents that claim to represent their interests.

As researchers, film-makers, and co-participants, we found ourselves quickly adopting the innovative bricolage demonstrated by our informants, sharing in the attitude that if a piece of technology is not versatile and robust, it is more hindrance than help. We would argue that our attitude towards our visual methodology has taken a similar turn towards demanding reflexivity and responsiveness. In our efforts to publicise our research process in the media we have taken objection to the misclassification of our informants, and, in the few instances where disconnection is not luxury but necessity, we have taken up the public cry for connectivity. Public ethnography presents such murky and often unfathomable waters, and often the surface churns like the waves beneath an island-bound passenger ferry en route to a remote island in British Columbia's Salish Sea. Added to the methodological discussion are layers of technological and ethical complexity that require interdisciplinary collaboration and patience to unravel. In weaving our field experiences into both the current representation and our final film, we acknowledge and rearticulate the emerging demand for ethnographers to exhibit a consciousness of their position within the communities in which they work. We share our experiences also in order to provide human characters on which to hang our narrative, and in doing so hope to further elucidate the ethnographic process for students of the method and for audiences beyond the academy. In documenting and revealing our trials and errors—both technological and social—we recognise that neither documentaries, ethnographies, nor any hybrid of the two, spring forth fully-formed and shining as if from the "dead hand of competence" (Stoller 2012). Of this reflexivity and complexity, we agree with Ruby (2000), that

> Once it is acknowledged that no one can speak for or represent a culture but only his or her relationship to it, then a multiplicity of viewpoints is possible and welcome—some from within and others from without, and all the marvelously gray areas in between.
>
> (Ruby 2000, 31)

REFERENCES

Barbash, I. 1997. *Cross-Cultural Filmmaking: A Handbook for Making Documentary and Ethnographic Films and Videos*. Berkeley: University of California Press.
Bourriaud, N. 2002. *Relational Aesthetics*. Paris: Les Presses du Reél.
Brand, S. 1986. For God's sake, Margaret: a conversation with Gregory Bateson and Margaret Mead, summer 1976. In Kleiner, A. and Brand, S. (Eds.) *News That Stayed News, 1974–1984: Ten Years of Coevolution Quarterly*. Berkeley: North Point Press.
Carey, J. 1992. *Communication as Culture*. New York: Routledge.
Coleman, S. and Von Hellerman, P. 2011. *Multi-Sited Ethnography*. New York: Routledge.
Crang, M. and Cook, I. 2007. *Doing Ethnographies*. Thousand Oaks: SAGE.
Denzin, N. and Lincoln, Y. (eds.) 1994. *The SAGE Handbook of Qualitative Research* 1st ed. Thousand Oaks: SAGE.
Denzin, N. and Lincoln, Y. (eds.) 2000. *The SAGE Handbook of Qualitative Research*. 2nd ed. Thousand Oaks: SAGE.
Denzin, N. and Lincoln, Y. (eds.) 2005. *The SAGE Handbook of Qualitative Research*. 3rd ed. Thousand Oaks: SAGE.
Edensor, T. 2009. Performing rurality. In Cloke, P. (ed.) *Handbook of Rural Studies*. London: SAGE.
El Guindi, F. 2004. *Visual Anthropology: Essential Method and Theory*. Walnut Creek: AltaMira Press.

Gans, H. 2010. Public ethnography; ethnography as public sociology. *Qualitative Sociology*, 33: 97–104.

Hardt, H. 2009. James Carey: communication, conservation, democracy. *Cultural Studies*, 23: 183–186.

Heath, C., Hindmarsh, J. and Luff, P. (eds.) 2010. *Video in Qualitative Research: Analysing Social Interaction in Everyday Life*. London: SAGE.

Heider, K. 1976. *Ethnographic Film*. Austin: University of Texas Press.

Ingold, T. 2000. *The Perception of the Environment*. London: Routledge.

Ingold, T. 2007. *Lines: A Brief History*. New York: Routledge.

Kwon, M. 2002. *One Place After Another*. Cambridge: MIT Press.

Lorimer, R. 2005. Cultural geography: the busyness of being "more-than-representational". *Progress in Human Geography*, 29: 83–94.

MacDougall, D. 1978. Ethnographic film: failure and promise. *Annual Review of Anthropology*, 7: 405–425.

Marres, N. 2012. Experiment: the experiment in living. In Lury, C. and Wakeford, N. (eds.) *Inventive Methods: The Happening of the Social*. New York: Routledge.

Moustakas, C. 1994. *Phenomenological Research Methods*. Thousand Oaks: SAGE.

Omori, Y. 2006. Basic problems in developing film ethnography. In Postma, M. and Crawford, P. I. (eds.) *Reflecting Visual Anthropology: Using the Camera in Anthropological Research*. Leiden: CNWS Publications.

Pink, S. 2006. *The Future of Visual Anthropology: Engaging the Senses*. London: Routledge.

Pink, S. 2009a. *Doing Sensory Ethnography*. London: SAGE.

Pink, S. 2009b. *Visual Interventions: Applying Visual Anthropology*. Boston: Berghann

Postma, M. 2006. From description to narrative: what's left of ethnography? In Postma, M. and Crawford, P. I. (eds.) *Reflecting Visual Anthropology: Using the Camera in Anthropological Research*. Leiden: CNWS Publications.

Ruby, J. 2000. *Picturing Culture: Explorations of Film & Anthropology*. Chicago: University of Chicago Press.

Ryan, M. D. 2012. Tips for generating a media release and media coverage: how the media ate up my research on Aussie horror movies. In Vannini, P. (ed.) *Popularizing Research*. Bern: Peter Lang.

Scheper-Hughes, N. 2009. Making anthropology public. *Anthropology News*, 25: 1–4.

Shove, E. 2003. *Comfort, Cleanliness and Convenience: The Social Organization of Normality*. Oxford: Berg.

Stoller, P. 1997. *Sensuous Scholarship*. Philadelphia: University of Pennsylvania Press.

Stoller, P. 2012. Ethnographic futures. Keynote address at Public Ethnography: Connecting New Genres, New Media, New Audiences, Victoria, British Columbia, 1 June.

Tedlock, B. 2005. The observation of participation and the emergence of public ethnography. In Denzin, N. and Lincoln, Y. (eds.) *The Handbook of Qualitative Research*. Thousand Oaks: SAGE.

Thrift, N. 1996. *Spatial Formations*. London: SAGE.

Thrift, N. 2008. *Non-Representational Theory*. London: Routledge.

Vannini, P. 2011. Constellations of ferry (im)mobility: islandness as the performance and politics of insulation and isolation. *Cultural Geographies*, 18(2): 249–271.

Vannini, P. 2012. Introduction. In Vannini, P. (ed.) *Popularizing Research*. Bern: Peter Lang.

Vannini, P. and Taggart, J. 2013. Doing islandness: a non-representational approach to an island's sense of place. *Cultural Geographies*, 20(2): 1–18.

Afterword

Video Methods beyond Representation: Experimenting with Multimodal, Sensuous, Affective Intensities in the 21st Century

Phillip Vannini

I received Charlotte Bates' kind request to write the conclusion to this timely collection of essays as Jonathan Taggart and I were en route back home after a week spent filming and doing fieldwork on the east coast of Canada. I hesitated to agree. Though I had been working with Jonathan for over two years on the making of an extensive video documentary production (see Taggert and Vannini, this volume), I had always held reservations about the academic establishment of both ethnographic film and video-based data collection methods. In my mind video has always had an enormous potential to affect its audiences—a potential to inform, educate, entertain, transform, and stimulate—but the people least qualified to actualise that potential, I had long been convinced, were academics. So I nervously agreed to write this chapter, presaging that it would inevitably end up being a polemical one focused on the shortcomings of video methods as currently practiced and the still largely unfulfilled potential of video-based scholarship.

My reservations weren't without their reasons. As a student I had sat through my fair share of projections of classic anthropological films—shaky, drawn-out, rough-sounding, clumsily-edited productions that simultaneously failed to meet my Generation-X-shaped expectations for entertainment and to inform my ethnographic sensitivity better than (often similarly drawn-out) written accounts. Later, as a scholar, I had become well aware of the prevailing social scientific attitude toward research-based film and video production, nicely epitomised by the following prescription:

> A static camera mounted on a tripod that does not tilt, pan, zoom, or in any way move is assumed to be the most "scientific" technique and one that is less distorting and more "truthful" in the recording of "natural" behavior than other camera techniques. Moreover the camera must be allowed to run as long as possible and used in as unobtrusive a manner as possible so that it records unaffected streams of culturally significant behaviour.
>
> (Ruby 2000, 177)[1]

In short, it wasn't unreasonable for me to have grown to believe that the same elitism, the same tendency to preach to the choir, the same realist compulsions, the same lack of imagination, and the same paucity of creative skills that had impacted much of scholarly writing had also severely impacted video-making for research purposes well beyond repair. So I accepted the invitation to write this chapter mostly as an opportunity to catch up with the latest cross-disciplinary developments in the field and perhaps as a way to push my own agenda on non-representational methodology (see Vannini 2014). Little did I know that an epistemological revolution, as manifested by the contributors to this volume, was actually already in full swing.

As Charlotte Bates points out in her introduction, video methods aren't what they used to be. And thank goodness for that! Across several disciplines, throughout disparate fieldsites, and alongside evolving theoretical and methodological traditions, the video methods of the second decade of the 21st century are as different from their filmic predecessors as HD DSLR cameras are from the tools of the silent film trade. Gone are the dominant realist and universalising pretensions to "capture" unbiased versions of reality, gone are the anxieties over aestheticising knowledge and experimenting with it, and gone are many of the most stringent limitations over dissemination and publication. Video methods are moving at full speed beyond representation, finally beginning to exploit their potential to evoke, communicate multimodally in a sensuous way, and to affect viewers in meaningful, arts-inspired ways. There has never been a better time to practice video methods and to push them to do what they haven't been pushed to do before.

BEYOND REPRESENTATION

If all the chapters of this book could be jammed into a word processor programmed to squeeze a single, synthesizing essence out of them then that essence might as well be this: video methods are less useful for "capturing" reality than they are for evoking distinct, multiple, competing, and often even contradictory aural and visual impressions. Allow me, in what follows, to tease out some of the different threads that are knotted through in this statement.

Evoking, Not Capturing

Following the crisis of representation of the 1980s the social sciences have experimented with a multitude of research traditions destined to evoke, animate, expose, impress, unsettle, and rapture reality, rather than "capture" it in older realist, objective, or supposedly authentic ways. Video methods haven't always been at the forefront of this epistemological revolution. Long condemned for being inferior to the written word, the use of visual imagery and sound in social scientific research has historically struggled to serve as little more than a supplement to print or as a teaching or conference presentation aide. Within ethnography, for example, "visual ethnography" has come to denote written ethnographic accounts accompanied by occasional photographs or (less often) video clips, as well as ethnographic film supported by written 'study guides'. For a long time the message underlying visual ethnographic knowledge has been simple: images are seductively dangerous and must be treated gingerly. Images—as the criticism went on—may appear to show truth and evidence, but therein lay their shallowness, for all images deceive and hide. The contributors to this book transcend this sceptical approach to the role of the audiovisual by finally abandoning the pretence of being capable of, and even being interested in, 'capturing' reality through images and sound.

In his research in London's St Pancras Station and Paris's Gare du Nord, for example, Simpson utilises multi-angle video recording and presentation techniques to 'approach', rather than 'capture', ephemeral ambiances and atmospheres. Ambiances and atmospheres—the research project's social 'reality' under focus—are by definition ungraspable, undefinable, and only perceivable as fleeting moods, diffuse feelings, and evanescent sensations. There is nothing, in other words, that can be objectively captured by a camera, by the written word, or any other mode of re-presentation. There the cameras are simply employed to give off a sense of the barely sensible, the intangible, and the un-captured. Cameras then work less as a 'recording' instrument and more as a heteroglossic device capable of creating (not *representing*, but *creating*) a feeling of multi-positionality which the technologically-unaided human body cannot otherwise achieve on its own. Thus a multi-angle video creation *makes up*—through the creative artifice of the montage process—a super-human, panoptic vision which rather than simply *observing* ends up *directing* and *composing*.

'More-than-representational' video methods—to borrow from Lorimer's (2005) useful moniker—are undoubtedly less the tool of the scientist, the security staff, and the bureaucrat and more that of an artist keen on allowing "the world to appear differently" (Simpson, this volume). I agree here with Simpson wholeheartedly: using video in a non-representational or more-than-representational manner helps us "see [and hear] the world differently from our habitual ways of looking and feeling" (Simpson, this volume). This is a simple lesson which every self-respecting visual artist—from photographers to film-makers—knows and understands very well: if all that the camera is employed to do is to see something the naked eye can also see on its own, then what is the value? Unfortunately this point has long been lost on social scientists. Boredom—a common response to many traditional social scientific video productions—is precisely the outcome of a viewing experience that discovers nothing new, nothing different, nothing surprising, unsettling, or imaginative in what the camera has been employed to see.

For these reasons I am sceptical about the word 'witnessing' (cf. Patchett, this volume). Though I agree with Patchett's claim—and before her, Dewsbury's (2003) and Lorimer's (2010)—that 'witnessing' and 'exposing' are ideas that transcend the boundaries of representationalism, the notion of witnessing is for me still too anchored in a view of the camera as a replacement for physical presence, sort of a testimonial eye and ear in absentia of the real thing. The video camera is capable of intensifying affect even when one's own eyes and ears are present—after all who hasn't experienced different sensations than they did in the field after playing back one's own footage?—and indeed rather than a witness I wish to think of the camera as a fabricator, a trickster, a storyteller. Video methods are indeed "primarily an art of illusion" (Gallagher, this volume, citing Chion 1994, 96) capable of manufacturing a hyper-reality of their own, not unlike the "enhanced" sound that we—in our hyper-mediated sound environments—have come to think of as high-fidelity, but which in actuality "may in fact be more accurately described as definition" (Gallagher, this volume).

In short, with the contributors of this volume I view the video camera's role in the research context not as a reproductive one but as a poetic one, "partly aligned but partly estranged" (Gallagher, this volume) with the subject at which it is aimed. And it is precisely in such slippage between the event-as-unfolded and the event-as-filmed that the non-representational excess comes to life, in all its enchanting power and multiple functionalities. It is in how it 'makes knowledge', in its production of an audiovisual *artefact,* that its evocation of a social "reality" can "facilitate an appreciation of the practical, sensual and affective dimensions" (Brown and Banks, this volume) of the practice of filming as much as an inchoate social reality itself.

Affective Experimentations

It was only a few years ago that Thrift and Dewsbury claimed that cultural geographies were "dead" and that only performative experimental approaches could re-animate them and make their subjects "flirt and flout, gyre and gimble, twist and shout" (2000, 412). At the time this pronouncement felt revolutionary to most geographers, but anthropologists and sociologists as well as communication and education studies scholars (e.g. Denzin and Lincoln 1994) had been preaching the same message for quite some time already. As a matter of fact, according to Denzin and Lincoln (2005), post-foundationalist research methods were by then already past the experimental moment, so Thrift and Dewsbury's incitation—if one is to judge by what was already happening—might have been nothing but a little guarded. Curiously, however, experimentation in video research methods has lagged behind the rest of the performative social sciences and so the calls made by contributors to this volume to be bold and experimental are still both innovative and inspiring.

I too "want to encourage video ethnographers to experiment"—to borrow from Garrett and Hawkins's words. Experimentation is not only "one of the key skill sets of video ethnographers" (Garrett and Hawkins, this volume) but I firmly believe that creative experimentation through newly-acquired video skills easily translates into learning new writing and data collection skills as well. Video is good to think with—as I myself have realised after learning to see fieldsites differently in light of the heightened reflexivity gained through the video camera. Indeed the socio-technological assemblages we operate within as social scientific researchers—whether these include nothing but pen and paper, or a fuller array of advanced digital devices—"are never static, and, as such, we can, and indeed should, work to stretch, extend and mould" (Garrett and Hawkins, this volume) these assemblages in order to devise new genres, styles, and goals for our fieldwork. Though we may occasionally fail, there is indeed "much to be gained for video researchers by experimenting with the relationship between audio and image" (Gallagher, this volume). Continued experimentation with diegetic and non-diegetic sound, camera angles, narrative linearity and un-linearity, and scene length and juxtaposition has the power to deeply "unsettle and rework" social realities, undoubtedly standing out as "one of the most intriguing and affectively potent aspects of the medium" (Gallagher, this volume).

Nowadays it is all too tempting to say that portable and affordable high-quality sound-recording HD video cameras and Final Cut Pro or Adobe Premiere make it easy to engage in video experimentation. Well, yes they do, but we need to remember that purchasing a brand new pair of parabolic skis won't turn us all into Olympic downhill skiers. The reality is that the greatest risk to experimentation is the embarrassing amateurism that comes from clueless optimism and excessive self-confidence. As Gallagher reminds us, then, the value of collaboration between specialists of different trades cannot be overestimated. Collaborating with professional visual artists—as I myself have learned—allows us to learn new 'languages' (to borrow from an overused but still effective metaphor) that can enable us academics to communicate with new audiences. As Jungnickel argues in her chapter, experimentations of various kinds can facilitate the production of courageously complex works that "resist the flattening of live, dynamic processes via a renewed interest in sociological description". Collaborative experimentations are thus in an advantageous position to animate the messy character of social life and "embrace 'impossible or barely possible, unthinkable or almost unthinkable' versions of reality" (Jungnickel, citing Law 2004, 6). Time-lapse videos (Jungnickel, this volume) or research videos that creatively borrow from the style of sleek music or adventure travel videos (Garrett and Hawkins, this volume) are but some of the possible styles likely to emerge from collaboration, cross-fertilization, and the search for inspiration across disparate fields and traditions.

Experimentation with video—to continue the argument presented in the previous section—can in particular play a key role in transcending the limits of representation. Several of the contributors to the volume find this to be a central benefit of working with video. For example, citing Whatmore (2006), Patchett argues that "in order for academic researchers to embody and enact more-than-human modes of working they must develop and follow an explicitly experimental methodological imperative" (Patchett, this volume) which supplements "the familiar repertoire of humanist methods (which generate text and talk) with experimental practices that amplify other sensory, bodily and affective registers and extend the company and modality of what constitutes a research subject" (Whatmore 2006, 606–607, cited in Patchett, this volume). It is outright difficult to disagree with this; as a matter of fact the mark of insanity, to borrow from Albert Einstein, might very well be said to be the attitude of someone (like a traditional scholar) who keeps doing the same thing in the same way over and over again while expecting different results. Going beyond the stale and conservative representationalism that has characterised the scientific method since its inception can allow us to *engage,* rather than merely investigate the world (Jungnickel, this volume, citing Lury and Wakeford 2012, 6), and thus reach out to new constituencies. And it can also allow us to connect to more-than-human subject matters that have hitherto been silenced or poorly understood, as several of the contributors remind us (e.g. Brown and Banks, this volume; Patchett, this volume).

An experimental sensitivity, or in other words a willingness to take compositional risks and deviate from the typical expository and overly rational mode of academic rhetoric, is also instrumental in intensifying the affective potential of research-based knowledge. Videos that attempt to "amplify" (Kullman, this volume) rather than merely *reproduce* the affective intensities that pulse through our daily lives can mobilise old and new audiences alike, with the explicit "potential to bring bodies, images and worlds into new relationships and, in doing so, transform understandings of the everyday" (Kullman, this volume). Video methods' affective intensity can then be felt with our bodies in their non-verbal sensual materiality (Latham and McCormack 2009), thus resulting in the opening up of thinking spaces for an "affective micropolitics of curiosity in which we can remain unsure as to what bodies and images might yet become" (Lorimer 2010, 252).

Making Conscious Technological and Aesthetic Choices

One of the key points emerging from the contributions to this volume is to be very careful with our tools. Though we may regard contemporary recording devices and editing software as user-friendly, spotting a first-time user is as easy as picking up an accent in someone who has only been speaking a new language for a week. Gallagher's call to caution on this count is particularly sobering and insightful:

> Professional film makers often remark that sound quality is one of the surest ways to distinguish amateur efforts from more serious productions, an observation easily supported by a brief trawl around YouTube. . . . In most cases, leaving audio to take care of itself or hoping

for some miraculous post-production quick fix for sloppy sound (if you ever find one, please let me know) is likely to be detrimental to the quality of video research.

(Gallagher, this volume)

Of course there is no need to despair. Even old dogs can learn new tricks with some patience, dedication, and a good teacher (or a good team of collaborators). The point, however, is that sloppy productions will bring negative light and will cause loss of attention not only onto the producer, but regrettably also onto the methodological field as a whole. Making deliberate, careful, and wise technological choices, therefore, is of the outmost importance.

As opposed to much of the available literature on visual ethnography, visual methods, visual anthropology, and related issues, many of the contributors to this volume aren't shy about discussing technical issues. Chief amongst their considerations, I found throughout my reading, is a concern with editing—arguably the most esoteric and least openly-discussed topic in visual research. Rather than a happenstance process, something to delegate to technical experts, or something to be epistemologically suspicious of, editing is a quintessential component of creative-analytic video research practice and is, as Garrett and Hawkins put it in no uncertain terms,

a mode of analysis . . . combining the aesthetic and informational in a suite of digital-material processes that are as much about research and analysis as they are oriented toward the production of outputs. Editing is of course a question of audiencing. Considerations of audiencing require that we foreground the productive force of films on the multiple audiences of the work, from the filmmaker as first field-based viewer, to myriad "secondary" audiences who encounter the film as it circulates.

(Garrett and Hawkins, this volume)

Editing, therefore, is a political and ethical practice within all video-based research no matter what the intended audience. It is a highly technical activity requiring an equally high level of reflexivity that allows us to come to terms with the symbolic, aesthetic, affective, and educational potential of our productions, as well as the possible mobilisations of our work by others with different goals than our own (see Garrett and Hawkins, this volume).

Making conscious technological choices in both the production and post-production phases is an aesthetic as much as it is a political process focused on constructing knowledge "driven by the practical and aesthetic challenges of the task at hand" (Garrett and Hawkins, this volume). Whether it is in the choice of a mode of data collection, a genre and style of editing, or a channel of dissemination, the practice of video research reminds us that doing research is not like following a cookbook recipe but rather a creative and often highly subjective and personal experience woven together by intersecting choices focused on "thematic excavation, the concentration of concepts, the intensification of ideas, and the refinement of trajectories" (Garrett and Hawkins, this volume)—all activities highly dependent on a level of intimacy with one's subject matter and trade that can only be gained over time as the result of failures, revelations, and reflexive choices.

All of these arguments may seem so common sense to professional video-makers to appear useless, but we must remember that at least within the tradition of ethnographic film aesthetic considerations and a preoccupation with recording and editing technology have long been considered to go against the plain style of observational film—the historically dominant genre. Thus for Heider (1976)—whose text on anthropological film-making has for years constituted the canon of the field—any aesthetically-sensitive intervention on the part of the film-maker/researcher throughout the editing process runs the risk of manipulating and distorting reality for expressive ends. Ruby (2000, 178) summarises this position thus: "there is an editing style that logically fits [the static camera style] to cinematography and is assumed to safeguard the scientific authority of the footage. If one does almost no editing except to slice rolls of film together in chronological order, then there is apparently little danger of introducing further distortion". It is precisely in juxtaposition to this plain style canon that the technological skills and choices—whether these be in the production or post-production phase of one's video work—advocated by the contributors to this volume can be understood as more-than-representational and thus ground-breaking.

The Sensuousness of Multimodality

Video-based methods of data collection and dissemination can be said to be 'multi-modal' and therefore superior—insofar as richness of modality goes—to the unimodal nature of writing. The evocation of multiple aural and visual impressions is a communicative achievement made possible by the technological affordance of video as a pictorial and sonorous medium. Video has the key advantage of relaying, for example, complex movements of various kinds—something which both the printed word and photography have difficulty with—and can therefore be part of a more choreographic, vibrant, and intense animation of the human and more-than-human experience. It is no accident that many of the contributors to this volume focus on subject matter influenced and inspired by the mobilities turn across the social sciences.

Video methods have developed from insights gleaned from a broader scholarship that over the last two decades has foregrounded corporeal, sensual, and affective matters. The evocation of experiences and practices of the human body—in all their non-representational excesses—is precisely where traditional methods, with their excessive emphasis on the discursive or the causative, have left much to be desired. The multimodality of video methods is then best equipped "in animating the vitality, movement, energies, and fluidities of more-than-human becoming, and coping with ways of being and knowing that take us beyond cognition and beyond the verbal into realms where bodily and multisensory grammars prevail, for which we have little established vocabulary" (Brown and Banks, this volume).

So, whereas writing and still photography run the risk of flattening action and experience (though, see Jungnickel in this volume on time-lapse photography), the aesthetic decisions made in the process of taking and editing video footage have the potential to integrate kinetic, musical, rhythmic, pictorial, luminous, textural, and tonal—only to name a few—dimensions of our and other species' and objects' existence. This is not to say, of course, that video methods have a greater likelihood to render actual experiences of reality in more faithful ways, but rather to suggest that the complexity of the impressions they convey has a unique semiotic power to affect viewers and listeners through their relationship with a screen and its speakers. Screens, as Kullman and Hatzius and Wakeford argue in their respective chapters, and sound speakers, as Gallagher would remind us, direct our attention to the material embeddedness and situatedness of audiovisual practice, opening a multimodal platform for the exploration of encounters with the life-world. Screens and speakers animate imagery and sound, functioning as a

> "portable sensorium" (Marks 2000, 243), mobilising images that contain not only pre-coded meanings in need of interpretation, but "blocs of sensation", that is, composites of "affects" and "percepts", or different types of pre-personal intensities, that have the potential to set bodies in new kinds of motion as they engage the attention of viewers (Deleuze and Guattari 1994, 164; see also van Alphen 2008; O'Sullivan 2001). Screens are one of the arenas where such intensive encounters between bodies and expressive materials are played out, often inviting unexpected responses in those who they bring together for the making and viewing of images.
>
> (Kullman, this volume)

Given all the above, I read the contributions to this volume to say that video methods are absolutely essential weapons in the research arsenal of sensuous scholars. As performative, narrative, reflexive, impressionist, embodied, and descriptive qualitative research traditions across the social sciences continue to evolve, the sensuous scholarship arising out of video methods has the potential to develop our understanding of and appreciation of knowledge *about the senses, through the senses, and for the senses.* Video methods' multimodality can—I believe better than any other methods—allow us to cultivate the meaningfulness of our somatic experience of the world, the performance of the skilful activities through which we actively make and remake the world through our body and senses, and the aesthetic evocativeness of our strategies of knowledge generation. The challenge of sensuous scholarship, according to its foremost proponent, Paul Stoller (1997), has traditionally consisted in re-learning how to rediscover the deep significance of sensations and in conveying the more-than-human nature of those sensations in evocative, passionate, carnal, and imaginative ways. As Stoller (1997, xi-xii) writes:

> stiffened from long sleep in the background of scholarly life, the scholar's body yearns to exercise its muscles. Sleepy from long inactivity, it aches to restore its sensibilities. Adrift in a sea of half-lives, it wants to breathe in the pungent odors of social life, to run its palms over the jagged surface of social reality, to hear the wondrous symphonies of social experience, to see the sensuous shapes and colors that fill windows of consciousness. It wants to awaken the imagination and bring scholarship back to "the things themselves."

More vibrantly than any other alternative then, video methods—as this book has made clear—serve as a brilliant set of exercises for our stiff bodies and our dull hearts. It is simply up to us to awake and take them on.

CONCLUSION: LINGERING LIMITS AND STILL-UNTAPPED POSSIBILITIES

I wish to conclude this chapter with a few brief practical considerations about video distribution—in my mind a topic not sufficiently treated by this book's contributors—and with an invitation to disseminate our work more ambitiously. Much too often, it seems to me, the production of video is still viewed as the end point of our work. Few academics indeed worry about little more than making a video "accessible" (by uploading it, for example, on their own website, YouTube, or Vimeo)—hence failing to truly actualise the potential of their research. It is true that not all video-based research studies are meant for broad viewing consumption, but those that are still suffer from a confusion between accessibility and publicity. Simply uploading a video on the Internet guarantees nothing: most of the academic videos I have managed to find and watch over the last few years have less than 200 viewers. Few have more than 500. Anything above 1000 or 2000 is a success. But while 2000 views are still probably more than a typical journal article garners, the thought of having one tenth or one hundredth the viewership size of a well-edited YouTube video about kittens is nothing to be proud of. The true strongest lingering limitation of video-based research is that it hasn't quite found a sizeable audience yet.

As academics we must consider far-reaching video dissemination a quintessential component of our scholarship, of our universities' broader mission in their communities, and an expression of our social and cultural role as public intellectuals. There are several ways to do this (for a review see Vannini 2012). We can strategically leverage the power of social media, for example (without facile hopes that somehow our work will magically go "viral" overnight, however). We can more intelligently and more frequently utilise electronic journals and the websites of print journals to link open-access video content with peer-reviewed material. We can do the same for book series as well, of course.[2] We can also seek audiences for our video productions at local, regional, or national and international festivals. We can liaise with local communities, organisations, and interest-based groups. We can make concrete efforts to have our video productions played—even if only in small segments—on local and national TV. And, more ambitiously, we can seek the assistance of professional distributors who can release our work on channels like Netflix and iTunes or in independent movie theatres.

All of these strategies require effort, skill, and, in most cases, intensive collaborations with professional specialists who know how to actualise the potential of video better than most of us academics do. For much too long the prevailing attitudes amongst scholars has been to legitimise our invisibility in public discourse by sanctimoniously invoking our refined taste and by belittling the polluting commercial formats and exigencies of popular channels. Such course of action has guaranteed us nothing but irrelevance. Now that more and more of us have learned to operate video cameras and editing suites in their full functionality and with a refreshed imagination, we truly can no longer afford to be so cavalier about the value of playing back our work.

NOTES

1. To be clear, Ruby's statement is an assessment of what he finds to be a common disposition in anthropological film, and not necessarily his opinion on how things should be.
2. See, for example, my own Routledge series on Innovative Ethnographies, which hopefully represents a step in that direction: http://innovativeethnographies.net/

REFERENCES

Denzin, N. and Lincoln, Y. (eds.) 1994. *The SAGE Handbook of Qualitative Research*. 1st ed. Thousand Oaks: SAGE.
Denzin, N. and Lincoln, Y. 2005. Introduction: the discipline and practice of qualitative research. In Denzin, N. and Lincoln, Y. (eds.) *The SAGE Handbook of Qualitative Research*. Thousand Oaks, CA: SAGE, 1–30.
Dewsbury, J. D. 2003. Witnessing space: "knowledge without contemplation." *Environment & Planning A*, 35: 1907–1932.
Heider, K. 1976. *Ethnographic Film*. Arlington: University of Texas Press.
Latham, A., and McCormack, D. 2009. Thinking with images in non-representational cities: vignettes from Berlin. *Area*, 41: 252–262.
Lorimer, H. 2005. Cultural geography: the busyness of being "more-than-representational." *Progress in Human Geography*, 29: 83–94.
Lorimer, J. 2010. Moving image methodologies for more-than-human geographies. *Cultural Geographies*, 17: 237–258.
Ruby, J. 2000. *Picturing Culture*. Chicago: University of Chicago Press.
Stoller, P. 1997. *Sensuous Scholarship*. Philadelphia: University of Pennsylvania Press.
Thrift, N. and Dewsbury, J. D. 2000. Dead geographies—and how to make them live. *Environment & Planning D*, 18: 411–432.
Vannini, P. (ed.) 2012. *Popularizing Research*. New York: Peter Lang.
Vannini, P. (ed.) 2014. *Non-Representational Methodologies*. New York: Routledge.

Contributors

Esther Banks worked for almost two years as a Research Assistant at the James Hutton Institute, where she was chiefly involved in projects exploring conflict in conservation and holistic approaches to land management, using a range of qualitative methods. She has a background in conservation biology and governance in conservation; however her research interests have evolved over time towards broader issues on the sustainability spectrum, which are more aptly interrogated using a mix of inspiration from the humanities and social sciences.

Charlotte Bates is a Researcher in the Sociology Department at Goldsmiths, University of London. Her work touches on the body and materiality, everyday life and sense of place. She is currently exploring the relationship between disability and the designed environment through the European Research Council funded project 'Universalism, universal design and equitable access to the designed environment'. As part of this project, she is continuing to experiment with video and sound as ways of researching lived encounters between people and place.

Katrina M. Brown is a Senior Researcher at the James Hutton Institute. A key aim of her research is to understand the role of formal and informal regulatory mechanisms in preventing and resolving land use conflicts. To explore embodied and geographically situated practice, Katrina and colleagues have developed innovative mobile and visual methods, with a focus on 'headcam' video techniques. She has used these methods to explore the key spaces of encounter and 'contact zones' of outdoor recreation, focusing on the role of the body, movement and emotion in the often-contested choreography of sharing space across mobile and species difference.

Michael Gallagher is a Research Associate in Human Geography at the University of Glasgow. His research involves experimentation with audio and other digital media as methods for ethnographic research. This work is driven by an interest in the sonic aspects of spaces and places, their affective potentials, and associated forms of power and knowledge. He currently holds an AHRC Early Career Fellowship, in which he is exploring the use of sound art and audio methodologies for research on sonic environments.

Bradley L. Garrett is a writer, researcher and photographer based in the School of Geography and the Environment at the University of Oxford. Brad has a particular interest in uncovering hidden places in soil, seas, cities and space and worked as a terrestrial and maritime archaeologist throughout the 2000s. His first book, *Explore Everything: Place-Hacking the City*, published by Verso Books in 2013, is an ethnographic account with urban explorers, photographers of off-limits urban environments.

Britt Hatzius is a visual artist and researcher working in video, film, sound, photography and installation. After receiving a degree in Fine Art Media at Chelsea College of Art, she completed an MA in Photography and Urban Cultures at Goldsmiths, University of London. While based within the Sociology Department she has worked on numerous international research projects including 'The Architecture of Contemporary Religious Transmission', 'Signs of the City' with Urban Dialogues, 'New Media Artists as Cultural Intermediaries of Technology', and various other experiments in ethnographic methods within Studio INCITE.

Harriet Hawkins is a Senior Lecturer in Human Geography at Royal Holloway, University of London. Her research interests include creative geographies and the geographies of art and aesthetics, including how these play out in methodological issues and discussions of disciplinary history and philosophy. Collaboration is an important part of Harriet's research practice and she has worked with a number of artists and arts institutions and organisations to create and commission work and produce exhibitions. Her first monograph, *For Creative Geographies,* was published by Routledge in 2013.

Katrina Jungnickel is a Lecturer in the Sociology Department at Goldsmiths, University of London. Her research explores mobilities, digital technology cultures, DiY/making practices and inventive methods. Her first book, *DiY WiFi: Re-imagining Connectivity,* published by Palgrave Pivot in 2013, ethnographically examines the cultures and practices of grassroots wireless digital networks. She is currently working on an ESRC funded project about inventive methods and modes of knowledge transmission which features new research into the history of women's cycling and cycle wear.

Kim Kullman is a Researcher in the Sociology Department at Goldsmiths, University of London, where he is currently working on the European Research Council funded project 'Universalism, universal design and equitable access to the designed environment'. His previous research has explored everyday practices of mobility, concentrating in particular on how these are learned, sustained and transformed across the life course. Apart from studying how children acquire mobility skills in urban environments, he has also engaged with topics such as adult cycle training.

Merle Patchett is a Lecturer in Human Geography at the School of Geographical Sciences, University of Bristol. Her longest-running research project to date has focused on critically examining the craft worlds and knowledge-practices of taxidermists, past and present, and the material culture of animal remains in order to re-think and re-present matter(s) of life and death and histories of human-animal relation. Merle has published on this research widely and has been a co-curator of taxidermy-art exhibitions at the Hunterian Museum, Glasgow and the Royal Alberta Museum, Edmonton. She is currently preparing a monograph entitled *The Taxidermist's Apprentice: On the Craft of Taxidermy and Histories of Human-Animal Relation*.

Paul Simpson is a Lecturer in Human Geography in the School of Geography, Earth and Environmental Sciences, Plymouth University. His research focuses on the social and cultural geographies of everyday, artistic and mobile practices and explores the complex situatedness of such practices in the environments in which they take place. He has recently been pursuing these interests through research funded by the Royal Geographical Society and L'Agence Nationale De La Recherche and has published on these themes in the journals *Area, Cultural Geographies, Environment and Planning A, Geoforum, Social and Cultural Geography* and *Space and Culture*.

Jonathan Taggart is a documentary photographer, a filmmaker, and a PhD student at the University of British Columbia's Institute for Resources, Environment and Sustainability. His visual projects have been published and exhibited internationally, and he has taught photography at Emily Carr University in Vancouver and Royal Roads University in Victoria, Canada.

Phillip Vannini is Canada Research Chair in Innovative Learning and Public Ethnography and Professor in the School of Communication and Culture at Royal Roads University in Victoria, Canada. He is author/editor of nine books, including *Ferry Tales: Mobility, Place, and Time on Canada's West Coast* (Routledge, 2012), *Popularizing Research: Engaging New Media, New Genres, New Audiences* (Peter Lang, 2012) and *The Senses in Self, Society, and Culture* (Routledge, 2012).

Nina Wakeford is Reader in Sociology at Goldsmiths, University of London and leads Studio INCITE (Incubator for Critical Inquiry into Technology and Ethnography). Along with colleagues at INCITE she is interested in the ways in which collaborations can be forged between ethnographers and those from other disciplines, such as engineering, design, visual arts and computer science. She is currently exploring how sociology might work with the openness and ambiguity of inventive methods. Drawing on her training in fine art she has also produced installations and interventions in academic conferences using film and performance. Alongside Celia Lury she edited *Inventive Methods: The Happening of the Social* (Routledge, 2012).

Index

Printed by PGSTL